PROPERTY REGIMES IN TRANSITION

For my three daughters Anneleen, Marleen, Marloes and their husbands

Property Regimes in Transition

Land Reform, Food Security and Economic Development: A Case Study in the Kyrgyz Republic

HENRI A.L. DEKKER

Routledge
Taylor & Francis Group
LONDON AND NEW YORK

First published 2003 by Ashgate Publishing

Reissued 2018 by Routledge
2 Park Square, Milton Park, Abingdon, Oxon OX14 4RN
711 Third Avenue, New York, NY 10017, USA

Routledge is an imprint of the Taylor & Francis Group, an informa business

A Library of Congress record exists under LC control number: 2003045157

ISBN 13: 978-1-138-71563-9 (hbk)
ISBN 13: 978-1-315-19744-9 (ebk)

Contents

List of Figures

List of Tables

PROPERTY REGIMES IN TRANSITION

Land Reform, Food Security and Economic Development: A Case Study in the Kyrgyz Republic

Henri A.L. Dekker

PREFACE

Many of the former communist republics strive to adopt a market economy in which the privatization of landed property is a key element. Generally it is expected that by doing so, economic development will take off improving food security and decreasing (rural) poverty. The relationships among changing land regulations, economic development and poverty are complex and, as yet, little understood. One can also refer to these phenomena as land reform, land market development, and livelihood of the poor, or restructuring of agricultural production, stimulating prosperity growth, and alleviating food insecurity. But that is just a matter of giving different names to basically the same phenomena. This book is the result of several assignments in various countries, mainly in Central and Eastern Europe. The text aims at providing more insight in the links between the mentioned phenomena in the context of land tenure and suggesting specific assistance with monitoring the effectiveness of projects that initiate land tenure changes.

Being educated as a land-surveyor and a registrar it might surprise some readers that in this book I do not put more emphasis on land registration and cadastral systems. They do not even appear as specific elements in the model I developed to monitor the progress of projects in which change of land tenure is a main goal. I have come to believe that land registration and cadastral systems are tools to support more important and all-encompassing social phenomena and human perceptions, like property regimes and land tenure security. In many cases these tools are essential, but not as indispensable as conventional wisdom leads us to believe. I noticed that several societies function perfectly well without land registration systems or cadastres. Land tenure security obviously does exist with and without written documents. In societies where communal land tenure is dominant, introduction of land registration systems might even be a threat to land tenure security of native people as recent research shows.

On the other hand, formal land registration and titling can be the best way to protect claims and traditional rights of native people against a government that wants to extensively exploit their natural habitat. No general rule or formula will provide the achievement of land tenure security. Like other social phenomena, land tenure security is a complex conceptual matter that will be accomplished best when it blends in with the historic, cultural and even the religious concepts of people. There is no standard desktop solution available to guarantee realization of the concept of land tenure security.

Many countries in transition seek to find a quick way out of economic stagnation by means of land reform. With successful land reform projects governments in transitional economies expect to achieve economic growth and thus alleviation of rural poverty. Nowadays there is ample research to prove that, to be effective, land policy reforms need to be complemented by policy and institutional reforms, and by effective rural development measures. However, this is not a new finding (Dorreen Warriner[1] had arrived at the same conclusion in the 1960s with her concept of 'integral' land reform). The necessity of application of such a 'total package deal' is still often ignored.

This book will not give clear-cut answers nor will it provide blueprint solutions for successful land reform and land tenure change projects. The ideal land reform project is one especially designed – idiosyncratic in character – for the specific country or region at hand. The aim of this book is to increase the awareness of links between land reform, food security and economic development. Moreover, it suggests use of a model for rapid assessment of project progress in which macro-economic indicators are applied in a systematic way to give insight in conceived phenomena like land tenure security and food security and to provide warning signals for less-desired developments as a result of project implementation. Although the data used in this book are collected in only a number of countries in transition, much of the contents of the book can be applied in all former communist countries now in transition from a centrally planned economy into a market economy.

Many sources have provided me with material for this book. Several of these sources can be acknowledged by mentioning them in the bibliography. A number of sources gave oral information or provided me with data, documents, and numbers. I like to thank all contributors and especially the ones that remain anonymous. Most likely, even without knowing, several local experts and fellow expatriate experts supplied data, useful thoughts, valuable considerations, and made information accessible to me that I have used here. Thank you all for sharing your doubts, your visions and your ideas with me.

This book aims at assisting in the accomplishment of more successful land tenure changing projects to improve the livelihood of the poor and to provide a positive change in the daily life for many of the inhabitants of post-communist countries.

---

[1] Doreen Warriner in 'Land Reform in Principle and Practice'. Oxford: Clarendon Press. 1969

Acknowledgement

Property Regimes in Transition has been in the making during and after the completion of an assignment in Kyrgyzstan.
I collected data and this was provided with indispensable support during the assignment and also at later stages knowingly or unknowingly by André, Carol, Carole, Edward, Edwin, Ernie, Fatima, Gavin, John, Peter, Rick, Theo, Tolobek, Valentina and supportive other friends whom I do not need to mention by name.

CHAPTER 1

INTRODUCTION

1.1 ALLEVIATION OF (RURAL) POVERTY

1.1.1 THE CONVENTIONAL APPROACH

There are many poor people in the world. Poverty is a persistent problem. Poor people often live in so-called less developed countries and the most poor of these live in rural areas of those countries. Mass media regularly remind us that these people live with continuous food shortages. If the reminder is part of the other 'news' we hear every day, it might hardly affect us. But for these people food insecurity is just part of daily life. The sad truth is that at least a great deal of it could be alleviated by targeted measurements and internationally funded projects when these projects are managed thoughtfully and responsibly. Consulting activities in economics, geodesy, and law carried out mainly in poorer rural areas in the world made me aware of such food insecurity as daily reality, not as a passing news item. Most of my assignments were in projects related to a change in rural land tenure (the 'how' of rights to land), linked with a (re-)distribution of land (the 'who' and 'what' of land rights: who controls what). Somc of these areas were clearly both poor and food insecure. The common expectation in the food insecure countries was that a change in land tenure would lead to higher food production, and thus to less food insecurity, a textbook, desktop-based, food insecurity reduction method.

However, a reduction in food insecurity was not always the chief aim. In fact, some of the areas where I worked were neither food insecure nor significantly poor. But changes in land tenure were expected to bring benefits there too: primarily economic development. The notion was that a new property regime would result in higher values of property, thus being an incentive for local people to improve the productivity of their landed property.

So basically two types of land tenure change can be distinguished in the traditional approach toward land reform, one to alleviate food insecurity and one primarily aiming at economic development. The two types of projects have much in common – they differ almost exclusively by their starting point (how poor or food insecure the area really is) and the ambition of their goals (strive for economic progress and prosperity or primarily improve food security).

The two different types of projects can be recognized in the Terms of Reference for projects in transition countries. Both generally contain assumptions of straightforward causality: change in land tenure leads to higher production which enhances food security or change in land tenure provides more certainty about land tenure – especially in combination with land titling and land registration – which leads to higher productivity and prosperity.

The assumption of straightforward causality has various corollaries. For example, an often-used notion in countries where customary property exists as the common rule, is that land reform should commodify the land – free it from most social obligations – because commodified land can more easily be transferred, and thus more easily reach its highest potential value resulting in economic growth. Similarly, another idea is that commodifying and privatizing land will lead to higher agricultural productivity. Having secure exclusive rights to land for long periods of time is an incentive for farmers to increase agricultural production.

1.1.2 CONSTRAINTS FOR SUCCESS

Recent research shows that most of the traditional assumptions only hold when several additional supportive measures are in place and certain conditions are met. In other words, the assumptions, and their corollaries, work in theory. They certainly do not automatically work in practice. Indeed, food insecurity is not only real; it is also very complex. The same goes for land tenure security. And although the effect of economic development – a perception of prosperity – is somewhat relative, the perception of tenure security is at least as important as the perception of food security to measure success of land reform projects, and all three are not directly measurable. They can only be estimated with the help of indicators.

The traditional assumption of straightforward causality quickly becomes problematic when it meets the socio-political reality in which actual projects are embedded. Mismatches easily develop between the project developed on a desktop and the reality on the ground. A divergence quickly grows between Western textbook food insecurity alleviation or theoretical economic development paradigms and political interests, practical pressures, and constraints 'on site.'

The problem starts with the very terms of reference that are used to guide project work. Because for whom, really, are they written? Terms of reference for projects generally aim at politicians to get project support at the various political levels. The result is that the description of projects on land reform is, above all, politically oriented and much less project implementation oriented. This often leaves project personnel with rather vague descriptions of their respective roles and responsibilities. There is a fixation on how property regimes should be oriented toward quick action. There is a neglect of the inter-relations between property rights, economic performance and ecologically sustainable resource use. And there is more. A workable new legal system is a necessary parallel development for any new 'western style' land tenure to succeed. Yet countries in transition do not have time to let new legal systems evolve in a natural way. Instead, 'off the shelf,' alien systems are imported and forced into institutional arrangements that carry some reflection of the concepts and practices of recipient countries, but they may remain an immature, artificial fit in many ways. A workable legal system is not enough for western style land tenure. An operational land registration system is another ingredient necessary for success. In the ideal situation a new land registration system should already be in place before privatized plots of land are distributed among individuals receiving rights to land this to ensure a proper and simple start of land registration. But, land reform is often driven by national politics, while land registration (being very costly and politically hardly beneficial) generally is donor driven, and international funding is almost always necessary for it to start. The result is a de-synchronization: the two developments do not run parallel and are out of sync with each other. Normally land registration institutions are established long after the land has been distributed. This causes difficulties for registration staff because of increasing discrepancies between realities and originally issued documents as more time has elapsed between the start of the actual registration and the start of the land reform project. It will also result in increased and costly litigation slowing down land transfers, and thus economic growth. Moreover, such a situation undermines people's willingness to register and stimulates their creativity to find ways to circumvent official registration thus frustrating the new land registration system.

Projects have fixed termination dates. These are seldom an incentive for local project staff to care much about the continuity of project benefits beyond the project duration, because they are generally only employed for the project duration. Limited project time and resources seldom provide a generous familiarizing process for local experts with the legal concepts and the legal system of a donor country. The disincentive works both ways: expatriate consultants assigned to a project experience similar disincentives. The limited duration of their assignment seldom permits any time to sufficiently become familiarized with specific circumstances, concepts, and cultural backgrounds in the recipient country.

1.1.3 AN IDIOSYNCRATIC APPROACH

In an ideal situation land registration and land titling projects should be of an idiosyncratic nature. No country is exactly alike any other; that is precisely the reason that there are separate nations. The historical, cultural and contemporary values of the nation's population must be reflected in the legislation that governs land registration if it is to become accepted and understood by them. It is my experience that there is always a trade off between available time and resources and carrying out project activities in an ethical and responsible way. After some years, more than half of the projects show no sustained benefits whatsoever. Of course, it is always difficult to know whether a certain project fulfills the requirement of future needs; criteria for success are difficult to define, while realistic, helpful assessment methods are time consuming. Moreover the surrounding world does not come to a standstill during a land reform project; what changes in that environment are a direct result of the land reform or what evolving circumstances did prevent the land reform to become successful? There are always justifications for failures as there are 'lucky' developments for success of a land reform project.

As mentioned before, an important constraint in assessing the success of land reform projects is that land tenure security, food security and economic prosperity cannot be measured directly. Although we use these terms as common currency, exchanging them as if they carry objective, universal meaning, land tenure security, food security and economic prosperity are complex subjective experiences. Without exaggeration, it can be stated that the experience of a new land tenure system (after land reform) and the security it provides, is extremely subjective. Its connection to the level of investments people will make in the productivity of their property is tenuous and unpredictable at best. Take the farmer in a war torn country whose sons, father, uncles and various other family members might have been killed in a string of civil wars of which he never even understood the purpose. Take the apartment owner in any town in the former USSR living in a dilapidated apartment building with missing windows in the hallway and a filthy smelling main entrance; or the house owner that cannot get the right materials to fix a leaking roof or to replace cracked and stained bathroom equipment. Look at a small farmer in Poland, for example, who was uprooted, placed here, then there. Or watch the farmer in Bulgaria struggling to indicate where the land of his/her ancestors was located on the vast tracts of land of the state farm that did completely re-landscape the rural scenery for miles and miles. How will such an heir be able to indicate the plot of ancestral land he or she is entitled to claim?
Land tenure security means something quite different to these people than it does to the farmer in Western Europe whose title to the land actually carries quite some weight. So how, really, do we know whether we are doing any good with land reform projects? In fact, how can the very people who run and implement these projects know? Most of the local experts assisting the expatriate experts are younger people without experience with individual private ownership issues, while the expatriates are trained and at ease in a conceptual world full of concepts that are often alien to the people in the recipient countries. One striking experience in this respect occurred to me when a native minister once said to me that I was talking about ownership rights to land in his country and that while most rural inhabitants of that country did not know more than a local landlord telling them 'This is your land, and this is his land' with nobody even thinking about challenging such decisions.

In this book, a tool for rapid assessment of effectiveness of land reform projects, whether they are focused on improvement of food security or on increased prosperity, will be developed. The model presented aims to support the work of project staff. It will assist them in assessing the effectiveness of a project, giving early warning signs of undesirable or non-sustainable project effects. The overall goal is to make project expectations more realistic and (foreign) project assistance more satisfactory. Use of the model depends on available macro-economic indicators, some of which are very general in nature. Use of indicators should be kept in perspective. It generally takes a generation before the effect of land reform projects can be observed with some certainty. In the meantime, all kinds of separate simultaneous developments will influence the effect of the land reform project, as well. Measuring indicators must not be applied in such a way that measurement accuracy surpasses the accuracy with which the issue at stake can be observed in isolation from other parallel developments.

1.2 LAND TENURE, FOOD SECURITY, AND ECONOMIC DEVELOPMENT

1.2.1 DIFFERENT ORIGINS

As mentioned, in many land reform projects a link between land tenure changes, increased land tenure security and improved food security and/or economic development is assumed. More recent research confirms the relation, but also emphasizes the complex character of the links. Land tenure, food production and economic development describe social processes, but they have their roots in different domains. Land tenure is primarily described in legal and institutional terms, while food security is defined in terms of agricultural production. Economic development is described with markets, goods, and scarcity and in terms of income generation and prosperity. There are quantitative and qualitative links among them. An example of a quantitative link is that increased access to land means an increase of food production and income growth and the even more obvious link that loss of access to land results in decreased food production and income loss in dominantly agrarian societies. A qualitative link is suggested in that increased long term guaranteed land access would intensify resource use, which shall result in more efficient and profitable agricultural production, leading to increased availability of food. In several project documents proposing land registration, it is suggested that establishment of a modern land registration system will enhance economic development. The assumption is that to achieve economic development, land transfers must be made easy by a reliable and clear description of titles and land objects in a registration system. It is similar to the general assumption that legal reform toward more individual 'western style' private ownership will significantly contribute to economic development especially when linked to the creation of greater legal security by land registration.

1.2.2. ECOLOGICALLY RESPONSIBLE STEWARDSHIP

There is nowadays a general awareness that increased agricultural production and ecologically responsible stewardship of land requires balancing. Exploitation of land resources at a level below the maximum potential can ensure sustainable future benefits. But, in economies in transition one often sees the emergence of many family type farms for which a (too) small farm is the main resource for their livelihood. Then there is sometimes a tendency to overexploit the land because the food produced is otherwise too meager to sustain the family need or simply out of ignorance.

On the other hand, individualized land tenure can be an important incentive for responsible stewardship. This matter of land exploitation is still widely debated.

To reach a state of sustainable food security, current food production should not be increased at the expense of future needs for food. Often it is necessary for the government to take action. Most new farmers focus primarily on the exploitation of resources and must be guided and educated toward responsible resource use. One of the most compelling aspects of land use is that, in many cases, land is not used to its full potential, but yet it is abused out of insufficient knowledge among farmers. The creation of extension centers in the agricultural areas of the country is an important condition that should be part of each and every land reform assistance program by international donors. Education in the use of fertilizers, but also in wise use of technologically improved seed can mean an important step forward in alleviation of rural poverty. This, however, is even a more hotly debated issue not only among agricultural scientists but also among politicians. And although mentioned, the aim of this book is different and thus it is not the place to elaborate further on such a controversial matters. Whatever the outcome in a particular country might be additional governmental monitoring of the use of natural resources should safeguard ecologically sustainable exploitation of privatized land.

1.3 LAND REGISTRATION

1.3.1. LAND REGISTRATION AND LAND TITLING AS PART OF LAND REFORM

Land registration and land titling are comparatively small elements of a land reform program. Neither land registration nor land titling are necessary elements of land reform, but to improve land tenure security, land titling and land registration are considered as complementary elements from the beginning of any given land reform project. Usually the actual preparation phase of the titling and registration component of a land reform project does not immediately materialize. Because land reform is politically motivated and land titling is often donor driven there is a misfit in synchronization between the two. Often the land registration component of the land tenure reform starts quite a bit later than the land reform activity. The time difference between the two activities generally results in the issuance of original title documents to the new owners before any registration activity could be deployed; there was simply not yet a land registration system in place. This often leads to a situation where land reform documents cannot directly be used for the creation of a solid land registration system. Generally, too much time has elapsed since the first land has been given into possession and documents showing rights to land may now differ from the actual situation on the ground because of boundary adjustments; (small) land exchanges between neighbors make it impossible to simply use those documents for the creation of land data in the land registration without an extensive investigation on the ground.

Many countries in transition do not have a long and strong history of land ownership. There is also a general lack of experience with legislation that focuses on protection of ownership rights to land. When most countries in transition aim at

establishing a free market economy they tend to look at the capitalist models of western countries. In all my land reform and land registration project assignments in countries in transition I have needed to introduce 'western' style legislation for rights to land. Land registration projects encompass all the institutional arrangements for establishment of a 'western style' land registration, including the importing of a 'western style' legal system and familiarizing and training of local experts and staff of land registration offices. As far as specific cadastral requirements are concerned, it also included the generating and implementing of ideas for cadastral surveying and mapping.
Most countries in transition have local experts familiar with registration aspects of real property; because, under communist rule, generally a system of data recording of users and use rights of real property was employed nationwide. The main task of the offices for real property registration was to monitor proper use of State owned real property by citizens who acquired use rights to it. Local BTI – Bureau of Technical Inventory – offices carried out this task in urban areas (as far as buildings are concerned, urban land was sometimes registered at separate offices of the Architectura), while in rural areas this task was part of regional offices of Land Administration (also referred to as Land Engineering offices).

1.3.2 LAND REGISTRATION; ONLY THE BASICS

Most land reform projects are set up with foreign funding and international donor assistance. Otherwise the projects create insurmountable burden on the, often-limited, governmental budgets in transition economies. Generally the new system for land registration aims at keeping the amount of collected data on land at a minimum. The scope of the collected data will reflect only the basic elements of a land registration. It should be unambiguous in answering simple questions about the Who, Where, What, When and How of each real right to an immovable property (more about this terminology in chapter 2). In the land registration offices, a clear and reliable link between the registered units and the geographical data of those units must be available. This requires a cadastral map for the area covered by the land registration office. For each registered right to immovable property, both alphanumeric as well as geographic-data will be made readily available.

Achieving quality cadastral mapping is a problem because of limited capacity in land surveying and the period of time and money it will require. This can sometimes be solved by the use of current topographic mapping providing topographic data rather than specific features of boundaries but nevertheless referred to as 'cadastral.' Such an intentional temporarily solution – although often extended – comes down to the use of geographical representations of real property units without much attention to topographic detail and geographical accuracy; (one of my fellow expatriate consultants suggested, in this respect, once to print on each 'map' that 'any similarity with reality is pure coincidence'). It is assumed – at least by the expatriate experts – that after establishing new land registration offices, existing 'cadastral' mapping will gradually be updated and improved with funding mainly out of the fees for registration.

In order to make economic transactions in land and real estate simple, inexpensive, and fast, it is necessary to remove existing bureaucratic hurdles, unnecessary fees and complicated processes. This involves analysis of existing laws, regulations and procedures and refinement of these for the benefit of the user. In addition, a public awareness strategy and a series of workshops and seminars for real estate professionals can help to develop the private market for real property. The future staff of new land registration offices should ideally assist the foreign technical team with providing input for new legislation and establishing the new system of land registration. This input is crucial to designing an operational land registration that protects the rights of new owners of land rights. The new system should be as closely familiar to the local people as possible to become successfully operational. Only with sufficient local assistance, it will be possible to adapt the imported 'western' system toward the cultural, religious and social perceptions of the citizens.

1.4 CONSTRAINTS FOR A LAND REGISTRATION PROJECT

1.4.1. LEGAL FRAMEWORK FOR LAND REGISTRATION

One of the main goals of a new land registration project is to design a legal framework for protection of individual rights to land. Most governments of countries in transition envisage reaching this goal by import of legal regulations, institutions and economic concepts to establish a 'western style' system of land registration. Combined with the development of a legal system for the protection of individual rights to land it should provide security of rights to land. This will give a positive impulse to the developing of a land market and that in turn will stimulate economic development. In doing so, there is an almost selective focus on property in its economic function: more efficient production and circulation of property objects to reach the highest market value. Because economic development is often badly needed, countries in transition cannot wait to construct a system of law for this purpose in an empirical fashion. The project must provide a, more or less, ready-to-implement system introducing individual private ownership of 'commodified' property (property that is stripped of most of its social functions – claims on the part of the community, neighborhood, and kinship group – and thus an easily tradable commodity for exploitation). Unfortunately but not unusual, the expatriate advisors are given little time to familiarize themselves with the receiving culture, and local legal experts in the country can seldom familiarize themselves sufficiently with the donor culture to always fully understand the proposals made by the expatriates. The result is generally a legal framework that can serve as a basis to start land registration in a, more or less, 'western' fashion, which is dependent on a rapid evolution toward a country specific system. A government should be open to accept several amendments on the proposed basic texts for law and regulations, and the local legal experts should be willing to face the challenge to adapt and propose implementation of adjusted legal regulations.

One of the differences within the former communist states is the situation of land tenure in the country before communism became the leading political power. The farther East from the Atlantic Ocean one travels in the previous USSR, the less knowledge the citizens have of private individual ownership of rights to real property. In some states there has not been private land ownership since losing their independence in the 1920s and 1930s. Many states in Central and Eastern Europe knew private individual land ownership before they became communist countries in the late 1940s and 1950s. Land there was owned by wealthy farmers and noble families in large estates and rented to small farmers, but there were also many small farmers who individually owned parcels of land. When the communists came to power in these countries, farmers were sometimes expropriated and their land became part of large state farms while other farmers 'voluntarily' joined cooperative farms and theoretically remained owners of the land. Over time, however, the management of the farm adapted the land parcels to be used for large scale farming without the consent of the official owners. Farm parcels in the cooperative farms were joined together, former boundaries got lost in the process of adapting the landscape into vast tracts of land, farm buildings were erected and irrigation works constructed. So, although still being owner of the land, many farmers practically lost their ownership to the management of what became the large collective farms according to the communist model of agricultural production. Many farmers could not give an accurate location of the land they originally owned because of the changes in the topography caused by many years of large scale farming policies.

After the political changes in the late 1980s and early 1990s, many former USSR republics adopted legislation to privatize the housing stock and the land. The result of the above is a distinction between the various former communist countries. On the European part of the continent, generally the newly formed states had to deal with former owners and with people facing hardship because they lived in apartment buildings or worked for many years on state or collective farms, but they could not claim property as heirs of former owners. Elsewhere in the former USSR there could be simply a distribution of land without taking into account re-adjudication (some authors refer to it as restitution of land).

Thus, in republics where private ownership of real property was almost abolished after World War II, several governments sought a solution to the distribution of real property among former owners and the general population along country specific rules. This was – as mentioned – to avoid homelessness and landlessness among that part of the population that could not claim to have ancestors or relatives that had previous ownership of real property. In countries where hardly any reminiscence of private ownership of rights to real property was present, this privatization generally meant a distribution of real property among the citizens according, again, to country-specific rules. There was no standard procedure, but some similarities can be observed. Except for some specific categories (apartments not meeting sanitary standards, houses listed for demolition, housing stock of state farms, etc.), all dwelling houses and apartments became objects of privatization and were transferred from State to private ownership. For rural land, the same privatization law generally limited privatization to distribution of land shares among individuals living on the land of state and collective farms that were subject of privatization. The land shares are a 'title' for a claim on part of the vast agricultural land – arable land – land planted with perennials, some hayfields and pastures previously in use by state of collective farms. Family members who wanted to start a single-family farm could pool land shares and apply for such a farm. The land shares could not be sold or transferred to people outside the farming community. When applied for, and initially only a few brave people did that, the area of land mentioned in the combined land shares had to be singled out of land of the state or collective farm and was initially often given in exclusive long term use to the single family farm.

1.4.2 VAGUE CLAIMS AND VAGUE LOCATIONS

People claiming ancestral land often had difficulties showing the extent of their claims because of the drastic changes some of the rural areas had seen during communist rule. The large-scale farming, so characteristic for the Soviet era, required large tracts of land, new large farm buildings and the removal or establishment of several natural and topographical features in the landscape. Some people claiming land owned by a father or uncle could not, any more, recognize the area where the land was supposed to be. Most cadastral maps were lost or deliberately destroyed in the process of collectivization of land. Often local commissions, specially intended and implemented to adjudicate former parcels of land, had a hard time selecting the claims and making a fair judgment about the rightfulness of vague claims. Added to the confusion of re-adjudication was the fact that during communist rule a quota system had been implemented for state and collective farms that made it beneficial to 'shrink' the size of the land of the farms on paper. This resulted in discrepancies between the sizes of land on paper and the actual amount of land available (See for more on this matter chapter 2.4.3)

Because of the fear for speculation with real property many governments also implemented a moratorium on real property obtained after the privatization; transfers to former citizens of the state, living abroad, were often restricted or limited. Foreigners were generally excluded from the privatization.

However, the moratorium was a constraint on the development of a so much wanted real property market, and in several new republics it was lifted or it became limited to short time periods only.

The above-mentioned circumstances complicated the land reform projects and hampered the land registration process, because to circumvent the limitations people started to avoid official registration. However, this situation differs from country to country.

It can be concluded that, in almost all countries in transition, obstacles for a straightforward land registration project activity can be observed. The earlier mentioned misfit in synchronization between land reform and land registration also negatively influenced the registration process because land registration could not be completed before most of the disputes and conflicts about land claims that erupted in the aftermath of the recent land distribution had been settled.

1.5 LIMITATIONS OF THE RESEARCH IN THIS BOOK

1.5.1 INDICATORS FOR MONITORING PROJECT PROGRESS

In this book a model has been developed to monitor the completion of land reform projects and the establishment of an operational and registration system. It also gives indicators for the progress of the battle against food insecurity and rural development. Because of the limited availability of reliable indicators on the household, the model uses mainly macro-economic indicators. So, although households and the household level are the main players in the linkages between land tenure security and food security, the research on the linkages between the two focuses primarily on the macro level.

It became obvious – other researchers in post communist countries confirm this in their reports – that statistical information (in English) sometimes contradicted itself. Discrepancies were noticeable in statistical data as well as in other sources of information, sometimes simply because of linguistics. For example (following VanAtta [95] his note 35 here), in Russian, any economic enterprise, farm or factory, is a 'khoziaistvo.' Agriculture is 'sel'skoe khoziaistvo,' but farms are often called 'khoziaistva,' literally translated as 'enterprise,' confusing the distinction between farm and factory. Another example is the term 'peasant farm' (krest'ianskoe khoziaistvo). This carries the connotation of a backward, subsistence farm. Supporters of the reform 'invented' the term 'farmer's farm' (fermerskoe khoziaistvo), to describe a large, modern, market-oriented but family-owned and operated farm. But (Russian) censors initially did not permit the use of 'fermerskoe khoziaistvo,' and 'krest'ianskoe khoziaistvo' had to be used in the USSR. So despite its name, the 'Law on Peasant Farms' was intended to promote the creation of American-style, family-run, market farms. So texts (provided after translation in English) were at times ambiguous in their translation, depending on the knowledge and the experience of the translator.

In most of the countries in transition, figures and data on the agrarian reform show ambiguities because of shifts in definitions used. I am aware that faulty conclusions are possible because of incorrect inferences about what one or another agency means at any given time by concepts, and definitions. Some examples of contradictions will be shown in the text of this document, detected by comparing data from different sources and my own observations. The original language of the country in transition often is not Russian, but Russian is widely spoken and understood. Russian has been the language in which most citizens received their (higher) education; almost all institutes of higher and academic education that the citizens of republics of the USSR could attend were in Russia. So, Russian is the language generally used in government circles and by 'educated' people.

1.5.2. OTHER LIMITATIONS

The research in this book is based on observations, field research and research of others found in literature, and as far as written documents are concerned, it is largely based on texts translated from Russian into English. Most documents were made available to me during my assignments.

Every effort has been made to double-check my own interpretations and observations as well as the reliability of data. Personally, I experience it always as both exciting and challenging to temporarily live and work in a country where citizens have different concepts and where the mentality is different from that region which one grew up. The most difficult issue is generally the translation or rather interpretation. It is usual to have the assistance of interpreters and translators during an assignment. Many of them do the job as best as they can, but also they have often the problem of being unfamiliar with the technical terms and specific language used by expatriate experts. One hilarious incident during my assignments was when we instructed local experts that they should teach the new staff of land registration offices to use a more customer friendly approach than the one normally exercised during communist times. In a manual we proposed to instruct staff to be friendly and attentive in approaching customers in the newly organized offices of land registration. This manual was translated in the national language and was circulated among the local experts for comments and amendments. After a few days, it returned amended on our desks. We asked a translator to give us an English translation of the obviously (slightly) adapted manual. One can imagine our surprise when we encountered the line: 'During intercourse with clients, special care should be exercised by the staff of the new land registration offices.'

Those who share with me the experience of working in former communist countries will recognize the observation that the Russian term 'DA' should not always be translated with 'YES' (as in the dictionaries). Remarkably often, it is more accurately translated with 'YES-BUT,' and similarly 'NJET' should not always be translated as 'NO' but with the more applicable 'NO-PERHAPS.'

During my first long-term assignment in Sofia in 1993, a high-ranking Bulgarian official kindly informed me about this subtle but important fact. Since then I have discovered the truth of the rule. And not limited to Bulgaria but also in most of the former Soviet countries and not only with the terms 'yes' and 'no.' People living under communist rule quickly learned not to express themselves too clearly in unambiguous ways, because that could easily being used against you. It was much safer to stay a little vague about opinions and intentions to avoid problems with the authorities. It might take another generation before people dare to speak out again without fear. This makes working abroad in post communist countries sometimes a little frustrating, but anyway very challenging.

1.6 A MODEL FOR ASSESSMENT OF LAND REFORM PROJECTS

1.6.1 A FIELD GUIDE

The model presented in this book provides a possibility to rapidly assess the effectiveness of a project, based on links between change of land tenure (by changing institutional arrangements) and economic development or improved food security. Because of my personal background and experience, the model and the method focus on countries in transition where land tenure reform aims at a (rather rapid and sudden) change toward individual tenure. And although the method in principle is applicable to any change in tenure, in cases of a (much) slower pace of tenure change, indicators for a rapid assessment might be more difficult to find because the effects of the land tenure change will take much more time to be noticeable. Many of the land reform projects carried out in other parts of the world did not pursue a sudden change in land tenure, but wanted to bring existing land tenure arrangements more in line with each other. It should also be borne in mind that in many land reform projects outside countries in transition, the need for rapid assessment of the effectiveness of changes is smaller because of the slower pace of reform, making an application of the model and the method less effective. The model is not only built on personal research and experience, but my findings are compared with research results of others in the fields of land and food security. The model has been designed to serve as a field guide to give rapid insight in the feasibility of a project concentrating on land tenure change. Use of the model depends on easily collectable macro-economic indicators. It provides an ad hoc appraisal of effectiveness for expatriate experts working in countries in transition.

1.6.2 'SNAPSHOTS' OF A DYNAMIC PROJECT

It seems contradictory to develop a model to assess the impact of 'change' in land tenure, while at the same time claiming that the model can be used for rapid assessment 'hic et nunc.' Change is per definition something that happens over time, and a certain course of time should be allowed to make an assessment. By using readily available statistical – macro (economic) – data and indicators, the time constraint is avoided, giving the model its possibility to provide insight 'hic et nunc' a kind of 'snapshot' of a dynamic process that is underway.

There are a lot of empirical expectations that surround land reform and land tenure change. It seemed important to use extensively proven evidence taken from research results by others to check if it converges with my theory. The complexity of changes in land tenure, economic development, and food security make it impossible to isolate the effects of a developing society and to consider the issues strictly on their own. The society in which they take place creates a whole new set of changing situations and possibilities while a researcher wants to observe just some specific effects. In other words, no researcher has control over the phenomena that are observed. When it comes to conclusions, data gathering in any research is very likely to be selective and should thus be supported by converging research results of others. There also is the danger of selective generalization to make them suitable for the results the research is looking for. Many expatriate consultants have a tendency – and sometimes an outright habit – to extrapolate 'logical' expectations. Finding similarities in other research can then be a comfort, although it is not a guarantee that the researcher does not fall into the same trap as the one he or she quotes.

1.7 STRUCTURE OF THE BOOK

1.7.1 THE CHOICE FOR ONE CASE STUDY

The theoretical research for this book started more than six years ago and contains experiences of a number of assignments in countries in transition. There are many similarities recognizable about the property regimes in the former Soviet countries, and that is why the title 'Property Regimes in Transition' has been chosen.
The practical application of the research in this book is related to an assignment in the Kyrgyz Republic, and so, the situation in the Kyrgyz Republic plays an important role in the contents of the statistics used to further investigate the usefulness of the model developed herein. Earlier it has been mentioned that sometimes data can be confusing and even contradictory. To limit oneself to just one country limits the complexity and the expected confusion that would arise by trying to compare such data collected in various countries. Although, under Soviet regime, human creativity provided regularly new terminology and standards to be able to polish the results of productivity and well being in an optical fashion, most dependent republics had to follow highly standardized methodologies in all kinds of procedures used by governmental institutions. Even with the badly standardized and documented data between the various republics and even inside one republic, experienced observers always will recognize similarities in most of the procedures of which a considerable number are still in use today in the now independent republics. Since there are so many similarities among the countries in transition, the research is not only applicable in the Kyrgyz Republic, but the research results and recommendations are suitable for use in most of the former communist republics.

1.7.2 A BOOK IN THREE PARTS

This book more or less consists of three parts. Part one contains the Chapters 1 – 5 and provides the reader with background information. This descriptive part is completed in Chapter 5 with building my model for rapid assessment of projects.
Chapter 1 contains an introduction into the research. Chapter 2 provides the terminology and definitions. Chapter 3 describes the Kyrgyz Republic, the Kyrgyz society, and the current economic situation. It provides details with respect to land tenure and ownership of rights to land in the Kyrgyz Republic before and after independence. In Chapter 4, a general introduction on land reform research and

land reform projects in countries in transition is given. This chapter closes with a description of the land reform experiences of China being culturally and ethnically not too far distant from several countries in Central Asia. It aims at informing the western reader with some of the ideas that dominate land reform in China. In Chapter 5, the model of linkages between institutional change and both economic development and food security is developed.

Part two is dedicated to an actual rapid assessment method with the model based on the situation in the Kyrgyz Republic. In chapters 6 to 13, the various elements of the model are described as far as relevant for the Kyrgyz situation. Per chapter one step in the model is assessed. Chapter 13 focuses on food security represented by the elements consumption and nutritional status. The development of the Kyrgyz Land and Real Estate Registration Project is described in Chapter 14.

Part three of the book contains two chapters. Chapter 15 describes what can be called 'second thoughts' or implications of non-evolutionary tenure change of importance for assessing effects of measures. Chapter 16 completes the book with some final remarks against the background of the situation in the Kyrgyz Republic but recognizable in most countries in transition.

CHAPTER 2

DEFINITIONS AND TERMINOLOGY

2.1 PROPERTY

2.1.1 PROPERTY, PROPERTY REGIME, AND PROPERTY RIGHTS

Bruce ([11] 1998) defines property as 'a set of rights and responsibilities concerning a thing; property also is the term for the thing itself.' When we use property as the thing itself, we can distinguish two different types of property: private and public property. Private property is held by private persons and includes property held by legal persons such as corporations or partnerships. Public property is held by any level of government.'

When we want to make it clear we are using property as a set of rules and responsibilities, we often say property rights. In Western law a distinction is made between two basic kinds of property. One is real (Anglo-American Law) or immovable property (European Civil Law). This is property in land and attachments to land like trees or buildings. The second is personal (Anglo-American Law) or movable property (European Civil Law), which is property in all other things. (The Dutch Civil Code states: 'Movable property is all that is not immovable property' – article 3.1.1.2 part 2).

Looking at rights and responsibilities, a 'property regime' is a complex of rules, principles, and procedures that in a specific community or society regulate legitimate control over, access to, and conditions of use of the means of existence and of production (resources), as well as the acquisition and transfer of such resources (Hoekema p. 78/79 [40] 2000).

Generally a property regime is considered to consist of four basic components; 'What,' 'Who,' 'How,' and 'When' – as a land surveyor I like to add a fifth component; 'Where.' 'What, Who, How, When, and Where?' How a land tenure system operates in practice depends on the types of relationships that evolved over time between the participants. Property rights and land tenure systems are far too complex to be explained in a few sentences. But it will be clear from what has been written above that the 'What' is the set of rights in the bundle held by any individual or distinctive group of people. The 'Who' refers obviously to the individual, the individuals, or the legal entity holding a particular bundle of rights (not necessarily the full bundle) and the set of individuals who are expected to respect those rights as legitimate. As can be expected, the 'How' describes the process used to exercise rights. 'When' of a right to land relates to the length of time involved in holding that particular right. 'Where' in the above context refers to the location where the right can be exercised. For real property the component 'where' can be added, because real property is immovable, and can thus be located by its position on the globe. Property rights incorporated in the institutional structure of a country are the building blocks of land tenure, but also are land registrations and credit structures. Property objects are vital for the existence of mankind; the field of property law and rights is one of the most important fields of research and theories in law and economics.

Von Benda-Beckmann (p. 21, [4]) states: 'Property is a sanctioned social relationship between persons – not between persons and objects – with respect to material and immaterial objects.' In [5] it is argued that there is a lack or neglect of anthropological approaches toward property rights in law and economics. The function of property is biased toward economic organizations with commodified property in order to be easily exchangeable to contribute to efficient and optimal allocation. The assumption is that legal reform toward marketable individual ownership rights would significantly contribute to economic development, by creating greater legal security, freeing the individual property holder from communal constraints. These constrains prevent him from becoming the 'homo economicus' capable and willing to pursue maximizing of his property as economic theory has laid out for him. In doing so, land will also provide a basis for collateral to obtain productive credit.

Modern 'western' people tend to see property as a means to exploit and use for private benefit and seldom at its functioning to establish social security. I observed in many projects that property is dominantly approached at the level of use and exploitation, in the field of private law. This while the legitimate authority to control, allocate and exploit property is one of the most salient elements of power through which people can be subordinated at all levels of socio-political organization.

In this book the term 'property' will be used to describe real property as we discuss the (dominantly material) objects. The term 'property regime' will be used for a complex of rules, principles, and procedures that regulate control over, access to, and conditions of use, of the objects and 'property rights' are the sets of rights and responsibilities that come with the object. Property rights in my text always mean a very general category and are not limited to, for example, private property rights, unless explicitly stated.

2.1.2 FROM COMMUNAL TO INDIVIDUAL PROPERTY

Originally most of the land in Europe once was held under communal rules in which land was primarily seen as a resource for survival for everyone belonging to the clan or the group dwelling in a certain area. There was a sense of belonging with the individual. Belonging to the clan, the group, the kinship, or the village was expressed by submitting oneself to the customs of the clan, the group, the kinship or the village. In early days there was also a religious colored respect for the most essential resources and this can still be found in some societies. A strict set of rules was in place manifesting the appropriate and respectful way to use and exploit the resource. Land was seen simply as too important a means of existence to give private persons any individual power of control, allocation and exploitation over it. The individual was tied to the explicit consent of the group or the clan, the kinship or the village. Use and exploitation of land was bound with a social mortgage on every tenure right. One of the most impassioned descriptions of the mystic relationship between man and land has been given in 1855 by Indian Chief Seattle [72] (third non-numbered page from the middle) of the Puget Sound tribes: 'Every part of this soil is sacred in the estimation of my people. Every hillside, every valley, every plain and grove has been hallowed by some sad or happy event in days long vanished. Even the rocks which seem to be dumb and dead as they swelter in the sun along the silent shore thrill with memories of stirring events connected with the lives of my people, and the very dust upon which you now stand responds more lovingly to their footsteps than to yours because it is rich with the dust of our ancestors, and our bare feet are conscious of the sympathetic touch.'

Hoekema [40] states (p.37): 'Once upon a time in Western societies, communal land tenure prevailed. Private property had a marginal status. In the course of the centuries, particularly in the 18th and the 19th centuries, private property took over, hand in hand with the rise of a market oriented capitalist economy'. Moore [57] (p.8) formulates this in 1968; 'Under the pressure of circumstances, the medieval notion of judging economic actions according to their contribution to the health of the social organism began to collapse. Men ceased to see the agrarian problem as a question of finding the best method of supporting people on the land and began to perceive it as the best way of investing capital in the land. They began to treat land more and more as something that could be bought and sold, used and abused, in a word like modern capitalist private property.'

2.1.3 SOCIAL FUNCTION OF PROPERTY

During the past centuries many economists and social researchers have focused on property regimes and property rights. There have been countless – sometimes violent – conflicts over this highly ideological and politically loaded issue in particular over justifications to change or to maintain a given property regime. Economists like Adam Smith and John Kenneth Galbraith have given numerous reflections on the economic significance of property.

Most publications about property rights focus on how property regimes should be, with emphasis on the future. But this is a one sided approach. A property regime governs the life of the people now, and although the future may be important, rules of a property regime should appeal to the current population of a nation because of the social function of property.

Denman also warns of a simple one-sided approach. He draws attention to the inter-relations between persons that play an important role in property regimes. These inter-relations are seldom recognized, acknowledged and taken into account in policy making. Nonetheless, they work away under the surface, often to the confounding of policies (1972) [21].

More recent is the accentuation on communal property regimes and their significance for some of the problems that, only in a poor way, can be addressed by private property regimes. Hoekema [40] (p.51) argues: 'The notion that only individual western style ownership provides enough individual security to promote an economic take off has been substituted by the opposite notion: only communal tenure (in areas where it still holds) provides enough security'.

Because of its less exploitative and more socially oriented nature, the practice of communal tenure has come to be seen as a possible solution for problems of resource depletion. It is a sometimes hotly debated issue.

Von Benda-Beckmann [4] (p.20-23) emphasizes in his theory of the various layers of property the sanctioned social relationship between persons with respect to material and immaterial objects. This social relationship can be observed in four layers of social organization of which the most relevant for this research are the cultural (and ideological) ideals, the normative and institutional regulations and the social property relations. (He also distinguishes a fourth layer, the social practices, less relevant in this context). Property should be attributed a social function, emphasizing that all property can serve a common good or has to be justly distributed among society's members. In many projects, I observed that property rights were mainly approached at the level of use and exploitation in the field of private law. Public authorities came in as an agency to regulate the property rights of private right-holders in such a way that at least some elements of the social function are safeguarded. The regime established by licenses, production quotas, and subsidies is an example. In matters of landed property one can think of zoning laws, environmental regulations, eminent domain, and laws that provide subsidized housing for low-income households. Although seldom explicitly referred to in donor-stimulated projects, it should be remembered that there are generally substantial public law constraints on private property in most Western societies. This sometimes goes so far that observers wonder whether there still is 'private individual property.'

Several decades ago researchers already described the merits of a more socially oriented approach for tenure regimes, but modern 'western' people continue to look at property at the level of use and exploitation and seldom at it's functioning to establish social security. Although not a central issue in this research, one of the questions raised is to consider the option of a land tenure system that does not primarily use the common exploit and use approach of property but goes for a more socially-oriented property regime. With many countries in transition looking for the most suitable property regime to import, there must be an opportunity for such a project.

2.1.4 LANDED PROPERTY

Some literature refers to 'Landed property' when focusing on property rights and the function of land being held under ownership rights.

In 'A Journey through Economic Time' Galbraith [36] reviews the roll of feudalism and capitalism (p.10 - 13).

> For centuries, political authority in Europe had been, to a greater or lesser degree, associated with landed proprietorship or, at a minimum, with landed aristocratic tradition. So also, and more markedly, had military power. .... There were notable consequences of this continuing role of the old feudal classes. One was the profound centuries-old instinct that war has primarily to do with landed territory. Once, indeed, this had been true: territorial conquest was the basis of both wealth and power. With land came economically productive peasants, public and personal revenues and men available to wage armed combat for their master'. ... 'It was to be one of the modern and welcome triumphs of the capitalism attitude and achievement to diminish the acquisitive need for more land. In the highly prosperous city-states of Singapore and Hong Kong, land has been shown to be wholly irrelevant. ... And when in the years after the Second World War many European nations ... as well as the United States, all shed their colonial possessions; scarcely a ripple was felt in their domestic economic well being.

However, this does not imply that landed property has lost its role as a generator of economic well-being and the development of a nation. In many less developed countries the process of industrialization is in progress or has hardly even begun. Still many peasants in rural areas have to rely on the land as the only source of sustenance for their living. Land has not, at all, lost it's meaning as a source of wealth and influence in these countries. In most of the countries in transition agriculture is the most important employer and source of income. It would be a gross error to underestimate the potential effects of the establishment of a new (imported) property regime there.

2.2 LAND

2.2.1 LAND AND REAL PROPERTY

Cadastral specialists use the term 'Land' to indicate real property as being the basic unit of registration in a land registration system. The terms land registration systems and land information systems nowadays are widely used to indicate systems containing data about real property, and the same goes for terms as land titling and land market.

In several former communist countries a specific twofold distinction of real property has been used. One is of land in use by state and collective farms such as land designated for agricultural production and land and real property in use for housing, for farm buildings, for the infrastructure of the farm and land on which agricultural installations were built. Another distinction is of land and real property outside the state and collective farms in urban areas and villages like dwelling houses, apartment buildings, parks, house-plots, and all other land and real property as roads, railways, canals, etc.

A specific regime of land tenure existed for the typical agricultural land parcels and often for land with agricultural buildings in use by the large farms that was different from the tenure of the other real property. The agricultural land was governed by special regulations and managed by offices of Land Engineering (also called Land Administration offices). As an important element in the economic planning, vast amounts of data on the agricultural land were stored and maintained in land data banks. Not at all surprising because the agricultural sectors of almost all economies (or nations for that matter), rich and poor, depend heavily on land. In most policy views, the function of rights to land is approached as a possibility of optimization of the productive use of resources.

One wants to have clear notion of whom is 'holding' certain rights to the land in a modern society. Looking at agriculture as a source of prosperity, it is important to know more about the rights to land of individuals, corporations and the State. The way the 'holding' of the land is organized and recognized may have widespread effects on agricultural production and the distribution of wealth and income.

In most legal systems, there is no difference in judicial approach to protection and registration of rights to real property whether it is an individual, a corporation or the State, owning the right. So, although the word 'individual' appears in the following paragraphs, it may well be meant as individualized rights, instead of explicitly referring to an individual as opposite of a corporation or the State.

2.2.2 RIGHTS TO LAND

The concept of land as used in legal systems is surprisingly difficult to define. The common concept is some form of the idea of terra firma or dry land, but this is inadequate. A good short definition is: 'Any part of the earth's surface which can be owned as property, and everything annexed to it, whether by nature or by hand of man' (Random House Dictionary). In legal terms, however, also a (thin) layer of earth beneath the surface of the object and a certain layer of 'air' above this surface is considered as the property and rights to land can also be executed as the same rights in those layers. Physical land is part of real property, the latter being property in land and attachments. So all things permanently attached to land can be defined as real property and often the land itself is also referred to as real property. In professional circles the term land is used for all real property. Land information, land information systems and land registration (systems) all refer to the term 'land' representing all real property objects. The owner of rights to one apartment in an apartment building will find the recording of this right in a land registration or cadastre, as will the owner of a right to a certain piece of agricultural land.

Land is divided into smaller portions and, in many societies, individuals hold exclusive rights to such a piece of land, but what piece of land exactly? With movable objects, there is often no doubt about the object to which rights are held. Possession is the common way of ownership for most movable objects and most movable objects are physically clearly identifiable.

With land and real property in general, it is often difficult to determine the relationship between an individual and the real property 'at first sight.' Real property does not always come in easy to identify separate objects. It cannot be physically possessed and normally it is connected to other real property to which other individuals are holding different rights. And to make it even more complicated, it is not uncommon that various individuals hold different rights on the same real property.

Even if the individual right to real property is made known, it still is not always automatically obvious where exactly on the land or in the real property object, the physical beginning and the end of the right of the specific individual and the object is, and where rights of other individuals begin or end. There is an invisible line where the different holders of a (real) right on the object change. There are several invisible lines or boundaries when more than one individual holds different rights on the same object.

The rights to real property may be recorded – according to the International Federation of Geodesists (FIG) – in a cadastre. The FIG statement on the Cadastre [34] (published in February 1995) describes a cadastre as a system that may record different forms of land tenure such as ownership, leasehold, easements, mortgages and different types of common, communal or customary land tenure. A more elaborate definition of a cadastre can be found in Henssen, J.L.G., (Basic Principles of the Main Cadastral Systems in the World, FIG Delft 1995): 'A Cadastre is a methodically arranged public inventory of data concerning properties (*separately and artificially made identifiable as 'parcels'; HD*) within a certain county or district, based on a survey of their boundaries. Such properties *(parcels)* are systematically identified by means of some separate designation. The outlines of the property and the parcel identifier normally are shown on large scale maps which, together with registers, may show for each separate property the nature, size, value and legal rights associated with the parcel.' As a side remark, I like to notice that Henssen uses 'value.' However this is often a very relative value, because generally cadastral systems record the selling price as stated by the parties involved and do not always provide for systematic updates of the value of parcels, unless the system is used for real property taxation. A similar remark can be made for 'nature.' Here also, updates of that element are seldom systematically pursued in most cadastral systems because of the (high) costs involved in such updates.

2.2.3 LAND TENURE

Land tenure is the institutional arrangement of rules, principles, procedures, and practices, whereby a society defines control over, access to, management of, exploitation of, and use of means of existence and production. Note the differences with property regime as defined earlier (A Property regime is a complex of rules, principles, and procedures that in a specific community or society regulate legitimate control over, access to, and conditions of use of the means of existence and of production (resources), as well as the acquisition and transfer of such resources).

Terms as property title, life-estate title, leasehold, usufruct, lease, (all the ways of defining entitlements to and use of the land), and all practices among people regarding what rights are held, by whom, and for what length of time determine the character of land tenure in a country. Change of the rules will change the access to land or will reflect the change in access to land already taking place and the citizens' perception of land tenure. Access to land thus has two forms: the formal and physical one, but also a perceived form. Land tenure can be defined in terms of a 'bundle of rights' – specific rights to do certain things with land or real property. In other words: Land tenure determines who can use what land, how much of it and how. The institutions governing land tenure answer the questions 'What, Who, How, Where, and When?'

In most modern societies real persons and legal identities can hold rights to land. Holding of rights to land can be captured by the term land tenure. As Bruce [11] (p. 6 – Glossary) states: 'Land tenure is: Right(s) in land.' The term 'tenure' comes from English feudalism. 'After their conquest of England in 1066, the Normans declared all previous land rights void and replaced them with grants from their new monarchy. Derived from Latin for 'holding,' land tenure means the conditions under which something is held: the rights and obligations of the holder. It is a legal term that means the right to hold land rather than the simple fact of holding land. In a society with well-documented rights to land, one may have tenure but may not have taken possession' (Bruce, 1998 [11] p. 1).

Land tenure is a term frequently used in the following chapters. The main reason for this is that one cannot think only in terms of land ownership if one wants to keep land registration in perspective. In several jurisdictions, the authority over land by the owner is not given to its full extent. In Anglo-American law, land ownership in its full extent is a prerogative of the Crown or the State. Individuals can obtain grants to inheritable and exclusive use of land although this is often experienced as ownership of land. Roman law, as practiced in almost all of continental Western Europe, theoretically recognizes an absolute ownership of rights to land. Theoretically, because almost every society knows of legal or customary provisions for the government to deal with land even against the will or the permission of the owner of rights to the land. In this respect it is interesting to notice that the French Civil Code sees ownership as the absolute right to dispose, while in the new version of the Civil Code of the Netherlands, this has been changed into 'the most complete rights one might have.'

2.2.4 SECURITY OF LAND TENURE

The philosophy of the World Bank for good governance policy for several decades has been that legal reform toward marketable individual private ownership rights will significantly contribute to economic development. This concept still is the most used scientific legitimization for restructuring of land laws. Development of institutional arrangements establishing a (new) system of land registration can be done without involving too much of a distinction between the various forms in which people enjoy rights to land. Proper development of land depends on 'security of tenure' rather than on the form in which people enjoy the ownership of rights to land. Rowton Simpson [69] (p. 8) remarks: 'A person has security of tenure if that person is secure or safe in the holding of land, but when ordinary man speaks of 'security of tenure' he is almost certainly thinking more of security of possession or occupation than strictly of tenure. To be adequate to encourage or even permit development, security of tenure need not amount to ownership, nor need it last all the time. A lessee has security for the time of the lease and, for as long as the lessee complies with its conditions, the law will give complete protection even against the owner of the land. '

For land tenure security my definition is: Land tenure security is tenure perceived as held without risk of loss except for customary rulings or formal expropriation with fair compensation. The term that would be appropriate in my 'definition' of land tenure security is 'sustainability of tenure.' If the question: 'Can I uphold the tenure against others in a sustainable way?' is answered positively, then there is land tenure security. Whether that security is achieved by effective protection by respected authorities or by customary recognition for property rights is not relevant.

It is important to bear in mind that security of tenure in many societies even today can be and frequently is enjoyed without any concrete evidence of title other than occupation. Security of tenure is a question of fact and, as a fact, it can exist whether there is documentary evidence to prove it or not. It does not necessarily rest on statutory title or on a system of written record. In several countries around the world, security of tenure of land exists without any formal record at all. Security of tenure describes the level of trust or certainty individuals have in the continuous protection of their tenure against 'third parties.' This trust is based on institutional arrangements whether or not backed up by state laws. Unwritten customary rules can provide a normative system that forms the basis for land tenure security because it is reliable, predictable and operational.

The tenure itself may be short, for instance, two months, but if the leaseholder can be certain that he or she will be able to keep the land for the two months, then the tenure is secure. It implies confidence in customary support (thus not necessarily a legal system!) and lack of worry about loss of one's rights. This is the narrowest usage of the term 'tenure security' common among legal professionals. According to Bruce [11], economists often use the term to include the confidence factor noted above and a second element: long duration. Any two-month tenure would be insecure because it is brief. The 'insecurity' used here relates to incentives for investment. Someone with a two-month lease will not plant trees, because there is no expectation of being able to use the wood or the fruits. Place et al. [67] (p. 19) describe land tenure security as follows: 'Land tenure security can be expected to exist when an individual perceives that he or she has rights to a piece of land on a continuous basis, free from imposition or interference from outside sources, as well as the ability to reap the benefits of labor and capital invested in the land either in use or upon transfer to another holder.' They distinguish three components in their definition: breadth, duration and assurance with legal and economic dimensions. Breadth of rights has to do with the robustness of the rights to land and is related to exerting the property right and the costs of enforcing the right. Duration has, in my opinion, mainly an economic dimension and thus is something to take into account when economic dimensions are important for the perception of tenure security. The economic dimensions are important as indicators of land tenure security perceived by peasants in relation to agricultural production. The duration of rights, the possibility of exerting the rights and the costs of enforcing the rights highly determine the choice of exploitation and use of agricultural land but have less to do with tenure security in a legal sense.

Although the relative character of the contents of rights under communal tenure is often seen as an impediment to security of title and thus security of tenure, Bruce [10] shows that, also under communal tenure, market oriented agrarian business could develop. As to security of tenure, the common outlook on western style ownership, only providing for tenure security has changed; and it is recognized that in areas where communal tenure still holds, it provides enough security.

2.2.5 LAND REFORM

The start of a non-evolutionary change in land tenure is often the result of a politically instigated land reform program, most likely supported by donor driven recommendations and funding. When speaking of land reform most people think primarily of agricultural land of which the land tenure changes. Most land reform research focuses on agricultural land, but the tenure of 'land' when used in the wider sense of real property is the subject of change in countries in transition. For urban property the reform is generally straightforward. The tenure changes from state to private individual right holders, and depending on the legislation, a certain amount of money has to be paid to become private owner of rights to urban real property. Changing the tenure of rural land makes most government hesitant to give full ownership rights, and one can observe that, often, conditions are imposed on new owners of rights to (agricultural) land.

Note that there is no general formula for land reform; nor does a 'best' system of land tenure exist. Dorner and Kanel [24] (p. 1) note that: 'Though ideological arguments on the best ways of organizing agriculture continue, no land tenure system can be adjudged best in abstract. Any judgments concerning a particular system must take note of the institutional and technological conditions in the society and the stage at which that society lies in the transformation from an agrarian to an industrial economy. Judgments should also consider what specific groups and individuals in the society are attempting to accomplish.'

The 1970 US-AID Spring Review noted that this strange animal called land reform is an animal that changes its colors, its appearance, its anatomy, and its physiology almost as often as much as other strange animals called democracy, freedom, capitalism. Virtually every author of our analytical papers apparently felt he or she had to define the term. Definitions vary according to whether you favor or oppose land reform, whether you treat it as an ideological symbol, or as an achievable goal, or look at actual results. Although this description does tell how difficult it actually is to determine the contents of land reform, one thing is obvious; land reform aims at changing the existing pattern of land tenure in a society.

It must be noted here that land registration can be a component of a land reform program, and this is highly recommended to avoid future problems and litigation. But land registration is not an element of land reform sine qua non. Since land reform is often politically motivated and setting up and maintaining a land registration is very costly and normally requires outside funding, several land reform projects start without the land registration component in place.

Land reform focuses on changing land tenure and redistribution of property; while in rural areas the distribution of agricultural assets and often the establishment of a system of land registration is also included. Together with a new legislation in which protection of new property right holders and the legitimate authority of public records of property rights to provide improved security in land transfers is regulated. The latter is seen as an important requirement for a land market to evolve to stimulate economic development. Land and agrarian reform puts emphasis on agricultural production. Land tenure is changed so that individual farmers are made responsible for the way in which they till the land expecting increased agricultural production.

2.3 FOOD

2.3.1 FOOD SECURITY

Food is the most important among the basic needs for human existence. Searching for food originally dominated human life. Providing for citizens a perceived food security is one of the main achievements in a society. Many people on earth are not food secure. The distribution of food over the globe is inequitable. With the rapid spreading of news, and the easy sharing of images from all over the world, most people nowadays in 'developed' countries are aware that many countries are food insecure.

During recent decades increased international attention has been given to food security. Donors have invested in food insecure countries, most of which are among the so-called 'developing' or less-developed countries, to improve food security. Foreign involvement often focuses on the distribution and the access to farmland in order to increase agricultural productivity, to increase food security, to improve the quality of rural life, and to reduce rural unrest. It is important to note that food production in itself does not provide for food security, although striving for increased food production is often the first and foremost political activity in food insecure regions. Food transfers can achieve food security and feeding programs, but the long-term political and macro-economic effects of such symptom-oriented interventions can have negative consequences for food security. Through the 1970s, food insecurity was used to increase food production or food availability, often at the national or global level. The work of Sen [73] draws attention to the critical access to food, particularly at the individual and household level, as distinct from food availability. Later a crucial third component was recognized: individuals' ability to utilize the food to which they had access. Hence food availability, access, and utilization are the three general components usually mentioned in definitions of food security today. In 'Determinants of Food Policy: An Attempt to Understand Government Behavior,' Michel Petit [64] demonstrates that countries have food security policies because the elite are threatened, or at the very least embarrassed, by famine. Such policies are implemented when acute problems develop and social order is at risk. But this does not provide a long-term solution. Long-term food security can only be achieved by substantial development of human, material, and technological capabilities giving depth and resilience to broad based food availability and access.

The definition used by the World Bank 'access by all people at all times to sufficient food for an active healthy life' (WB report 1986) [98] does not mention sustainability. Food security must, at least, be sustainable to be qualified as 'sufficient and at all times'. A household cannot be food secure if it has to use its endowment of resources to stay food secure. If a depletion of the non-labor resources takes place, the household is not food secure. So, I prefer a slightly adapted definition: Food security can be defined as sustained and assured access by all social groups and individuals to food adequate in quantity and quality to meet nutritional needs – to live an active and healthy life.

A food system offering security should have the five following characteristics according to the Food and Agricultural Organization of the United Nations (FAO 1979) [28]: 'The capacity to produce, store and import sufficient food to meet basic needs for all. This includes maximum autonomy and self-determination in order to reduce vulnerability. Furthermore it covers reliability, meaning that food supply should know minimal seasonal or cyclical variations, sustainability while protecting the ecological system, and equity in order to give access to adequate food for all social groups.' Some argue that food security is a utopian concept (See Molnar [56]); it reflects an ideal or value-laden state of well being unlikely ever to be fully attained. For many, food security is a moral imperative of the well nourished (Lappe and Collins 1986 [46] and Aiken and LaFolette 1996 [1]). Implementing long-term policies engendering strong institutions, enhancing the widespread availability of sustainable livelihoods and instilling a capacity to withstand food shocks requires a high level of social organization. To achieve food security, markets have to work; property rights to (rural) land must be distributed among the population and policymakers must act also.

Maxwell and Wiebe [55] introduce the term vulnerability for the level of ability to cope with exposures to shocks in food access. Exposures as can be caused by predictable seasonable influences (a dry season for example each year leaving people hungry for a period of time), or by chronic circumstances and during a period of civic unrest or war.

2.3.2 ACCESS, AVAILABILITY, AND UTILIZATION OF FOOD

The definitions for food security as used by the World Bank, the Food and Agriculture Organization (FAO) of the United Nations and the U.S. Agency for International Development (US-AID) (USAID 1992, p. 1) do not explicitly mention two other important determinants of food security; availability and utilization. As far as availability is concerned, the problem has been almost solved according to Table 2.3.2.

Table 2.3.2 Global food availability

	Actual output		Projected output
Output in calories per day	1969-1971	1990-1992	2010
Developed countries	3190	3320	3390
Developing countries	2140	2520	2770
Average for the world	2440	2720	2900

Source: FAO report 1996 [29]

The average supply of dietary energy seems to be sufficient and this makes availability of sufficient food not an overriding constraint anymore. Despite the world food supplies being more than adequate per capita as an average to provide food security for all, altruism is not widespread enough to enable sufficient transfers of food over the globe.

Access to food meaning the ability to acquire available food from earnings and transfers is the major constraint to food security. For most people living in the rural areas of a great number of countries, food availability is closely linked to buying power. Food consumers outnumber food producers in every country. Some researchers argue that raising prices of food, for whatever reason, will first reach the food producers and might even result in increasing food insecurity for the majority of the consumers. However, eventually higher prices will stimulate production and thus benefit everyone in the longer term. The opposite is even truer, lowering food prices will in the short run benefit all consumers, but will eventually lead to diminishing production and increasing food insecurity. I could observe a grim example of that in the 80s in Burkina Faso where grain – a gift from the people of the US, as was clearly marked in English on the bags – was sold at the market in French speaking Ouagadougou. The influx of relatively cheap grain on the market resulted in lower prices for the domestically produced rice, and several domestic producers changed to the more favorably priced cotton instead of food crops. The predictable, but of course never intended, result was a decrease in domestic food production and an increase in food insecurity that could only be alleviated by additional import of food products in the coming years.

The third critical element in food security is utilization. If people do not or cannot utilize food properly, access to sufficient food will not alleviate their food insecurity. This is, for example, the case when food cannot be prepared properly (insufficiently cooked by lack of heating sources); when their only source of water causes intestinal parasites because it is unsanitary water or when they suffer from eating disorders (foreign imported food, or too one-sided diets).

2.3.3 FOOD SECURITY AND LAND REFORM

One of the ways to combat food insecurity is by land or agrarian reform. Land reform research shows that the battle against poverty and the evolution of economic development in developing countries can be more effectively won with equal distribution of assets, than with more equal income distribution. Equal income distribution, by means of social safety nets or redistribution of income by taxes, generally has short term and not long lasting effects for the poorer segments of the population. Besides, it is costly to implement a properly functioning social security system or an income correcting tax system in developing countries; it is also difficult to maintain and to keep it corruption free. In an analysis by Deininger and Squire [20] (p.38-41;1997) almost no association between income inequality and economic growth was found. They note; 'Even when income inequality has worsened, its negative effect on the poor has been more than outweighed by the positive effect of growth.'

Land is the most fundamental resource for agricultural production and many governments of prosperous countries have sought an involvement in increasing agricultural production in developing countries. For this reason, land reform has been promoted by international development agencies the world over. Change of patterns of land tenure has been the starting point for programs aimed at improvement of agricultural production. But there is a danger here. Land reform should not be an isolated activity to combat food insecurity. Emphasis on increased agricultural production and the assumption that this will result in increased food consumption will most likely provide disappointing results. Improving (rural) livelihood and the research on the relationship between food production and food consumption in the specific regional circumstances must be a part of national food policies.

Barraclough [2] (p.130) notes that in countries where rural poverty is widespread and closely associated with power of a land owning class: 'Land reform becomes the only option for improving rural livelihoods rapidly and substantially.' A review of land reform experiences by the author does suggest several tentative conclusions concerning land reform's suitability as a political instrument to alleviate food insecurity. It has been highly effective in some situations and much less so in others. Broader socio-economic and political processes determine the success of implementing land reform because it directly challenges established class relations. The greatest contribution of land reform according to Barraclough, has often not been economic but social and political. Nevertheless, where land reform has been implemented, it almost invariably improved access to food although the longer-term production and distributive impact of land reform is difficult to untangle from the broader process of which land reform is only a part.

The World Food Summit in Rome in 1996 made access to sufficient and adequate food a human right of everyone. This makes food security a legitimate national concern for all countries. A predictable and stable trading system should be a central element in global and national food security. Some countries suffer from high national production costs of food. Under ordinary circumstances, it would have been most cost efficient to rely entirely on the world market in order to provide food for the population of these countries. Based on historic experience and due to the uncertainty associated with future international supplies and prices, national production policies will always be a central element in national food security policy. But as a difficult supply situation might be long-term, a national stocking in high cost countries can only partly compensate for such a risk. The risk of a rupture in supplies, as a result of war or insurgency or a crisis in peacetime (ecological disasters, diseases in plants and animals, radioactive fallout), can cause substantial changes in international demand and supply. Even if these risks are small, policies to secure food supply could be seen as insurance, and the public costs of higher national production are a function of the population's risk aversion and its willingness to pay for 'the insurance.'

2.3.4 PROSPERITY FOCUS AND FOOD SECURITY FOCUS IN LAND REFORM

When the goal of land reform is primarily to bring about a development of the land market to stimulate economic and prosperity development, such a land reform can be categorized as a land reform aimed at prosperity. As a result of national revolutions driven by populist forces, other land reforms were initiated as a response by the government to ensure food production and to avoid food insecurity. In this type of land reform, alleviating food insecurity is the main aim, often combined with the goal to improve rural living standards.

Countries in transition do primarily seek economic development because of disappointing results of the communist doctrine in society. Nevertheless, it seems that in several countries in transition improvement in food production is at least as important. The availability of sufficient domestically produced food is a matter of national independence and a safeguard against food insecurity among the population. It is generally difficult to find a clearly documented motive for land reform in donor assisted projects, which only makes the consulting in projects more difficult. The development of a model to assess the progress of a land reform project will be done while using the two separate goals. However, it will be shown that it is possible to combine both paradigms into one model, in which the various elements or steps may have slightly different accents, but also show remarkable similarities.

2.4 NON-EVOLUTIONARY CHANGE

2.4.1 INSTITUTIONS

Institutions are the established rules and customary relationships of a social organization. They govern the behavioral relations among individuals or groups as a set of constraints. Changing institutions means changing the social organization. Several reasons can be found in literature as to why governments embark on such an adventure. It is an adventure. Experience shows that the results are difficult to predict and the success of land reform projects is dependent on several other complementary factors and measures that should be implemented as well. With land reform an important problem is that, as a major intervention in the society, it does not deliver quick results. It takes at least half a generation to build up a farm but it takes a full generation to see the results of land reform, let alone what it takes to restructure a society. In this book I will not attempt to answer the question of what is the most appropriate institution to combat food insecurity. Nor will I try to formulate the best institutional arrangement to guarantee land tenure security. Should land be privately, cooperatively, or state owned? Should agricultural production and, in particular food production, be organized in private farms, cooperatives or collectives? Is a market economy the best way to improve economic development or must central planning be applied in famine prone regions? I am convinced that only dogmatic answers exist and no straightforward pragmatic solution can ever be offered.

Nevertheless, I certainly will encourage land reform. Natural resources should not lay wasted or should not be insufficiently used. It is hard to accept that some of the world population lives with food shortages and threat of famines and that nothing might be done to alleviate their hardship. It is interesting to speculate about a utopian model and discover possible steps that can be taken in the real world toward this utopian concept. The result of research on land reform and food production is that achievement of food security requires social transformations. The model I will develop starts with institutional change, change of rules and non-evolutionary change of customary relationships. Many governments have followed this path.

2.4.2 LAND REGISTRATION AND LAND TITLING

Changing legislation to introduce western style land tenure will encounter the question of whether or not to introduce land registration and land titling. Land registration is the official recording of legally recognized interests in land and is usually part of a cadastral system. Knowledge and public record of land tenure in several modern societies is relatively simple because of the recording of the tenure in registers. The situation becomes more complicated where individual rights to land are rooted in local customs or in customary rules. Local customs are generally not documented but are known to inhabitants of a certain region or village. There can be many customs governing the use and the access to land and these customs certainly do not always easily translate into Western concepts of legislation or even in the conceptual interpretative frame of Western experts and advisors. Nevertheless, these rights are respected and are of great importance for local communities and indigenous people. Their non-perceptibility for the non-trained Western mind make them easily overlooked in the process of drawing new 'Western style' legislation, leaving indigenous people with uncertainty about their rights and causing insecurity of tenure for them. (See on this subject Von Benda-Beckmann [3] and [5], Carter [13], Doolittle [26], Hoekema [40], Lastarria [47], Lynch et al [53], Platteau [65], Tshuma [90], Wheeler [97] and many others).

Platteau [66] suggests that a change in land tenure might be pursued because there is a doctrine of a misfit between embodied tenure systems and the requirement of agricultural production. If this argument is followed, a drastic alteration of customary land rights under supervision of determined authorities is a viable option. But the World Bank endorses another more dynamic doctrine according to Platteau. It denies the empirical validity of this type of state intervention, but promotes a more or less autonomous evolution of indigenous land rights under pressures of market forces, with government guidance and support to formalize and consolidate the newly emerging land tenure system. One pre-condition Platteau finds, is that the state needs to implement a land registration and titling program without jeopardizing sufficient access to land for the mass of land tillers.

Western style registration requires clearly described rights related to surveyed physical plots of land and distinguished from other plots of land to which different rights are attached. In modern societies the boundaries between real properties are recorded in Land Information Systems and Land Registration Systems. These are the institutions and the materialization of the political decisions on the very existence of invisible lines that form the boundary of real property ownership between two or more owners. Land Information Systems have to be set up to provide publicity of invisible lines, to mark them on maps and to describe the rights that go with them in registers or documents. However, in several societies rights to land are respected and secured without any form of Land Information System or Land Registration System. Bruce Chatwin [16] gives in 'The Song Lines' an account of the way Aborigines in Australia know the boundaries of their land with certain lines of ancestral songs. The song describes the land and, by traveling over the land while chanting the song, makes the land recognizable for aborigines. Chatwin discovered that when he was normally driving over the land accompanied by an aboriginal male, the native man was made to chant the ancestral song at a breathtaking speed, but when the car was slowed down to almost walking speed, the song changed into more normal 'singing.' Knowing the song and the lines of the song that are yours, gave aborigines their titles to the land.

2.4.3. LAND REGISTRATION AND LAND DATA

Land tends to be forever, one cannot hide, or as a rule, destroy it completely. Ownership of rights to land – when duly protected – can give mankind the feeling of long lasting security. The requirement of security demands careful managing in the administration of data about the plots of land the rights refer to. Although recorded on paper or in electronic files, the property should be directly related with the clods of earth, the bricks and the buildings of which it consists. An accurate survey of the property by a professional surveyor as part of the description in the records and a reliable administration should give this guarantee. For a modern computerized land registration a primary condition is integrity of data. The earlier mentioned 'Who, What, How much, When, and Where' should translate into data that seamlessly provide answers to these questions without ambiguity and contradictions. Increasing use of computers for managing land related data makes it relatively easy to carry out cross checks on data on land. In several modern societies actual cross checks between different land registration systems are used as a means to maintain or restore the integrity of the data (see also 5.3). The requirement of integrity of land-related data is not always understood well. In several Eastern European countries, for example, under communist rule, land was treated as an area simply on paper. One piece of land could be exchanged for another by writing only numbers in registers. The land record was not connected anymore with the clods of earth of which it originally consisted, thus creating invisible land. In many cases this practice becomes a source of conflicts and uncertainty when land is returned to original owners or redistributed on the bases of the recorded size.

In 'The Elasticity of Land' by Katherine Verdery [96] (p. 1083) an account of this practice can be found (in Transylvania a region in Central-Romania):

> In the village of Vlaicu one clerk was a notorious drunk and he could readily be persuaded for a bottle of brandy, to reduce the recorded size of one's holdings. The system used by the government was to set quotas to be produced and handed over to the state by farmers depending on the size of their farm, quotas whose magnitude increased exponentially with the size of the holding. Sizes of holdings were based on village registers (not on a Cadastre). Any holding thus dipped in brandy shrank, invalidating the area reported in the 1950s. (One farmer could show seven different recorded figures for the size of the farm, each figure responding to a particular need of the time, and each as the result of liberal applications of brandy). Such shrinkages have effects in the present, as owners of shrunken fields often find it difficult now to stretch them back out to their former dimensions. But, this situation gives way for officials (as insiders) to use the remaining land for their own purposes.

CHAPTER 3

THE KYRGYZ REPUBLIC[1]

3.1 KYRGYZSTAN

3.1.1 GEOGRAPHY AND DEMOGRAPHY

The Kyrgyz Republic is an independent Republic; a small land-locked country in Central Asia with a population of 4.8 million, 60 per cent of it rural. It borders Kazakhstan, Uzbekistan, Tajikistan, and China's Xinjiang province. It encompasses 198,500 square kilometers (76,641 sq. mi.) of territory. Administratively, the Kyrgyz Republic has 7 regions (oblasts)[2] and within each oblast a number of rayons (districts), 42 in total. Unlike Uzbekistan and Kazakhstan, two of its neighboring countries, the Kyrgyz Republic lacks oil resources and depends heavily on natural gas imports from Uzbekistan. Bishkek, the capital of the Kyrgyz Republic, is situated in the North of the country. The Kyrgyz Republic stretches between 69 to 80 degrees East longitude and 39 and 43 North latitude. Most of what is now the Kyrgyz Republic became a so-called autonomous district on 14 October 1924 and a dependent Republic in the Union of Soviet Republics on 1 February 1926. It joined the USSR as a Union Republic on 5 December 1936 and declared itself an independent sovereign state on 31 August 1991.

The Kyrgyz Republic is a mountainous country with high peaks and several mountain ranges, Mount Pobeda at 7.439 meters (24,406 feet) is the highest peak in the country. Ninety per cent of its territory lies at least 1.000 meters (3,300 feet) above sea level. Only 28 per cent of the total territory has an altitude relatively favorable for population and land cultivation, and more than 60 per cent of it is rough terrain. The Kyrgyz Republic has an extremely limited resource of useable land, while the harsh continental climate and extreme range of altitudes increase considerably the basic energy costs required to maintain minimum living standards. Large parts of the territory are difficult to cultivate with unstable yields. Agriculture is possible only in the lower areas of the country in the valleys and

---

[1] Both the names Kyrgyzstan and the Kyrgyz Republic are officially used.

[2] Until 1999 the Kyrgyz Republic had six oblasts: Chui, Talas, Djalal-Abad, Osh, Naryn, Issyk-Kyll oblasts and a special territory of the capital Bishkek (formerly Frunze). The seventh, and smallest, oblast being Batken oblast, was established in November 1999 after a small-scale war there between government troops and Islamic fundamentalists infiltrating the Kyrgyz Republic from neighboring Tadjikistan and Afghanistan. It reduces the size of the Osh oblast.

generally requires irrigation because of the dry climate. Transport in the country is difficult due to the highly mountainous terrain with the majority of roads in poor condition. The railway infrastructure of the Kyrgyz Republic is very limited; the only passenger line of some importance is between the capital Bishkek eastward to the city of Balykchy at Lake Issyk-Kul. That lake is the main Kyrgyz vacation resort. Westward from Bishkek a railway line connects the capital of the Kyrgyz Republic via the towns of Kara-Balta and Taraz (formerly Djambyl) with the capital of Uzbekistan, Tashkent. The second largest city in the country, Osh, has a railway freight connection with cities in neighboring Uzbekistan. A road trip between Bishkek and Osh takes fifteen to sixteen hours of driving time through various mountain passes (a new road is currently under construction and will reduce driving time). Positioned in the heart of the Asian continent, the country's geographical location is also rather unfavorable and far removed from harbors and shipping lanes. Branches of the great silk route run through the Kyrgyz Republic.

In 2000 there were 4,850,700 people permanently living in the Kyrgyz Republic of whom 35.3 per cent live in urban and 64.7 per cent in rural areas. During the years of newly gained independence, population increased with 50,000 per annum (before independence the annual average growth was 80,000) and almost 90 per cent of this growth came in the rural population. The Kyrgyz Republic has become a more mono-ethnic country as shown in Table 3.1.1:

Table 3.1.1 Ethnicity of the Kyrgyz population

Percentage of the total population	1990	2000
Ethnic Kyrgyz	52.4%	64.9%
Ethnic Russians	21.5%	12.5%
Ethnic Germans	2.4%	0.4%
Others (Byelorussias, Tatars, Ukraines etc.)	23.7%	22.2%

Source: First National Census and TCA of 01-11-01

According to the statistics, the birthrate has decreased from 29.4 per cent to 21.4 per cent over the last ten years, with a tendency toward smaller families. From the viewpoint of gender there are slightly more women than men (respectively 50.6 per cent and 49.4 per cent).

The Government of the Kyrgyz Republic is open to experimentation and to engaging international expertise in reforming the economy. The Kyrgyz Republic has obtained real economic assistance – more per capita than any state in Central Asia, or even in the CIS. Currently, more than 1,500 NGOs (Non Governmental Organizations) have registered in the Kyrgyz Republic focusing on social, economic, and humanitarian issues.

A privatization program for the use (not all real property was given into ownership) of real property started in 1991. The tenure of apartments and dwelling houses was transferred to private individual owners who became private owners of the property. An interesting and confusing feature of privatization of apartments was that the apartments became privately owned, but that the apartment building itself remained property of 'Minkomkhoz' to be managed by the Municipal Property Administration. One of the difficult problems to solve, due to lack of funds with Minkomkhoz (most of its revenues disappeared after privatization), is to properly maintain and clean the building, the commonly used areas, the stairways, and elevators. The new private apartment owners hardly feel responsible for those areas, but they should be urged to solve the problem together and take a shared responsibility.

For land designated for agriculture a different transfer of tenure took place. That land (the 'Ugodia') was distributed generally among the rural population by issuing land shares, giving right to exclusive long term or even permanent use. Eligibility for land shares was originally limited to people living and working on state and collective farms only. The land shares were only paper shares and did not correspond with actual pieces of land. All the 'Ugodia' land remained in State ownership.

The introduction of the local currency (the Kyrgyz som) in 1993 has been important in bringing down inflation from the destructive hyperinflation level of 1,259 per cent in 1992 and 1,210 per cent in 1993 to 450 per cent in 1994 and about 50 per cent in 1995. An October 1998 referendum granted private ownership of land and ensured legal protection for a free press and freedom of expression – another first in the region, as well as in the CIS. The Kyrgyz Republic was the first state in the CIS to enter the World Trade Organization (WTO). Since this event, the Uzbekistan and Kazakhstan customs officials have been raising tariff rates. Borders between Central Asian republics have long been problematic. Tensions exist between the villages on the Kyrgyz and Tajik side of the border regarding the allocation of land and water. Any deterioration in relations between the ethnic Kyrgyz and the ethnic Uzbek populations in southern Kyrgyzstan is a concern; in 1990, riots over irrigated lands erupted between the two groups, resulting in over 200 fatalities.

A weak economy, massive unemployment and poverty (especially in rural areas), and increased crime and corruption are the greatest causes of social instability in the country. The spectacular mountains and beauty of the countryside in the Kyrgyz Republic offers a potential for tourism, but it remains doubtful that the proper infrastructure can be developed to attract foreign tourists in large numbers.

3.1.2 IMPORTANCE OF AGRICULTURE

The most radical reform in the Kyrgyz Republic is the privatization of land because of the dominantly economic significance of agriculture in the country. Conflicts arose in the Chui Oblast during experimenting in pilot projects with privatization. There were false or real rumors about privileges for the well connected, land picking by insiders (because of the 'elasticity' of land some insiders could indeed manipulate documents) and priority treatment for the former elite. As a result, the land privatization process has been more carefully implemented in the Osh and Djallal-Abad Oblasts, especially in regions with ethnically mixed populations. Rumors of ethnic discrimination (real or imagined) would have easily provoked conflict. The distribution of land and water are considered the main reasons for potential conflict in the Southern part of the Kyrgyz Republic.[3] There is a general concern that the risk for conflict will increase once private land ownership is fully introduced. Discussions between international, governmental, and non-governmental organizations and farmers have shown that existing laws, rules, and regulations are sometimes confusing and that the farmers do not always understand them.

As mentioned earlier, the Kyrgyz Republic is dominantly an agrarian country with the most important sector in the Kyrgyz Republic being agriculture and agriculture-related industries. During the Soviet period, the state and collective farms (sovkhozy and kolkhozy) were ineffective, centrally planned, and heavily subsidized. Since independence (1991), the socioeconomic crisis has had more impact on industry than on agriculture. Kolkhozy and sovkhozy were liquidated without preparation and in an authoritarian way. Liberalization of agricultural land policy and de-collectivization were accompanied by a decline in agricultural production. The majority of rural people were unable to generate income through agricultural activities. Many of them migrated to cities. Nevertheless, over 60 per cent of the population still lives in rural areas, and about half of the able-bodied population is engaged in the agricultural sector. The average income in agriculture (about 200 Kyrgyz som, or, 50 US$ monthly) is three times lower than that in industry and construction. It is the lowest among all categories of working people. Agriculture will remain the engine of growth and the main source of household income in the foreseeable future, particularly in the rural areas where most of the population resides. In 1996 agriculture accounted for 48 per cent of the Gross Domestic Product (GDP) and 49 per cent of the employment. Agriculture and agro-industry constituted 38 per cent of exports and 23 per cent of imports. The share of food in the household budget is rising; in 1990 before independence, it was around 30 per cent and in 1996 this had risen to 57 per cent. Agricultural production bottomed out in 1995 but grew over ten per cent in 1996 and 1997. Crop production has increased more than livestock production, which still remains depressed. One of the reasons for this is that livestock can easily be distributed and sold for cash or used for private consumption in times of reduced food supplies. Another problem with statistical information on livestock is that distribution among private farmers most likely results in quite some undercounting in statistics.

[3] In June 1990 – before land reform and independence – ethnic tensions erupted in Osh oblast, with more than 200 people killed, over the distribution of water in this part of the Ferghana Valley where the majority of the people is Uzbek.

3.1.3 ECONOMIC TRENDS

After the declaration of independence, the Kyrgyz Republic embarked on a reform program aimed at creating a market economy. Prices were liberated, most capital controls were eliminated and the government introduced a liberal trade regime. The Kyrgyz Republic was the first of the Newly Independent States (NIS) in the region to present the national currency (the Kyrgyz Som) as convertible. This brought progress in establishing macro-economic stability. Although the GDP saw a dramatic decline during the first years of independence, it started to increase in 1995. As in many of the other Newly Independent States, the Kyrgyz Republic has faced continued financial problems; the national budget has been relying on international donor aid and World Bank financing. In 1998 an enhanced structural adjustment facility agreement with the IMF was reached.
Macroeconomic and financial improvement in the last years of the nineties has been less than expected.

The negative trend has been largely due to the Russian crisis resulting, among others, in decreasing imports from Russia of agricultural assets and lower export levels to the still dominant Russian market. The development of the rate of exchange between the Kyrgyz Som and the US Dollar as depicted in Figure 3.1.3 reflects this trend (bearing in mind that the US dollar showed an international appreciation of around ten per cent in the final months of 1999).

Exchange rate KGS/US $	
1993/1994	08.04
1995/1996	11.15
1996/1997	17.38
1999/2000	47.07

Figure 3.1.3 Rate of exchange between Kyrgyz Som and US Dollar

An indication for economic development in the Kyrgyz Republic is the development of the number of transactions in real property in the capital Bishkek. However, it should be borne in mind that it is impossible to give the 'normal' or expected level of transactions in a city like Bishkek because of the relative short time of independence and the existence of a market for real property. The numbers give an indication and not more. To eliminate most of the monthly variations, Table 1.3.1 uses six-month averages expressed per month.

The table is based on data, which I collected from a source at the Bishkek BTI office. It shows the date and under that the average number of transactions registered at the BTI office (The number 1744 under 01/07 – 01 July – represents the average number of transactions between April 1, 1999 and October 1, 1999):

Table 3.1.3 Number of real property transfers in Bishkek

1998						1999		
01/07	01/08	01/09	01/10	01/11	01/12	01/01	01/02	01/03
1744	1722	1800	1807	1693	1634	1643	1600	1568
1999 (cont.)								
01/04	01/05	01/06	01/07	01/08	01/09	01/10	01/11	01/12
1500	1589	1530	1484	1386	1277	1176	991	995

Source: BTI office Bishkek

The six-months average number of transactions in real property in Bishkek, with a population of over 600.000 people, decreases from a level of around 1700 - 1800 in mid 1998 (the first time these data were available in computerized form) to just under a 1000 at the end of 1999.

It is interesting to note here that the average life expectancy in Bishkek is around 60 years. There are 600,000 inhabitants in the capital generally living in apartments for which they have a registered inheritable right of use (or newly acquired ownership rights), the number of transactions resulting from inheritances could easily be around 3,000 - 5,000 per year or several hundreds per month at an average. With less than 1,000 transactions monthly around the change of the millennium, this indicates that economic transactions of real property in the capital Bishkek not being for inheritance, mortgage, or first time registration, had almost come to a standstill by the beginning of 2000. Registration officials at the Bishkek BTI registration office have confirmed this conclusion. I was told that most of the registered transactions resulted from inheritances, second were first time registrations (citizens having acquired a ownership rights to real property and now processing an application under the new rules or now able to pay the fees involved for registration).

Inflation trends in the Kyrgyz Republic have been dramatic in the first years of independence, but are more or less under control by now. The actual rate of inflation in 1998 was less than 20 per cent, but showed a dramatic increase in 1999 (one of the most difficult years for the national currency) to almost 40 per cent. But the newspaper 'Slovo Kyrgyzstana' published on 24 February 2000, states that one of the key macro-economic objectives of the government and the National Bank of the Kyrgyz Republic is to maintain the rate of inflation in 2000 under 20 per cent.

The population growth is, in particular, negatively influenced by migration of ethnic Russians out of the country during 1998 and 1999. There is a general tendency to discriminate against ethnic Russians in employment in newly created institutions and enterprises. However, this does not yet go as far as in neighboring Uzbekistan where all government officials (also the ethnic Russians among them) were obliged to master the Uzbek language by 1 April 2000 in order to keep their jobs. Interesting is to note that the statistics suggest that migration from rural areas to urban areas in the Kyrgyz Republic is, as a whole, negative. It has to be borne in mind, however, that there has been a considerable migration of ethnic Russians – mainly urban dwellers – out of the country. Obviously the influx of ethnic Kyrgyz to the cities could not make up for that. In 1999 the population of the Kyrgyz Republic increased over 13 per cent compared with 1989. Urban population growth was four per cent and the rural population grew with 19 per cent. There is a trend of migration from regional cities to rural areas and to the capital. The increase in the population of Bishkek (including its suburbs) was more than 25 per cent between 1998 and 1999 according to 'Slovo Kyrgyzstana.'

3.1.4 FOOD AND AGRICULTURAL PRODUCTION

At independence the Kyrgyz Republic inherited a pattern of dependence on large food imports from other FSU Republics, mainly wheat and sugar. As the 1999 report on National Food Security Policy [44] describes, the country has successfully met the challenge of achieving basic national food sufficiency in the eight years since independence. In monitoring the food security situation in the Kyrgyz Republic, both wheat production and wheat trade are important indicators because bread is the basic food commodity. Since independence, wheat production has dropped to about 650,000 tons per year in 1994 and 1995; thereafter, the wheat production policy resulted in a current production level of 1,250,000 tons per year while imports were reduced to almost nil. While living in the Kyrgyz Republic it was interesting to observe how much emphasis was put on wheat production. It was an almost daily news item on the national television during the prime time of news broadcasts.

In 1990 just before reform, livestock and livestock products accounted for almost 60 per cent of the nations' gross value of agricultural products. Cultivated land (winter wheat, barley, maize, winter barley, spring wheat, and non grain crops in the southwest tobacco, cotton, fruits, and vegetables) encompassed an area of around 1,500 million ha (± 3,750 million acres), summer and winter pastures an area of around 9 million ha (± 22.5 million acres). In 1993 the per capita gross domestic product was estimated at an all time low of 680 $US.

Agricultural production shifted steadily to (almost) self-sufficiency since 1990. An economic recovery seemed to start in 1995. Annual inflation was 1,000 per cent in 1993, 450 per cent in 1994 and in 1995 about 50 per cent. Primary agriculture employs about 1/3 of the labor force and accounts also for 1/3 of the GDP. In early 1994 agricultural pricing was liberated, but there was no immediate response. In 1995 the interest rate was about 30 per cent yearly and institutional credit was available, but a severe drought masked any evidence of improved productivity (Land Tenure Center research paper # 128) [8]. The year 1995 seemed a turning point in economic development, but the economic recovery stalled. Current reports neither do show (yet) a significant recovery of the economy nor a considerable economic development.

Some statistics need to be examined in detail and compared with other data. For example statistics show that wheat production has grown 164 per cent between 1990 and 1997 due to a 185 per cent increase in sown area. But average yields have declined 8 per cent. An expansion of wheat area replaced other crops such as barley, corn and fodder. Although justifiable during the first years of transition to build up a situation of self-sufficiency with this staple food that is easy to store for longer periods, one can question a continuation of the expansion of wheat production. With a limited land base, the Kyrgyz Republic cannot afford to allocate almost half of its total sown area to one crop that is not highly competitive (as compared to crops like potatoes, vegetables, sugar beets, oilseeds, and cotton).

3.1.5 FOOD SECURITY IN THE KYRGYZ REPUBLIC

The report of the National Food Security Policy estimates a national wheat surplus of around 300,000 tons per year after 1998 if agricultural production is normal, but as far as I could find out, that surplus never materialized. Official exports are reported to be 13,000 tons, but there is evidence of (unofficial) export to Tajikistan where wheat prices are considerably higher than in the Kyrgyz Republic and some border trade with Uzbekistan and Kazakhstan. All wheat flour consumed in the country originates from domestically milled grain, which is done partly in former kolkhozy, and partly by a large number of smaller mills. As far as observed in the capital, bread is available daily everywhere at affordable prices (3-6 Kyrgyz som per loaf, or less than around 0.07 - 0.15 US$). The 'Times of Central Asia' [88] reported in April 2000 that the forecast grain harvest for 2000 was 1,145 million tons, which spurred the Ministry of Agriculture to take some urgent measures because national food security required 1,260 million tons of grain for 2000.

As for the second basic commodity in the Kyrgyz diet, mutton and beef, there seems to be sufficient quantities available to meet basic nutritional requirements (National Food Security Report 1999). The negative effect of the decline in official livestock numbers – it is supposed that the privatization has lead to some undercounting in the official numbers – since independence is somewhat compensated for by advantages. The features of Soviet husbandry of overgrazing and overfeeding (with heavily subsidized grain) represented a challenge to human food security. In that respect, the decline in livestock numbers in the Kyrgyz Republic can be seen as a positive development because it diminishes over exploitation and overgrazing of the nation's pasture lands. Overall, the country has become self-sufficient in wheat and wheat flour, and also in meat and meat products. There is a theoretical buffer due to some surplus export to meet possibly less favorable harvests in future years. The biggest risk is that price, which influenced by the free market policy, might rise as a result of demand from neighboring Tajikistan to reach a price level above an affordable one for the poorer segment of the Kyrgyz population.

Contrary to the national level, household food security has worsened since independence especially in the lower income households. A demographic trend with high birthrates has recently been slowed down by an increasing mortality rate. Under the Soviet system social benefits were guaranteed to every citizen, regardless of economic or financial cost. Under the rules of a free market economy, social benefits are decreasing rapidly resulting in a decrease of industrial production because of lack of demand, also causing widespread unemployment. The rapid fall in living standards creates an increasing awareness at the Government level, resulting in a socially oriented policy. The effects of decreased household income and increased sharing of food supply give insufficient purchasing power for poor families, and thus problems to maintain an adequate food intake.

The country's food security situation is mainly determined by two factors: namely, the dominant position of agriculture in the macro economic picture and, secondly, the isolated geographic situation of the country. The latter hinders internal logistics and makes external transport links dependent on neighboring republics. Import and export are very sensitive to variations in energy prices because of its effect on transportation costs. Although the country, on a national scale, is almost self sufficient (except for sugar imports), importation will be very expensive in times of failing harvest, requiring high subsidies by the government. However, that would be unaffordable and the country would have to rely on food aid, bearing in it the danger of creating disincentives for local production. The result could be a rapidly developing downward spiral of food security.
Also the over-emphasis on grain production as the main crop and the subsequent one-sided use of arable land could result in deterioration of land, threatening land resource conservation.

3.1.6 FOOD SECURITY POLICY IN THE KYRGYZ REPUBLIC

During a National Food Security Policy Seminar in Bishkek in July 1999 the policy toward food security was unveiled. The core of the government's policy will be to develop the agricultural potential of the country to ensure that all people have access to adequate food at all times, in all regions and in all households. This policy is based on the four basic principles of food security as they were formulated in Bishkek, i.e.:

- Availability (from domestic production, from stock or from imports)
- Stability (daily food needs must not suffer sudden or important changes)
- Proper use (assurance that food is safe, of acceptable quality and apply to balanced nutritional habits)
- Accessibility (both in physical terms as well as in terms of household acquisition power)

The four principles should apply everywhere at all times. So it is essential for the government to verify that people's food security is assured at three levels of concern: the national, regional and household level.

Four major priority policy elements were selected on the basis of primary and direct relevance to the four food security principles. These four policy elements are:

- Agriculture: Promote an adequate quantity of basic domestic crop and animal production at competitive cost against imports and strongly stimulate the economic growth of the agricultural sector. It should be made the pulling force for the overall development process of the country. Promote production of food commodities for which the country has comparative advantages and other measures in direct support of improving the long-term competitiveness of Kyrgyz agriculture both in domestic and export markets. Land and agrarian reform, crop and livestock production, rural finance, extension services, natural resources management, reform of agro-industries, institutional reform in the Ministry of Agriculture and seed development are key policy issues included in this element.
- Marketing: Stimulate internal and external trade in farm produce and processed food items. A key policy issue is to support the overall effort to remove physical barriers (transport infrastructure).
- Social protection and health care: Guarantee that all people at all socio-economic levels have access to basic and healthy food. Key policy issues are to support the overall efforts aimed at employment/income generation (industrial restructuring, private sector development etc.)
- Macro-economy and public finance: Create and maintain a macro-economic and public finance environment favorable to ensure food security to all citizens.

The seminar report concludes that a structural food security situation in the Kyrgyz Republic is still non-existent: 'What exists is a volatile and basic national food security situation with imbalances at regional level, and a high and growing occurrence of food insecurity at household level. The most urgent issue for the Kyrgyz government is to achieve structural food security during the years to come.' The government of the Kyrgyz Republic acknowledges that the path toward reaching structural food security is closely interrelated with the overall economic development of the country. In term, the selected priority policy elements cannot be isolated and should be seen as part of an integrated and coordinated reform effort. Priority areas include:

- The emergence of commercially viable farms through consolidation of the present fragmented structures created through the process of land reform, next to and above the layer of small-scale subsistence farming (post privatization restructuring);

- Further gradual diversification into products with a longer-term and more sustainable competitive market positioning both on the domestic and export markets.

For the government of the Kyrgyz Republic this has been translated into the following policy issues:

Land and agrarian reform

Establishment in the long-term of a secure and well-functioning market in land and other immovable assets based on free market principles. Through stimulating the process of farm restructuring, consolidation and development of commercial transactions in the sector will contribute to the overall economic development of the agricultural sector.

The results of the irrigation strategy to be ready by 2000 to be taken into consideration in further land reform developments.

Agricultural marketing

Through stimulating the development of well-performing agricultural commodities, markets facilitate agricultural recovery and growth, and raise rural incomes.

Financing private rural enterprises

Through the establishment of a sustainable system of mostly private rural finance, increase the efficiency and profitability of the agricultural sector and the living standard of the rural population

Extension services for crop and livestock production

Through technical support by the Ministry of Agriculture, promote farm reform and adaptation of private rural operators to market economy requirements and to extend the knowledge and advice through private agencies.

Management of natural Resources

Set rigid standards to avoid overexploitation of the three basic natural resources, farmland, water and range land for sustainable domestic food production, while optimizing their use in order to maintain food stability during future years. A policy of preservation of the nation's vast natural capital is considered to be a guarantee of a continuously stable National Food Balance.

Agro-industries

To support the development of a competitive private food processing industry in the country: to guarantee food is processed, conditioned and preserved properly to contribute to import substitution and to take, in the longer term, full advantage of the export potential of the sector.

Institutional reform in the Ministry of Agriculture (and Water Resources; MAWR)

To continue the process of institutional reform in the MAWR in conformity with the Government free market policy.

Seed development

> To support the development of available domestic seed industry which will provide farmers with a range of quality seed and develop the possibility of exports.

Furthermore, the government will pursue policy issues directed at establishing a sustainable social safety net: Provide a minimum guaranteed income to vulnerable groups, institute balanced nutritional habits among the population and ensure that accessible and available locally produced and imported food commodities are safe, healthy, and in conformity with common international quality standards.

The overall policy of the government is to ensure permanent food security by unifying and coordinating monitoring instruments and study the feasibility of a national food reserve. By consolidating the overall economic reform program, a macro-economic environment will be in place to enhance or maintain food security. Key pillars are the budget and monetary policy, trade and customs policy and fiscal policy.

The national report concludes that the Government's National Food Security Policy is based on the following major strategy components:

- Privatization of property of all means of production, including land;
- Promoting the emergence of a class of true rural proprietors;
- De-monopolization and decentralization;
- Development of a demand- and offer-driven market for means of production, such as investment (including real estate), financial and credit resources, working capital, and labor;
- Updating of the legislative framework to introduce open competition in all spheres of the economy;
- Organizing tax collection so as to ensure sufficient means to the revenue part of the budget in support of the food security policy measures;
- Creating or modernizing and adapting its tools for emergency preparedness.

A World Bank report on Strategy for Rural Growth and Poverty Alleviation for the Kyrgyz Republic (WB discussion paper # 394) [58] (p. 1) states; 'In addition to creating a policy environment that provides positive incentives to the private sector, a handful of other factors also have important implications for efforts to increase growth and improve the productivity, profitability, and sustainability of agriculture. These relate to the country's highly diverse and less favorable agro-ecological conditions; low rainfall and irrigation-dependent crop agriculture (over 80 per cent of arable land is irrigated); water logging; salinity; nutrient-deficiency, and erosion in soils problems; overgrazing and poor management of pasture land (45 per cent of the total land area); inadequate number of all-weather roads and lack of efficient transport network; long distances to world markets; and the legacy of the centralized planning, resource allocation, input distribution, and state procurement of agricultural output.'

More than anything else it shows that there is still a long way to go before the population in the Kyrgyz Republic will be food secure. There are a number of conditions that will determine the possible implementation of the food security policy. The most important ones are favorable harvests for several years, increasing resources for the government to fund the policy, and substantial donor aid.

3.1.7 RURAL LIVING IN THE KYRGYZ REPUBLIC

The Kyrgyz people originally were herdsmen. They used the vast mountainous pastureland as grazing land for their herds; the lower parts of the mountain slopes in the wintertime and the higher parts in the summer, living a nomadic life in their yurts (wooden framed 'tents'). The yurt is such an important cultural element in Kyrgyz heritage that its characteristic open top is represented in the national flag. Many valleys in the Southern parts of the country are not the dominant domains of the Kyrgyz. This is Uzbek country, people traditionally more inclined to agriculture and horticulture, resulting in some Uzbek enclaves in Southern Kyrgyzstan. Nevertheless, it is the limited number of valley regions of Kyrgyzstan that have the highest population density and are intensively used for agriculture and horticulture by Kyrgyz citizens of whom several have an Uzbek heritage (Uzbek is one of the languages in school curricula in the South).

Of the Kyrgyz population about 75 per cent is rural (excluding Bishkek) and almost two-thirds of the rural population lives below the poverty line. Poverty allocation is the second most important development challenge (after agricultural improvement) for the nation, and agricultural and rural development must lead the effort (WB paper # 394) [58]. Poverty has increased during the transition period. Poverty is more severe in rural areas in the Southern oblasts. Indicators of declining living standards are the increase in the incidence of malnutrition, particularly among children, the greater difficulty of residents in rural areas in receiving pensions and other social benefits, in part because of the inadequate banking system in rural areas. The Kyrgyz government has recognized the poverty problem and has declared 1998 'the year of rural development and fighting poverty.' It launched the National Program for Poverty Alleviation, which seeks to increase employment, improve access to basic social services, improve the targeting of social assistance, and ensure the timely payment of pensions. The program stated that the development of an efficient agricultural sector is fundamental to the alleviation of rural poverty.

Zvi Lerman notes in 'Agricultural Land Ownership in Transitional Economies' (1994 edited by Gene Wunderlich) [49] p.54-57):

> Socialist agriculture was characterized by large collective and state farms, which were introduced in the Soviet Union mainly in the 1930s and extended to the dependent Republics (like the Kyrgyz Republic). These agricultural production units evolved into core institutions regulating virtually all of rural life, from political and civil order to social services, welfare and retail trade. From the beginning the collective or state farm was more than just a production unit; it also served as local government and social community. The chairs of kolkhozy controlled the budgets for schools, clubs, roads, and similar infrastructure and facilities. Resident permits and internal passports

were issued to and held by farm authorities so that until the late 1950s peasants could not leave without the chair's permission. Farms, not the local communities, designate building lots and household plots on which members can keep livestock and/or grow subsistence crops for their households. The yields of these auxiliary plots tend to be a great deal higher than on former collective and state farms, not only because this land grows higher-value crops and is better tended, but also because the farm management can, if it wishes, permit petty pilfering of inputs from the collective. The situation in the Kyrgyz Republic on most State farms in the post World War II era is similar to the situation in Russia as described by VanAtta in 1994 [95] (p.7). 'The chairman controls the lives of his farmers: he chooses whether or not to provide them with transportation to the city when they get sick, he can evict them at will, and he and his subordinate bookkeepers and brigadiers can assign the farmer good-paying or poorly paid jobs or simply cheat him his pay. ... The job tends to make even the most democratic managers dictatorial. (The chairman's cultural taste also determines the kind of entertainment available on the farm. See: Govorukhin 'Prikaz, igrat na balalaike!' 1988; 'I order to play the balalaika!').

3.1.8 CHANGES IN RURAL LIVING AFTER INDEPENDENCE

Initially the declaration of independence and the resulting transition period had a marginal influence on rural life in the Kyrgyz Republic. In many rural areas the first years of independence showed some bureaucratic activity reorganizing state and collective farms into new legal entities maintaining the original management structure (mainly 'cosmetic' changes) and without much effect for the workers on the farm. On some of the farms certain families were allocated paper land shares theoretically corresponding with individual plots of land. But rarely did these paper shares lead to actual distribution of specific land parcels. Families continued to work on collective farm lands and did not work their own land. After obtaining their shares, as an exception, some families together pooled the shares and were registered as peasant farms (a legal requirement), but in most cases the entire farm continued business as usual. Peasant farms of this type flouted the legal definition, but little attempt was made to enforce adherence to the law. Later in the transition period, owners of land shares could apply for land certificates, or in the case of (small) multi-family farming enterprises, State Acts, which could be registered with notaries with permission of the local authorities in local land administration offices. In this case actual land allocation out of the land of the former farms was often pursued.

Use rights in urban areas could likewise be converted into ownership rights at the BTI offices for buildings, or at Rayon Architectura offices for urban land (a confusing situation anyway). But since this registration involved payment of fees and generally a lot of time to be spent while waiting in the office it only occurred sporadically.

The process of registration of the land certificates is still going on today in the Kyrgyz Republic. Progress is slow, mainly because there are no obvious benefits and only costs involved. In rural areas it is not always clear to the people where to register, and many peasants rely on the notary deed of registration of the land certificate as sufficient proof of authority for right to land. So, unless a transfer of the land is at hand, registration is seldom actively pursued.

One could wonder about the low response among the peasants on this challenge. But it is important to realize that the agricultural employee had no responsibilities for management of the farm and that information about the operation of the farm and marketing of its produce is generally out of reach for peasants starting their own farm. A few peasants were brave enough to ask for their own plots of land and to actually create a privatized farm, as a result of the distribution of land shares, but this was rare. The allocation of land was mainly from the lesser productive parts of the collective farm, unless the request came from a person with good ties with the former management. For agricultural supplies and sales the new farmers still needed the cooperation with the former collective farm for seeds, agricultural tools and to market their harvest. They had to rely heavily on the existing large state and collective farms because of total lack of support in this respect for private individual farmers. All this did not encourage large scale quitting of the existing farms.

3.1.9 REAL PROPERTY IN THE KYRGYZ REPUBLIC

Before the Kyrgyz Republic became independent in 1991, generally all land and real estate was owned by the State. State institutions took care of registration and inspection of the immovable property and all legal occupants or exclusive users of real property had the obligation to register. It was simply a matter of existence. The registration provided proof of residence and with that document the citizen could obtain an 'internal Kyrgyz passport' at the local office of the militia (the police). This passport was proof of citizenship, and a document to be shown at any occasion when requested by police or other authorities. It was one's proof of existence and residence. In urban areas the local Bureau of Technical Inventory (BTI) had the authority to provide proof of residence and, in rural areas, Land Engineering offices registered residence and controlled use of agricultural-designated land (actually the 'Ugodia') and carried out surveying of land plots.
Private land ownership did not exist in communist times. All arable land was state property and most of the mountain pastures were commonly used as grazing lands for the livestock of state and collective farms, also as common pastureland for herds of the population.

The 1991 privatization law signaled the start of tenure reform in the Kyrgyz Republic. Between 1993 and 1999 various laws and decrees initiated private ownership of immovable property. As a result, the Kyrgyz Republic has been engaged in the process of a massive change of real property tenure. Immovable property units are being transferred from institutions for 'public' decision making into private hands to a substantial degree. The moving force behind the global privatization trend as seen in many former communistic countries nowadays is that it is believed that privatization of land management supports the development of dynamic market economies and stimulates economic development.

As the management of land becomes privatized, the institutions of land administration (understood as the processes of recording, maintaining and disseminating data on land ownership, land use, land location, land quality and the value of land) must also change. The creation of private ownership rights to land has been erratic in several of the transition countries. All attempts for a quick and simple solution to the task of establishing private ownership to land have shown significant problems and misunderstandings in countries still full of concepts of a centrally planned economy.

A particularly interesting aspect of the transition in the Kyrgyz Republic is that the initially issued land shares established rights to exclusive use of 'Ugodia' land by private individuals. In November 1998 (after a long period of parliament debates) an amendment on the Constitution changed the land share documents of land use rights into documents providing ownership rights to land.

In 1995 the president of the Kyrgyz Republic initiated a Land and Real Estate Registration Project. The latter aims at establishing a 'Western' style land registration to protect the rights to immovable property of individuals in the Kyrgyz Republic. In 1999 the preparatory phase of the Land and Real Estate Project actually began with 'western style' individual private ownership of rights to real property in urban areas having existed since 1991, but private ownership of arable land did only exist for a number of months in the Kyrgyz Republic.

3.2 OWNERSHIP OF RIGHTS TO LAND BEFORE INDEPENDENCE IN KYRGYZIA[4]

3.2.1 OBTAINING USE RIGHTS

People could obtain the exclusive right of use for a specific real property object in Kyrgyzia. This right was not unconditional. Generally people had to pay a nominal rent for this use, and an important condition the state put on the use right was an obligation of proper use to be controlled by government officials. For farmland, the main condition was the obligation to use it to its full potential, which generally meant use according to recommendations and expectations set forward by government officials. Apartments and other residential structures were in exclusive use and most inhabitants enjoyed an inheritable right of use of them. Land was State owned both in urban and rural areas, and rural people were allocated a house plot to be used as a vegetable garden.

Before independence in 1991, private ownership of real property (whether apartments, other residential structures or land) did exist in Kyrgyzia, as an exception and only marginally. Some residential, single-family homes were owned (as a structure) but the land was only in use.

---

[4] Kyrgyzia is the name under which most of the territory of the current Kyrgyz Republic was known in the time it was part of the USSR.

Most of the existing apartment buildings, multiple housing structures and single-family homes were state owned and given in use with a strict regime of control and inventory by government agencies. The latter also applied for agricultural land. What is now the Kyrgyz Republic was a dependent Republic in the Russian Federation from 1924. Between 1930 and 1990, there were basically four ways to obtain the exclusive use of an apartment or residential property in Kyrgyzia:

- One way was to try to get permission from the local authority office to obtain or buy that right;
- Another was via your employer, who would enlist you as a potential candidate for the exclusive use of urban real property. In due time you would obtain permission to take possession of an available apartment or other real property structure;
- The third way was via a cooperative that collected money from its members and then tried to obtain land and a building permit to erect an apartment building. Any member of the cooperative eligible for an apartment could receive a life long use right, which also became inheritable in a certain sense (see further);
- The fourth and hardest way was to obtain permission to build your own home on a piece of land. If successful, as explained before, the structure became yours, but the land remained State property. The problem was not only to obtain permission, but also to collect building materials; therefore only a limited number of citizens could follow this route to home ownership.

The right to exclusively use land, or a structure on it, or even to own the structure without any other right than that of exclusive use of the land – as long as it suited the government officials – did provide a specific kind of land tenure security. Furthermore, the strict control on proper use exercised by government agencies contributed to the feeling that one received a favor of exclusive use of the real property.

At each transfer of the real property BTI inspectors carried out an inspection on the ground (requiring a site visit); or if the real property was located in rural areas inspectors of the Land Register of the State Inspectorate on Land Engineering – as the Land Engineering offices were officially named – were responsible.

3.2.2 'INHERITABLE' USE RIGHTS

The most common way of using real property can be described by the 'inheritable use right.' People received an inheritable right of exclusive use to real property. In urban areas this was limited to an apartment or residential structure, while in rural areas it was common to have a residential structure plus adjacent to it a house plot generally used as vegetable garden. All arable ('Ugodia') land was held by a state or collective farm and used according to the indications in the five-year economic planning system of the USSR. Pastureland was state owned, but when not in exclusive use by large state and collective farms, also available for communal use. The 'inheritable use right on real property' consisted of a right of exclusive use of a real property unit by descendents, but not necessarily in the same premises as the deceased. For example, if parents and one or more descendents lived in a rather large apartment and the parents both passed away, the descendent(s) could receive an order to move to a smaller apartment. The condition was that the descendent(s) had to be registered as living in the apartment – this showed in their domestic passport[5] – to benefit of this 'inheritable right.' Registration was important anyway and was also required by the police. If the former tenant of an apartment died and there were no heirs registered as living in the same apartment, the apartment would be freed for a new applicant. The same happened if someone living alone in an apartment was convicted and sent to jail for longer than six months. The property and all its contents were simply confiscated and given in use to others. Relatives of the convicted could also be ordered to move to a smaller apartment in the neighborhood.

The local authority office of the municipality gave permits for people who then could obtain such an inheritable use right to real property. In urban areas the process to obtain such a right was often initiated by the employer who provided lodgings on a first come, first serve basis. (But 'political capital' could assist enormously in being first served). As soon as someone gained employment, he or she could sign up for lodging and over time lodging was provided. As mentioned earlier another way to become a legal lifetime user of real property was via a cooperative. The cooperative collected money of its members and after obtaining approval of the responsible authorities started building suitable lodgings for which the members could apply.

Although moving in general was restricted and occurred only occasionally, if this happened, the Architectura office of the municipality had to approve the move in order for the people to obtain new living quarters in the new area. Since this was a rather difficult procedure, the general practice was that it happened only if there was a possibility to exchange real property. People indeed could exchange real property with people from other regions after approval by the local authority in either regions or towns. So, if you wanted to move from Bishkek to Osh and you knew people who wanted to move from Osh to Bishkek, you could apply for permission to exchange your lodgings. Farm workers who wanted to move generally needed permission from the management of the state or collective farm to do so.

5 This passport should always be carried and shown on demand to officials. It serves as a document to proof identity. It is in general not valid for foreign travel. Prior to travel abroad, a citizen has to apply for a special extension to this passport permitting to leave the country for travel outside the (former) USSR.

3.2.3 PROTECTION AND REGISTRATION OF PROPERTY RIGHTS

Prior to independence, little attention was paid to the question of protection of rights in land and other real property because land and real property was owned by the State. However, vast records on real property were maintained. Information on land and other real property was collected and managed by a number of different agencies, but the data were primarily used for purposes of planning and control by the State. As mentioned earlier, technical and legal data on residential structures in urban areas were collected and maintained by offices of the Bureau of Technical Inventory (BTI), but also the Architectura offices of local governments maintained a system of data on real property. Building and zoning data on land and real property was collected and used by municipal offices associated with the Ministry of Construction (in urban areas).

On several occasions, I was assured that during communist times hardly anyone could use a plot of land (or another real property object) without somewhere being registered and recognized as having a certain right to it, except as stated before for grazing of (domestic) livestock on communal pastureland and collecting some hay from it.

In rural areas the use of state owned land (virtually all land) was controlled and organized by the Land Engineering (also called land administration or land management) offices. These offices also carried out surveys of plots to determine the size, the location, and to assess the soil quality. In all areas of the Kyrgyz Republic local authorities maintained and updated – sometimes yearly – the inventory they had of data on real property. This official activity certainly contributed to a perception of tenure security and to the perception of secure property access. Several other agencies and departments all kept data on land for various purposes of state control and planning. A department of the Ministry of Agriculture maintained a land cadastre of agricultural lands (actually not a cadastre[6] as in the Western concept but more an inventory for agricultural planning purposes suitable for the national economic planning; see for example [33] p.15 and p. 187).

Like elsewhere in the USSR, the Kyrgyz Republic had a specific land registration in its rural areas. This land registration confusingly referred to as a 'cadastre,' contained a vast amount of data on the 'Ugodia' (all land designated for agriculture). To assist the five-year central planning cycle of the USSR, data were collected at local, district (rayon) and provincial (oblast) level, and submitted to the national level. Not only alphanumeric data but also maps of the land of state and collective farms were provided indicating the areas and also the soil quality of the

---

[6] See '*Nationale Grondboekhoudingen*' ISBN 90 6110 108 5 (in Dutch) by Henri Dekker. A review of cadastres and land registration systems in English will be published by Ashgate Publishing in 2003 under the title '*The Invisible Line*'.

various land plots. Apart from data on distribution of land and its quality, data were also collected and maintained on climate and topographic details. In several areas of the Soviet Union even data on the agricultural productivity of the farm employees were added to the data set. There was a whole institutional arrangement to provide these data of which offices of Land Engineering formed the core. Scientific research on soil quality sometimes went as far as providing ten different soil classes, and within these a subdivision of again ten classes for each main class, resulting in almost one hundred soil qualifications (as I observed in Bulgaria). Map production to keep track of soil classes and farm boundaries provided maps to determine crops and quota to be produced on each farm. Currently these data are still used in the Kyrgyz Republic to determine proper use of agricultural land, although most of the data are outdated by lack of funds for updating and maintaining the system since the cease of the USSR five year economic planning cycles. But as mentioned before, the offices of Land Engineering are still involved in collecting and maintaining data on land in rural areas in the Kyrgyz Republic.

3.2.4 REGISTRATION OF USE RIGHTS

Most of the political support for the introduction of a new system for land registration came from the fact that transfers of real property were cumbersome and time consuming. It is a well-known fact in Kyrgyz society that in order to speed up the procedure at each window some extra cash would speed up the job and this increased the costs of transfers considerably. Some of the most relevant offices and their tasks with respect to real property can be summarized as follows:

Rural sector:

State institute for Land Resources and Land Management (Kyrgyzgiprozem).

This institute is responsible for maintaining an inventory of all land resources in the Kyrgyz Republic. It compiles an annual inventory of land resources with detailed figures on land holdings of each agricultural user. Every five years, a cadastre is prepared on the basis of the annual reports. During Soviet times with a total of only 500 agricultural users (state and collective farms) this was a reasonable task, with the more than 24,000 users in 1995 and a staff reduction of 75 per cent by lack of funding, the likelihood to continue with this task is small.

Land Engineering offices at the rayon level.

These offices collect data on land use in rural areas on behalf of the rural councils. It takes care of the land administration by providing data to Kyrgyzgiprozem on population figures, area of land in yards and gardens, it carries out surveys of lands and manages and administers the (domestic) passport regime of the rural villages. (These offices are also referred to as Land Management offices after The Committee for Land Reform and Land Management established offices of Land Management Service) The Land

Management Service was put in charge of land use, land monitoring, land cadastre, land management organization, topographical and geodetic mapping, and soils, botany, agrochemical, and other land management research with financing from the budget of the Kyrgyz Republic.

Urban sector:

State Committee on Architecture and Construction (Gosstroi)

This is the state agency for city and regional planning. It has the responsibility for privatizing apartments and other urban properties. The Architectura offices at the rayon level register urban owners and users of real property and report this information to the local tax offices. It submits data to Kyrgyzgiprozem for compilation of the annual land register.

Bureau of Technical Inventory (BTI)

BTI collects all data on immovable property, such as location, area, and owner of rights to the property. It maintains an archive for all blueprints, construction plan of houses, apartments, and other immovable property. It is subordinate to the State Committee of Communal Affairs.

This cycle needed an urban area in order to complete a conveyance of real property (i.e. buildings) is given in Figure 3.2.4 :

1.Start at BTI to obtain approval and authorization of documents that exist on rights to real property

2. Go to Local Administration (includes Land Engineering & Architectura offices) to obtain a valuation of the real property

3.Go to Notariat (part Of Ministry of Justice) to prepare deeds of transfer and pay the 7 per cent tax on the value

4. Back to BTI to register the new situation!

Figure 3.2.4 'Cycle' to register real property

In rural areas a slightly shorter procedure must be followed, it begins at the Land Administration and ended there. Differences between rural and urban areas are mainly in the nature of the property rights. In urban areas it is mostly ownership, in rural areas it is only ownership of dwelling houses, apartments, and house plots. For all other real property areas one needs always permission to convey real property (at the land engineering offices of the local authority). All land designated for agriculture remained state owned until the amendment to the Constitution allowing private individual ownership of it.

The legal base for the Land and Real Estate Registration Project is laid down in the Law on State Registration of Rights to Immovable Property as adopted by the Legislative Assembly of the Jogorku Kenesh of the Kyrgyz Republic on 26 November 1998. (An English translation was provided by US-AID on 22 December 1998). The preparatory project aimed at land and real estate registration started in 1999 by the World Bank. It focuses on the functions of the in 1998 newly created office (GosRegister) in which the existing offices of Land Management and BTI will be combined. It is clear that this causes tension, with still unsolved competence questions, between GosRegister and the Architectura offices that now have a certain responsibility for registration of rights to real property. It is the aim of the new organization within GosRegister, to reduce all the cumbersome stages of registration of real property and to establish one integrated procedure in one office, where clients start with the application of a transfer and leave the same office with their approved new land title(s). The distribution of data among the government offices involved now becomes one of the responsibilities of GosRegister.

3.3 LAND AND AGRARIAN REFORM

3.3.1 THE LEGAL FRAMEWORK

Land reform in the Kyrgyz Republic is also referred to as 'land and agrarian reform' in the Kyrgyz Republic. As mentioned before, in 1991 a privatization law was implemented. The situation in the rural areas initially confused observers. There seemed, perhaps, to be a hurried response to implement reforms that resulted in an obvious lack of definitions and careful planning. In article 4 of the Constitution [44] it is clearly stated that although private ownership is recognized, all land belongs to the State. Would this also imply that only an inheritable exclusive use right to plots of land is possible? According to the Law on Peasant Farms of February 1991, land was granted to individuals in either rent or lifetime inheritable tenure. A 1994 attempt to improve the progress of land reform started with a presidential decree [44]. Holders of land shares could now pool their shares with others and heads of households could obtain land use certificates in the form of a 99-year lease. If the farm was multi-family and registered as a farming enterprise, a State Act was issued. A November 1998 amendment to the Constitution recognized private ownership of land and converted the land certificates and State Acts into documents showing ownership of rights to land.

Before 1991 there were two kinds of real property in urban areas. One was the apartment and the other was the private (dwelling) house generally government

owned, but also sometimes privately owned (built by the owner with collected materials on state owned land). The latter could be sold and transferred even in USSR times (not the land!); the use right of government owned lodgings normally could not, unless permission was obtained from the local authorities.
After introduction of the privatization law, the apartment or single family home one used and possessed at that moment could become one's own, that is to say, with written permission of all (adult) inhabitants. This transfer from state controlled to privately controlled and managed property had to be approved by a special local commission. A fee or purchase price had to be paid to the local authorities, of which the height was also determined by the local commission.

For the 'Ugodia,' the initial cost paid for the right to exclusive use of the land could pose a problem (25 times the tax rate) for new peasants. As in rural areas, urban area residents could not always pay the required amount. There were a number of exceptions to the rule that one had to 'purchase' the premises (for example war veterans, invalids, and heroes of the revolution were exempted of paying the purchase-money[7]). It also meant that one could be fortunate if one possessed, at that time, a large apartment; most of the purchase prices were more or less adapted to the situation – although still out of reach for some – and did not always reflect the actual value of the premises.
Of course there were some irregularities, especially at the sale of state controlled property to private organizations or persons. Sometimes the (re) valuation was much lower than usual because of political capital or special relations possessed by prospective buyers.

The struggle of the Kyrgyz with the changes during the transition, while trying to maintain agricultural production levels, has been documented in July 1996 by the Land Tenure Center of the University of Wisconsin (LTC research paper #128) [52]. I will more or less follow, that document here.
Research on the evolution of the agrarian structure by LTC showed ambiguities in shifts and definition of land reform concepts and inherent confusion (peasant farm, private farm, cooperative farm and reorganized enterprise). The legislation that underpinned farm restructuring in the Kyrgyz Republic in the first years of transition is listed:

- Law on Peasant Farms (2 February 1991)
- Law of the Kyrgyz Republic on Enterprises (6 February 1991)
- Law of Kyrgyz Republic on Land Reform (19 April 1991)

The law on Land Reform of April 1991 [44], envisaged two steps of reform; to provide appropriate legislation and land regulations and the creation of a Land Fund under the local council of people's deputies for emerging private farmers, lessors, and farm cooperatives. Land tax and land use payment schedules would be

[7] Article 4 of the Law of 20 December 1991 'On privatization of housing stock in the Republic of Kyrgyzstan' lists a number of exceptions (See Annex A for most of the text of this Law)

developed and boundaries of administrative units would be demarcated (not yet the boundaries of individual parcels!).

The privatization of farmland in the Kyrgyz Republic was initially dominated by fear of the Government about possible adverse equity effects of land markets. This led to hesitation and inconsistency over legal land rights. Rural committees, rural enterprise managers and farming households became confused regarding who held which rights. The introduction of a number of restrictions on land transfers like an absolute restriction on the sale of land shares and land transfers, and a maximum amount of land to be held by one family further contributed to the confusion.

During the early stages of the reform, land shares (also called land passports or land certificates) were issued to farmers and land users in accordance with the Law on Land Reform. Land Reform was made the responsibility of the Committee on Land Reform and Land Management of the Council of People's Deputies with participation of the appropriate ministries and agencies. The share system is widely used in the former USSR. Under this system state and collective farms issue paper shares of their land and non-land assets to workers and other residents of rural areas who can pool these shares to form new farming enterprises. The theory is that state and collective farms will be transformed into a variety of smaller-scale, collectively- and individually-managed farm units. Decisions regarding the operation of the new farms – from sowing, using fertilizers, size of livestock, obtaining credit, to marketing of farm products – will be made by the workers and members themselves and not by the state. However, as mentioned before, most of the new farm units continued in practice to operate under (part of) the former management with or without explicit involvement of workers or members in decision making.

According to Bloch [8], three phases of land reform for agricultural land can be distinguished. The initial phase or early reform in which introduction of small-scale farms took place (in 1991), a second phase of restructuring unprofitable farms and distribution of their lands occurred (1991 - 1993) and a third phase of restructuring the state and collective farms. It should be borne in mind that the following description focuses on land designated for agriculture (the Ugodia). The importance of agriculture in many countries in transition justifies this special focus. Once again in urban areas real property was privatized as well, but in a much more straightforward fashion than seemed appropriate because of the political and economic significance of agricultural land.

3.3.2 FIRST PHASE OF LAND REFORM (1991)

The law on peasant farms encouraged individuals to petition the local Rayon Council of People's Deputies to set up a peasant farm. The farmland came from areas deemed to be underutilized or from a collective or state farm marked as unprofitable or of low profitability. There was no ceiling on the amount of land an individual could apply for and a variety of farms emerged with sizes ranging from less than ten to over hundred hectares. Persons who managed to establish a farm in this stage of the reform were generally well off. They kept access to state supply and marketing channels, low interest on credit and state support system (low) prices for agricultural inputs. Mostly the well-connected people (employees of the farm administration for example) succeeded in establishing such farms.

Under the Law of Peasant Farms (PF) of February 1991 article 2, a peasant farm is an independent farming complex comprised of family members, relatives, and other individuals jointly operating the farming unit. Establishment is voluntary (art. 6), ownership restricted to one farm per family and the farm could be inherited by will (art. 7), but all other transfers (buying, selling, granting, mortgaging and unauthorized exchange or allotment) were strictly prohibited. All members had a right to compensation when leaving the farm, the amount to be determined according to labor and property share assigned to the PF during its organization (art. 8). Terms of compensation had to be established according to mutual agreement but payment terms should be within five years. The PF was taxable by the government, depending on land quality and location at rates determined by law (art.17). Rights of ownership in the PF were to be forfeited in cases of voluntary withdrawal, failure to make necessary land improvements within a designated period, and failure to pay land taxes and other charges on time (art. 20).
The land of a PF came from the lands of former collective (state) farms, with land shares distributed according to labor contributions of farmers during their time at the collective farm. On other state farms, land grants were to be assigned on a rental basis, with an option of purchase later, taking into account the farmers income (art. 6). Maximum farm size was to be set by the rayon council of people's deputies taking into account soil fertility, population, public land reserve, number of members and degree of professional ability of the farmers – all aimed at ensuring maximum livestock and crop efficiency (art. 13).

The head of the PF is responsible for all management activities and for production and marketing (art.4). The same article forbids interference by the State except in cases of law infringement. The land must be used for the intended purpose and must achieve minimum productivity (according to the cadastral evaluation) and must be kept environmentally 'clean' (art.14). Land allotments were carried out after application by the village. In this stage land was allotted on a competitive basis (later all citizens were made eligible); preference was determined by the length of farm experience, necessary qualifications, and capability to manage the PF. State and collective farms producing above the rayon average were exempted from privatization (as was land for research and scientific use). With consent of the PF, people could move over the PF lands, fish, camp and bathe. Labor contracts (stating length of the working day, days off, paid vacation, wage rate, meals, and any other condition that might apply) are obligatory in peasant farms and the peasant farm must pay social security insurance into a state fund. The peasant farm is eligible to obtain agricultural assets and tools, pedigree seeds, utilities, and materials from the state logistical support system (at state set prices). It all looks convincing, but it should be noted that the reform initially was a debacle, hardly any real progress was made with the reform. Only a few peasant farms emerged during the first phase.

3.3.3 SECOND PHASE OF LAND REFORM (1992-1994)

Subsequent laws and regulations to completely liquidate unprofitable state and collective farms gave way to the next phase of reform in the Kyrgyz Republic. About 60 farms were restructured and got new organizational forms. Generally it was the manager of the existing farm who decided upon the new organization and an array of types of agricultural enterprises appeared. Under this arrangement, peasant farms, associations of peasant farms, agricultural production cooperatives, and joint stock companies were established.

Peasant farms were a continuation of the peasant farms of the first stage of reform, but only a few families took their share of land and assets and attempted to farm individually.

Associations of peasant farms are voluntary associations of farmers granted land and property shares. It formalized a practice of continuation of the former large-scale farms, often with a new name, but with the same old structure and management. Sometimes two or three associations were formed on the land of the former large-scale farm.

Agricultural production cooperatives are restructured large-scale farms where former farm managers became the 'elected' heads of the cooperative and where farm workers carried on with their duties as before. Also here a split of the very large-scale farm into two or three cooperatives was not uncommon.

Joint stock companies are closed corporates in which shareholders, defined as the farm residents, now hold the assets of former large-scale collective or state farms and where the management and production structures remained mostly as before.

Again on paper the impact of the reform looks impressive. The number of peasant farms on 1 January 1994, was 9,764 and their land measured 3,640,600 ha (land designated for agriculture). But the figure has to be interpreted. Peasant farms and associations of peasant farms were counted together in official statistics.

3.3.4 THIRD PHASE; REVITALIZATION OF AGRICULTURAL RESTRUCTURING (1994 ->)

The third land reform phase is based on a series of presidential decrees, government orders and ministerial regulations on land and agrarian reform of 1994 and 1995. The process started with a presidential decree 'On measures for enforcement of the land and agrarian reform' of 22 February 1994. Responsibility for the farm restructuring was transferred from the State Property Committee to the Ministry of Agriculture. The Ministry has set up within the Ministry itself a Republican Center for Land and Agrarian Reform (CLAR) with offices at oblast, rayon and local levels. With the exception of certain specific farms (for seed and livestock breeding) all state and collective farms should be replaced with smaller management units using the land and assets of the former large-scale farms. Pastureland remains under state control and 25 per cent of arable land should be put in a National Land Fund. This National Land Fund should use the 25 per cent of land of state and collective farms to develop agricultural entrepreneurship, and prioritizing farming enterprises. Land that is taken into the fund is used for seed production, experimental farming and to be distributed among new settlers, pensioners and health workers in the community. Remaining land can be leased on a profitable basis in a competitive way. Most of the land for the fund came from insufficiently used lands, like land provided to agricultural industries but not utilized within one year, and other land not used within a predetermined time or for which the five-year performance was lower than a norm set by cadastral assessment. Specific inventory programs were carried out to identify these lands. Once the land was in the Land Fund, the Council of People's Deputies was to determine appropriate future use of it, whether to continue use by current owners, withhold lands, re-distribute land to new landowners and tenants or introduce conservation programs on degraded lands. Inefficient collective farms, state farms and other agricultural enterprises would be reorganized into agricultural cooperatives, and (associations of) peasant farms with priorities set by the Cabinet of Ministers. The village, town, settlement or district council of People's Deputies would issue an ownership document to re-register such lands. A presidential decree of 3 November 1995, created an Agriculture Lands Redistribution Fund with 327,000 ha from the National Land Fund of which, in June 2000, almost half was leased to various types of farms. Auctions for sale of land from the fund resulted in selling of almost 2,500 ha. The rest of the land is used for haymaking, leaving land fallow and for short-term use by individual farmers (obviously without lease agreements). The collection of rents from these lands is sometimes problematic and reveals economic problems in the country. In 1999 less than 80 per cent of the rental payments in the whole country were received; in this period in Talas oblast only 22 per cent of all rental payments for leased land could be collected. The general aim now seems to be to sell as much of the land that currently is still in the redistribution fund.

The Committee for Land Reform and Land Management established offices of Land Management Service (also referred to as offices of Land Engineering, because the staff was largely taken from those offices). These offices provide yearly cadastral documentation, land monitoring, inspections and issuance of 'passports' to landowners and tenants. They carry out land monitoring, topographical and geodetic mapping, research on soils, botany, and agro-chemicals, with financing from the budget of the Kyrgyz Republic. Any land improvements, however, were to be carried out at the initiative of landowners and tenants at their own expense.

Initially, this third phase of the land reform was a frontal assault on state and collective farms which had ignored previous restructuring edicts. Implementation came after the planting and harvesting season in the fall of 1994. The presidential decree of 22 February 1994 gives all citizens living on the territory of state and collective farms a right to a share of land and all Kyrgyz citizens could transfer the right of use of real property. One could pool shares of land getting 49 years (a presidential decree of 3 November 1995, extended this to 99 years with preferential right to renewal) of guaranteed tenure with preferential rights to extension. New maximum land holdings for households were set; 20 ha, 25 ha, 30 ha, for intensive agriculture, semi-intensive agriculture, and mountainous pasture lands respectively; and plots must be used for agricultural production according to standards set by government officials. Consolidation of multiple household holdings into larger enterprises is allowed and no maximum size for the new enterprises has been set. A regulation of 4 January 1995, requires re-registration of all economic enterprises with the following definitions:

- Private farm (labor of one household)
- Peasant farm, presumably two or more families (no definitions given)
- Agricultural cooperative, no definition, but sizes between 30-100 ha (50-150 ha pastures)
- Collective farm (kolkhoz) farm size above 100 (150) ha (no further definition given)
- State farm (Sovkhoz or Gozkhoz) state property, farm size as for kolkhozy.

Although this regulation was designed to systematize the situation, there still is a lack of definitions, questions and confusion. It causes a problem with statistical information because of the lack of a clear conversion of farm types before and after this regulation.

The heads of rayons (districts) were charged with developing programs for farm reorganization and setting up rural committees in the rayon. Local taxes on real property could be increased to a maximum of twenty fold the old (nominal) tax, with 50 per cent coming to the rayon itself, but in February 1995, this was changed to only 25 per cent for the rayon (and 75 per cent to the state budget). A regulation of 22/08/94 made farm reorganization obligatory for all enterprises. On every farm to be re-organized according to the new regulations, rural committees are established more or less as executive instruments of the rayons. Implementing the reforms still turned out to be difficult and a regulation of 23 January 1995, establishes a new style commissions on land and agrarian reform to help realize the reforms. Each commission, one on every not yet re-organized farm, includes the head of the rural committee, representatives of the Ministry of Agriculture, the Kenesh (village head), oblast and rayon representatives, bankers and statistical experts and representatively chosen farmers (but not more than 15 people in total). These commissions look similar to the rural committees, but they are now more an umbrella group of all interests.

Regulation of 22 August 1994, opens the possibility to buy land shares. Land share certificates can be purchased at the rural committees for 25 times the tax rate and they are to be registered in the local registration of deeds. Farmers should have a notary deed made up by the notary employed in the offices of the local authority where registration also takes place. Transfer of shares is not limited and could be done among the registered owners of shares. In practice, purchase of land proved to be difficult. High interests due on loans and mortgages, lack of resources and funds, and a failing banking system severely limits the practical implementation. Collective and state farms may be:

- Divided into peasant farms (regarding the maximum size per household);
- Reorganized in a joint stock company;
- Declared bankrupt, with the property sold by auction to other agricultural producers.

Restructuring former collective or state farms must at least encompass accurate measurements and the establishment of legal boundaries. It also must cover a valuation of the assets, taking into account the size of the population, number of farmsteads and work force, future land use possibilities, the way to distribute the shares, with details of the process, valuation of lands and rights of succession and leaving the farm. The restructuring plan is to be voted upon and implemented by the rural committee after approval by the rayon head. Debts incurred by the collective or state farm before 1 October 1994, should be paid out of the property of the reorganized farm; remaining debt is transferred to the newly formed enterprises (recently with a period of repayment of fifteen years).

In an update on the situation in December 1998, the Center for Land and Agrarian Reform under the Ministry of Agriculture reports the following numbers: At the end of December 1998, the Kyrgyz Republic has 21,226 private farms, 27,169 peasant farms, 348 cooperatives, 331 (new smaller) collective farms, and 45 (old style) state farms. As a result of the reform, 406 state and collective farms were re-organized. (Source: report of the Center for Land and Agricultural Reform)

3.3.5 OVERALL PROGRESS OF THE REFORM

According to art. 4 of the Constitution of the Kyrgyz Republic, the land, the subsoil, water, air space, fauna, flora are the property of the State. Land may be given in private possession to individual citizens in accordance with the law. Nevertheless the Republic 'shall defend the right of its citizens and legal entities to own property.' The size of the share is determined by the labor contribution on the old farm. When pooled shares comply with the rules for the farm size they can be redeemed for a land certificate (for a one-family farm) or State Act (for farm enterprises) of land use right to be issued by the rayon administration. The rayon land management office along with the rural committee carries out actual land allocation. Social-cultural units (stores, workshops, garages, oil-stations etc.) are managed by the rural committee for all shareholders. Rural committees can form agro-industrial enterprises such as veterinary clinics, land reclamation projects etc. The Ministry of Agriculture can organize joint-stock companies as seed farms, livestock breeding stations, hippodromes, fruit nurseries, educational farms etc. According to the Law on Peasant Farms, land was granted to individuals in either rent or lifetime inheritable tenure. Land shares generally did not refer to a specific parcel of land. Land share definitions and rules for giving out certificates for rights to land are given in provision # 632 of 22 August 1994. With exception of land in the National Land Fund, pastures and populated areas with private plots and forests, all collective farmed land (state and collective farms) should be distributed to eligible interests. Present workers, retired workers, health workers living on the farm, those born on the farm and coming back permanently are eligible for shares free of charge. The size of land shares has to be determined by the rural committee and depends on the family size at the time of reorganization as approved by the rayon administration. Shareholders have the possibility to pool their shares with family members to form individual single-family farms or with others to form larger farm enterprises. Rural committees are responsible for replacing the combined shares by issuing land certificates to household heads or in case of multi-family farm enterprises to issue a State Act in the name of the enterprise. Land Use certificates provide the holders with land use rights for a 99-year lease term. Land use certificates must be registered at the rayon land management offices.

In a June 2000 report to the World Bank the Director-General K. Kadyrkulov of the Ministry of Agriculture and Water Resources, states that of the 1,496,300 ha of agricultural lands (excluding pastureland) 1,081,800 ha have been distributed in the form of land shares among citizens. All land shares have been replaced in the meantime by land certificates in the proper format for registration for more than 510,500 families or 3,481,800 individuals residing in rural areas. This indicates that a family has an average area of arable land of just over 2.1 ha and each individual an average area of about 0.31 ha. The small average size of 2.1 ha implies that several of these families have to farm together in cooperative farms or in new style collective farms. Land share size depends on the amount of land designated for agriculture of the former state or collective farm and on the number or rural residents. In Osh oblast and Djallal-Abad oblast and in particular in the fertile Ferghana valley in the South of the Kyrgyz Republic with its relatively dense population the smallest areas per individual (0.1 - 0.3 ha) occur. Driving through the valley and talking to farmers there, one could observe that most families had no other choice than cooperative or collective farming to make a living. An interesting feature of that type of farming is that with some crops each family still had their own number of rows of crop pegged out in the fields. While traveling through the valley one could see various families scattered over the fields but each tending their own rows to prepare for a good harvest. In Chui and Issyk-Kul oblasts in the North of the country population density is much lower with less mountainous and more fertile land individual sizes of arable land ranged from 0.75 to 1.0 ha.

3.4 INTRODUCING OWNERSHIP OF RIGHTS FOR ALL LAND

3.4.1 AMENDMENT OF THE CONSTITUTION

An important decision made by the government of the Kyrgyz Republic occurred during the third phase of the land reform. I hesitate to see it as the fourth phase of the land reform, because on the one hand it is a considerable change in property rights, but on the other hand it is not as much of a change in the land reform process to be classified as a sequential new phase. LTC senior researcher Peter

Bloch states in an unpublished paper on the situation in the Kyrgyz Republic (used in a small seminar in Washington DC in April 2000) that it took years of hesitation and debate in Parliament on the issue of private ownership of rights to land designated for agriculture ('Ugodia') to determine a final situation. In October 1998 an amendment on the Constitution [44] was approved by referendum that essentially converted all land use certificates into ownership documents. With this decision all real property transferred to citizens by land shares, land certificates and State Acts was from now on held in ownership (Some 'Ugodia' land was transferred in lease and that remained unchanged as leased land with lease contracts). For the Kyrgyz Republic this finalized – for the time being – the process of legal adaptation to a new property regime in the country. The tenure of all privatized real property is now in ownership rights according to the typical 'western style' land tenure system.

3.4.2 THE LAND REGISTRATION PROJECT

Reference to a new 'western style' land registration system in the Kyrgyz Republic has been made several times in the previous paragraphs and in particular in 1.3, 1.4 and 3.2.4. In November 1998, Kyrgyz Parliament adopted the 'Law on State Registration of Rights to Immovable Property.' This law establishes the legal basis and the procedures for a new registration system of rights to land in the Kyrgyz Republic. The purpose is to provide protection of registered rights to land. It is the registration law envisaged in the Civil Code of the Kyrgyz Republic.

As a consequence of this law, the preparation phase of the Land and Real Estate Registration Project earlier referred to began in June 1999. Local experts on legal matters, on cadastre, on surveying, and on mapping worked together with three expatriate consultants for the development of the procedures and to develop a practical manual for registration. Furthermore, several (paper) forms for registration were designed and discussed with staff of GosRegister.

To implement the new system of land registration two regulations on procedures and on local registration offices were prepared. GosRegister staff was trained in Western style registration methods and after approval by GosRegister, training in the process of registration for prospective staff of the new offices took place. Various visits were paid to sites selected for new offices, to provide advice for refurbishment and to assist in the preparation for opening of new offices. In this phase three offices 'new style' were opened. Most of the existing data at the BTI and Land Engineering offices in the area were used after careful examination. Mapping was produced to supply new office staff with a set of alphanumeric and geographical data on the units to be registered. Thus before the end of the preparation phase three new offices were officially operational to serve the public in a new way for land registration. The three new offices were located in Kant, Kara-Suu and Sokuluk.

3.4.3 SOME SPECIFIC LAND REGISTRATION DIFFICULTIES

As mentioned in 3.2.3 during communist times little attention was paid to the question of protection of rights to land. Land tenure security was not an important issue and most of the population did not care about it, especially not in urban areas strengthened by yearly inspections and inventory of urban real property carried out by the authorities. It gave people a feeling of security about their rights to use the property as they did.

In Kyrgyzstan as well as in most other former communist countries, the documentation of the BTI and the Land Management offices has been used for the initial privatization activities. In most of the rural areas the privatization of farmland progresses smoothly. New parcels are not always pegged out on the ground because of the fact that agricultural production in several areas continues to be on a co-operative basis with sharing of the parcels of land. In such cases marking of boundaries would hinder agricultural mechanization and most boundary markers would soon be destroyed anyway. The more or less provisory process of minor surveys during the privatization of rural property had the initial advantage of a quick fix, but it may cause future problems and there are signs that in Kyrgyzstan the number of disputes over property rights in rural areas is rising.
Due to the low level of actual surveys during the privatization process, a specific problem in Kyrgyzstan with urban property now appearing with the registration activities in the new land registration system is the fact that during communist times people were rather certain of the limits of their use rights and they had hardly reason to bother much about it during privatization. What they used became their new privatized property.

However, during the still obligatory 'inventory' – used as a source of income by the new offices – on the ground carried out after claims of rights by first registrants or by registrants wishing to transfer their property sometimes (unintentional) encroachments of real property may be exposed. Building without the proper permission or correct approval of the authorities during communist times might have caused such encroachments that are now being revealed. In exceptional cases it even might have been an intentional encroachment by (former) users of the real property. In such cases the official documents show a different approximate size than actually in use by the current user and new registrant. It is estimated that in some urban areas in Kyrgyzstan this happens with a considerable amount of the number of applications (recent reports even mention a percentage of up to 50%) for urban land registration. The current user of the real property immediately loses security of tenure in such cases sometimes turning the new land registration into a real nightmare. Lots of time and perhaps money must be spent and several bureaucratic steps must be taken to officially regulate the situation while any encroachment or incorrect building could well be caused not by the current user but by someone previously using the real property.

During the project assignment expatriate experts have successfully defended the introduction of a provisional title to be issued when the presented documents for first registration were incomplete or contradictory. The provisional title will over time become a full title when no contradictory claims for the land are made during a pre-determined period of time. Such a provisional title does in itself not resolve the problems mentioned but will often lessen a feeling of complete land tenure insecurity (which is a serious set-back for the introduction of a new registration system). It is strongly advised to undertake systematic registration and directly resolving problems as much as possible in setting up a new land registration to prevent issues arising during registration at transfers of land. By giving registration officials authorization to correct 'mismatches' between oral claims and documents or between actual use of real property and documented rights also making it possible to register the 'de facto' situation can avoid a strong perception of land tenure insecurity for many urban residents.

A systematic (and for the citizens totally or almost free of charge) registration process to deal with found discrepancies between de facto situations and documented ones is in former communist countries the best way to deal with privatization and it will considerably speed up the land registration process.

CHAPTER 4

LAND REFORM IN COUNTRIES IN TRANSITION

4.1 FARMING AND POLITICS

4.1.1 INTRODUCTION

Galbraith [35] (p. 47) states: 'For socialists, property was and in some measure remains not only the decisive but the sole source of power, the integument that held and holds the capitalist system together. As long as it remains in private hands no others can possess power. The theory of the Communists may be summed up in the single phrase: Abolition of private property.' And on p. 87 he continues: 'In non-socialist doctrine, by contrast, property is so important as a source of power that it cannot wisely be concentrated in the hands of the government ... But there remains the question of how extensively the state should intervene to get a wider distribution of property (and associated income) and thus of the power emanating there from.'

Thus land reform is a revolutionary step; it passes power, property, and status. It should be realized that land reform in countries in transition is somewhat different from land reforms elsewhere. Land reform in a transition period is often linked with privatization of property, not only of plots of land, but also involving urban real property.

In chapter 5 the model for rapid assessment of land reform related projects will be developed. In this chapter research findings on land reform are reviewed in their relevance for countries in transition. Research on land reform generally focuses on rural areas and that will be the emphasis in a review as this is. Nevertheless, as far as relevant, some remarks will be made about the changes for urban dwellers. This overview provides background information and summarizes motives for land reform as currently practiced in countries in transition. It is not always easy to determine the motives behind a land reform project especially for project staff, unless the motive is clearly stated in the terms of reference of a project. But then again, does the stated motive cover the actual activities to be carried out on the ground? Are these activities effective in view of long term sustained project benefits? The model in this research is a tool for assessment of effectiveness, but it should be used with relevant background information.

Employing it will provide early warning signals of possible non-desired side effects or of failing supportive measures to reach the project goals.

4.1.2 POLITICS AND AGRICULTURE

The continuous agricultural attention among political leaders all over the world is remarkable considering that the role of the farming population is decreasing in most societies. Although the proportion of agricultural labor is relatively and increasingly smaller, agriculture is not a marginal issue in political life. In spite of the agriculture's lesser economic contribution to national economies in the industrial era, agriculture has been able to conquer regularly the front pages of newspapers and to get the interest of leading politicians. This is particularly true in the former USSR influenced by Russian leaders who appear to worry more about harvest failures than politicians elsewhere. Perhaps they cannot forget the riot in a food line that sparked the February 1917 revolution and the victims of Krushchev's attempt to increase food prices – peaceful demonstrators shot in Novocherkassk in 1962. (VanAtta [95] p.2). Domestic agricultural production can be, and in many countries where agriculture is the dominant production factor, is the backbone of domestic food security. There also is another effect: rural society has left its mark on culture and mentality, a factor in supporting policies that favor agrarian interests. In dominantly agrarian former Soviet countries not the politicians in the capital, but the managers and the bureaucrats running the state and collective farms were seen as the real rulers of the country. VanAtta ([95] p.7 by quoting Sokolov) states about the chairman (of the farm board): 'A dictatorially-inclined chairman – and the job tends to make even the most democratic managers dictatorial – can impose his own punishments and even jail people with little opposition or review. Even now when they have internal (domestic) passports, villagers are formally prevented from moving to major cities by the retention of the residence permit ('propiska') system.' Most of these farm managers continue to use their political endowments after independence. In many cases they are the only people able to manage agricultural production, the acquisition of seed, fertilizers and agricultural assets, the marketing of products, and to warrant the continuity of government support.

4.1.3 CENTRALLY PLANNED AGRICULTURAL PRODUCTION

Several decades of central planning in agriculture have left their traces on the concept of farming among the workers on collective farms. In this respect, I witnessed an interesting scene in Bulgaria where I oriented myself for an assignment in the Bulgarian land reform project. On a cold but sunny November day in 1992 the Minister of Agriculture officially handed out the first land ownership documents to re-adjudicated farmers near the town of Pazardzhik about 20 miles west of Plovdiv. After the ceremony a lunch was served (including lavish servings of Rakija the national strong drink). After lunch many speakers took the floor and one of the last ones was a representative of the farmers in the region. He addressed the Minister as 'Comrade minister,' causing some hilarity, but that was a minor issue compared to the final words of his speech. The last sentence was a question, translated to me as: '... and Comrade minister when are you going to tell us what we will have to grow on our fields?'

After a short uncomfortable silence the Minister explained the new situation to the farmer. And during his discourse everyone noticed that the farmer got more and more distressed with his obviously unexpected newly acquired responsibilities. As an expatriate observer I suddenly realized how the concept of land ownership could differ among farmers from different countries. Subsequent discussions with farmers in Bulgaria revealed that most of them had no idea about how to manage a farm. In particular the planning of crops without market information, the purchase of seeds and fertilizers from often still state dominated suppliers, the absence of suitable mechanization for small scale farming, the general lack of market information and an inadequate infrastructure made individual private farming a kind of a gamble. It explains why most farmers in former communist countries feel uncomfortable taking up responsibilities for matters they cannot (yet) manage. It also explains the continuation of old structures of farming in which experienced agricultural managers take care of matters knowing their way in the often still-present bureaucratic maze of post communist government agencies.

I have to admit however that sometime later I witnessed a contrasting scene. I was invited for a similar ceremony in another part of the country. Here again a high-ranking official was handing out ownership documents to re-adjudicated farmers. When one elderly lady farmer came up to the table to receive the title to her ancestral land, the official kindly asked her: 'And what are you planning to do with the land?' She replied harshly: 'That is none of your business,' and grabbing the document from his hands she stalked right out of the meeting hall holding tight to her just received papers.

It was not uncommon to see some emotional scenes as well. I do remember a very cold windy and snowy day when some members of our expatriate team witnessed the staking out of the location of ancestral land parcels on a low hill near the Black Sea coast. Here an old farmer was so overcome with emotions that he sank to his knees in the middle of the just indicated parcel of ancestral land and stayed there for some time in his definitely not very suitable clothing for this weather in silent tears before he was helped up and led to one of the waiting cars.

4.1.4 CONDITIONAL PRIVATIZATION

Political concern for the level of agricultural production and fear for speculation with agricultural land has spurred governments to condition the transfer of rights from the state to private owners. In several former communist countries stipulations are set to use the transferred agricultural land for specific purposes within a certain time after the transfer, or to complete a specific type of building on the land within for example three years after the transfer. (The latter stipulation caused numerous problems in Russia for new owners that were faced with excessive monetary inflation while trying to purchase building materials). Non-compliance with the conditions would normally result in expropriation with only limited rules in the legislation to protect the position of the one being expropriated, hitting hardest those without political capital because they seldom can fall back on different resources. In several countries in transition, the right to land designated for agriculture is conditioned on proper use of the land and this proper use is generally narrowly described, mentioning an amount of specific agricultural products to be grown in compliance with 'cadastral' standards.

An often-used limitation – another condition – is a moratorium on transfers of rights to agricultural land for a number of years. However, this condition severely limits the establishment of a dynamic land market and is as such contradictory to the economic development motive of privatization. Thus privatized property in urban areas is generally excluded from a moratorium on sales because the land market is expected to start primarily in urban areas. Nevertheless economic theory also wants rural land to reach its highest potential value. The result is that in many former Soviet states the limitation on transfers has been removed again or is drastically reduced in time.

Many researchers have stressed continuous government concern for specific negative developments after privatization in countries in transition, but little research has specifically focused on the effects of privatization on the urban population. Most research shows that the effect of privatization – even with conditional privatization – is a growing inequity among the population, with possible dramatic consequences for the 'losers' because of absence of the alternative adequate social safety institutions. For urban residents the assumed economic development should bring the benefits of the land reform/privatization process. If the economy does not grow or grows only very slowly, as is currently the general condition in most post communist states, privatization can have considerable negative effects on the living conditions in the urban areas. Observations in cities show a decline of upkeep and maintenance in residential neighborhoods, mainly caused by absence of funds and interest also typical for many of the State managed buildings as well. I do pity children in school buildings with boarded up windows, dilapidated furniture and poor bathrooms. Their daily environment at school does not provide an incentive to 'clean up' and with the increased messiness of residential areas as well, one can only worry for their future concept of care for the environment they live in.

Is there another approach possible? If Platteau [66] is right in his observations that there is an evolutionary development towards more individualized property rights, then introduction of a limited individualized and more socially oriented property regime should be considered rather than a sudden non-evolutionary change as a large-scale and sudden land reform. The social impact of that type of land reform is now well-known and research has shown that such reforms always results in gainers and losers. Such a more evolutionary or incremental land reform could give a minimum protection to the 'losers' in the process and avoid sudden changes. The studies of Platteau point to population growth as the main cause for pressures initiating the evolution toward more privatized land ownership, they do not exclude other causes. Exposure to western lifestyles and exchange of ideas with western scholars could be a logical – albeit so far less researched incentive for evolutionary changes. Especially in most of the transition countries where limited resources severely constrain the economic development, a more socially focused property regime gradually evolving from a collective property regime could prevent too many people from becoming dependent on rapidly decreasing social safety nets.

Why not apply an incremental approach towards privatization in which the land is given in conditional exclusive use rights to citizens instead of almost unconditional ownership? It can be observed that a limited type of property right like the use rights to agricultural land, as initially issued, did not significantly hamper the land and agrarian reform project. It obviously does not matter too much to farmers whether full ownership or only exclusive longer-term use rights to land are obtained. They felt evidently secure enough to continue agricultural production and to even make improvements during the initial years after privatization. Besides, many farmers have very limited, if any, experience with private ownership rights to real property.

It is important to realize that farmers initially received 'only' privatized use rights to their land while the State retained the ownership of land designated for agriculture. And so the question arises whether it would have been possible to consider long term, more socially oriented and perhaps more equitable property regimes instead of making the cultural jump toward the typical imported 'Western style' of commodified property.

4.1.5 LAND REFORM AND LAND TENURE SECURITY

In most Western countries, the Land Registration or the Cadastre is the main base for land tenure security. The offices of the registration and their data provide physical proof of an institutionalized system for the protection of rights to land. Research shows that the population generally has a high degree of trust in such registrations. Besides, several countries have legislation explicitly sanctioning the data as proof of title – the so-called positive system of land registration.

The above system of land registration in Western countries is often referred to as a 'legal cadastre.' It is aimed to benefit the landowner by protecting his legal interests and facilitating transfers by providing easy proof ownership of rights, their extent and limitations. It simplifies obtaining credit using the legal interests as security. This indirectly benefits society by leading to an improved and efficient land market.

Other types of cadastres that can be distinguished are the fiscal and multipurpose cadastres. They are largely orientated to the direct benefit of government organizations for the raising of taxes and control of land use and development. In some countries the various types of cadastres are combined in one multi-purpose organization.

In Eastern Europe, particularly during the communist regimes, land cadastres were designed and established as tools for central (agricultural) economic planning. Therefore these land cadastres tend to include a large range of information without consideration of user needs and of the cost of collecting and maintaining such information bases. In several former communist countries, much of the information in the State controlled Cadastre may be incomplete when considered on a countrywide basis and has not been maintained. There is an unfortunate continuing tendency to retain and computerize these centralized, complex information bases even though they are unlikely to be required in a society no longer centrally planned. There is also the danger that the perpetuation of the old command economy cadastres in a multipurpose cadastre will deflect the focus away from the legal protection of rights in land, which needs to remain the main concern for the years to come. These remarks by Platteau [65] (his chapter 5) about 'cadastral' systems should be warning signs for countries in transition.

In former communist countries local authorities carried out yearly inventories both in urban areas and rural areas to ensure that registered data stayed up to date. These state activities to control and actually manage the use of real property during communist times resulted in trust that the inspecting authorities were aware of and implicitly approved the current situation of use of the real property. It made most owners of rights to real property feel pretty secure about their use rights, although the biggest threat to their rights was the State. The government not only maintained all data on land but could actually expropriate owners of rights to land because of inefficient use, illegal use of the real property, or careless use. The reverse of governmental actions, as done after independence, is another source of insecurity. It is one thing to reverse most decisions of former governments by questioning the legitimacy of their actions. But at the same time, this can be applied also to actions of current governments. The questioning of the legitimacy of past governmental acquisitions and allocations of land through review and possible reversal leaves present occupants of land with doubt about the security of their current claims.

Today in countries in transition, new land claimants sometimes have problems in claiming the adjudicated land or, if they do so forcibly, what will the consequences be over the coming years. Under such conditions, violence might become a serious problem in both rural and urban areas. Recent information about the situation is not reassuring in this respect. Although cases of violence have not yet been reported, there are an increasing number of disputes over land occurring in the last few months. The discrepancies as a result of the 'shrinking of land' to reduce production quota between land shares on paper and the real pieces of land they presumably refer to, contribute to this. There is also conflict between the theoretical exercise of distributing land (by paper land shares) with the actual possessing and cultivating pattern by the current occupants. There is evidence that in certain areas present occupants of land react angrily to the threat of eviction while claimants (i.e. holders of land shares or certificates) attempt forcibly to reoccupy the land, producing a conflictive situation, which can only jeopardize the long-term investment process required for economic progress in the country. A strong perception of tenure security will only be reached after several years of continuous commitment of a government toward the protection of private rights to real property.

Harold Lemel (1998) [48] (Chapter 3 p. 27-49) argues in 'Rural Property and Economy in Post-Communist Albania,' that the perception of land tenure security is based on four different aspects of institutional arrangements provided; land titling, land registration, maps and boundaries and that ownership documents appeared to contribute very little to people's sense of tenure security in those areas in Albania where pre-collectivization rights had largely been restored.

4.2 LAND REFORM EXPECTATIONS

4.2.1 MOTIVES FOR LAND REFORM

Max Spoor [78] (p.1) argues: 'Privatization of land and other assets and the restructuring of the previously dominant state farms (sovkhozy) and collective farms (kolkhozy) has been a focal point in many 'transitional strategies' of countries of Central and Eastern Europe and the FSU. There is broad acceptance about the reasons behind the stagnation of agriculture during the final stages of the Soviet regime.' The privatization or land reform took place in various forms of distribution of land. It could be distributed among workers, re-adjudicated to former owners, or by sales of assets and leasing arrangements. Often additional measures were necessary to protect the 'losers' in the process of privatization. For example, in Bulgaria where the emphasis was on re-adjudication of ownership rights to land, many former state and collective farm workers were facing joblessness after the land reform. Many new landowners expectedly would not need them and if they needed them it was doubtful whether they would be able to pay them after they started their new small individual family farm. The government had to interfere to provide these people with some land to start their own little farms and to continue tilling the earth and making a (small) living.
The main reasons for land reform are:

- The large farms, although formed to benefit from advantages of scale, suffered from low productivity and were inefficient in the use of resources (particularly capital);
- Free rider behavior was dominant, and income had to be complemented by the produce of household plots with much higher productivity (partly by using subsidized inputs provided by the state or collective farm);
- The farms were taxed through the state order system with lower than market prices and this system did not provide a strong incentive for the farm management.

Land reform has been practised the world over. In Africa the motive has been mainly to implement 'western style' land tenure, replacing communal land tenure that does not fit well into western legal concepts. Reasoning is the – proven disputable – assumption that a more western style land tenure would improve land tenure security. In Asia it has been emphasized that small farms may produce higher yields per unit of resources, and in Latin America the distorted distribution of land (the bimodal structure) has been the target of changes by land reform. Generally speaking, research on the link between tenure security and food security has in Africa focused on changes in customary tenure, in Asia on 'land to the tiller' programs and in land scarce Latin America, on redistribution of land. It is not always easy to determine the motive behind land reform. An important political motive for land reform has been the fear of insurgencies. Inequities associated with land tenure have been the cause of rebellion of peasants. The French Revolution, the American Civil War (also over slavery), the revolutions in Mexico, Bolivia, Somoza's overthrow and that of Batista in respectively Nicaragua and Cuba, as well as the civil war in El Salvador and the continuing turmoil in the Philippines all have their origin in land tenure systems that favor a small group of wealthy families at the expense of millions of impoverished rural people. Landless peasants have caused most of the great twentieth-century revolutions – those, in particular, of Mexico, Russia, China and Vietnam.

Barriers of communication between the countryside and the city break down, and those between domestic and international information gathering are breaking down. The peasantry has increased possibilities to come in contact with urban intellectuals, with images of other societies, with foreign ideas and ideologies and that all can lead to revolutionary ideas and movements.

Until the mid 80s land reform had been considered one of the main tools available to increase land access and improve agriculture. Then the focus shifted from land reform and other interventions toward promotion of land leasing, land titling and land registration to develop land markets or make them more efficient. (Binswanger et al. in a World Bank working paper (1993)) [99]. Shifts in focus by international donors, political motives for international support, and the eagerness of governments to secure funds for national programs have increasingly clouded the real issues of land reform. The motive is even more difficult to determine in the increasing number of programs that only address a part of a land reform program, like a program only for institutional reform, a program to promote individual ownership of real property, or one to stimulate land market development.

Agricultural production is not a static process, but it adapts to changes in methods, technology and product demand. It is likely that, a few years after a land reform project in some areas, land parcels need change again. Such projects are commonly referred to as land consolidation projects and these are generally smaller in scale and do have a more regional character. Nevertheless land consolidation is an important tool for rural development and for increasing agricultural production. Recently emphasis in land consolidation projects is put also on the development of rural living by improving the rural scenery and taking additional measures to protect the environment. Another reason to draw attention to land consolidation is that such a process might be a fair way to share the impact between all farmers in a certain area of (large) infrastructure measures disrupting agricultural production possibilities, that otherwise might only affect a few farmers out of proportion.

4.2.2 THEORETICAL CONSIDERATIONS

Many former republics of the USSR have a society dominated by agriculture and livestock breeding, so it is not surprising that agriculture is an important issue in politics in the countries in transition. What scenario out of the vast experience with land reform all over the globe is suitable to those countries when taking into account the interest of agriculture first and foremost? In an analogy by Peter Dorner in 'Latin American Land Reforms in Theory and Practice; a retrospective analysis' (1991) [25] (Chapter 2) a comprehensive review of some viewpoints can be given to assess the situation in republics in transition.

Structuralism

Structuralism is a reaction on rising doubts about the neoclassical economic view of international free trade. Under the existing structure of division of labor, countries on the periphery produced and exported raw materials to countries in the center that specialized in manufacturing goods. As a result, the periphery was always behind in terms of trade and had a chronic slow down in domestic capital accumulation. Gains of free trade were concentrated in the center. Backwash effects might even lead to worsening conditions in the periphery. A similar conclusion has been made by Myrdal [59] in 'Asian Drama' (1969) where he describes the situation of South Asian countries and their 'free' trade with Western countries (Part Three, chapter 12). 'It is generally believed that in the early stages of industrialization in Western Europe the income distribution became more unequal and that only later, with the diffusion of spread effects and rising production, and later as an effect of social legislation, this tendency was reversed. From this point of view, increasing inequality may be thought to be symptomatic of economic growth and dynamism' (p. 571). And earlier he mentioned (p. 567) that 'even if the degree of over-all inequality were comparable to that in the Western economies it would have much more adverse consequences in the countries of South Asia since a given degree of inequality wreaks considerably more hardship on the less developed economy.'

Observing these phenomena paved the way for two distinct reactions. A country could decide to import and stimulate substitution industrialization, or it could start a battle with rising food prices on the periphery by land tenure reform to increase domestic agricultural production. During the USSR time, most of the dependent republics in Central Asia served as an area to produce for markets in Moscow and other cities in the USSR. The break-up of the Soviet Union caused a loss of monetary subsidies from Moscow, a cessation of valuable agricultural imports (like for example concentrate feed, farm machinery, and fertilizers) and a loss of export markets for almost all export products.

Dependency theory

In dependency theory a dependent relationship exists when a country can only develop as a response to the expansion of dominant countries. The metropolitan centers will extract surplus from the hinterland. It is sometimes called internal colonialism. This term describes pretty accurately the situation in the former USSR where most of the countries on the periphery served as supply centers for the cities and population centers in the center of power in the federative republic. In the peripheral countries symptoms of underdevelopment can be observed because of the dependence of the center from where the resources and the agricultural planning came. After breaking free of the center land reform seemed the answer to raise agricultural production and create local incentives for better farming methods. But the well related and relatively well to do agricultural managers of large farms operating in countries in transition had nothing to gain and a lot to lose by a drastic land reform. The general result was a deliberately slow progression of land reform because of lack of action by the managers and obstruction to measures taken by the government to restructure farm enterprises. An alliance between those farm managers and some of the political elite showed mainly restructuring on paper only.

Institutionalism

Institutionalists reformulate development theory by indicating that both growth and equity should occur together. This theory can work, see for example Gunnar Myrdal [60] (p. 50) where he states:

> The conclusion I have reached is that inequality and the trend toward rising inequality stand as a complex of inhibitions and obstacles to development and that, consequently, there is an urgent need for reversing the trend and creating greater equality as a condition for speeding up development. Traditionally Western economists for the most part assume, on the contrary, a conflict between economic growth and egalitarian reforms. They take it for granted that a "*price has to be paid*" for reforms and that often this price is prohibitive for poor countries.

Creating greater equality requires the necessity of state intervention in a systematic and enduring way. In several of the former USSR countries it can be observed that state intervention is not working, either by lack of supportive institutes and respected enforcement bodies and/or by lack of resources. Part of the theoretical support for land reform is based on the observation that an inverse relation exists between farm size and productivity. Smaller farms produce relatively more than larger farms and thus a change in demand for agricultural supplies and labor will occur among the low-income rural majority as a result of land reform. However there is an important condition, which is not yet fulfilled in most of the republics in transition; there should be sufficient attention to agricultural innovation. Dorner and Kanel [24] formulate (p. 5 and 7) the condition as follows:

> Less developed countries need a labor-intensive, capital-saving approach with heavy reliance on yield-increasing technical innovations in earlier phases of agricultural development, followed by a capital-intensive, labor saving approach only in the later phases ... This policy approach both produces the required increases in agricultural production and avoids displacing labor prematurely from agriculture. It is a prescription for agricultural research, for large increases in the use of yield increasing inputs such as fertilizer, improved seeds, insecticides and pesticides, for increases in irrigation facilities, and for extension services, marketing, and credit. It is also a prescription to minimize mechanization, especially when it serves to displace labor.

This condition of agricultural innovation is difficult to meet in countries in transition especially for those in Central Asia. Before the break-up of the USSR much of the indispensable agricultural imports came from Russia and these imports almost stopped after independence. The effect of an expected large overall reduction in farm size did not come about because the necessary tools and institutions to make small-scale farming efficient were not available. There were not sufficient assets for small-scale farming, there hardly was any institutional arrangement to assist farmers with purchases and marketing of produce, and there was a general lack of extension services for training and education in new agricultural techniques.

4.2.3 REVITALIZATION OF LAND REFORM

Researchers like El-Ghonemy [37] (p.1) promote a revitalization of land reform programs: 'Among the major issues in development policy, malnutrition, poverty, and inequality in the distribution of wealth and opportunities are well known to interested observers. However, it is on the inter-relationship between them and the role of the state in quickly alleviating poverty and inequality not by the market-mechanism, but through land reform that different schools of thought and ideologies conflict. Since 1980, this conflict has been further intensified to the disadvantage of land reform policy and the rural poor.' Support for land reform also comes from other sides. Increasing concern for the environment is a relatively new incentive for efforts to push land and agrarian reform. Although the link between land tenure change and resource conservation and how they relate is still heavily debated, this nevertheless has fuelled new attention for land tenure change. Increased concern for the environment has strengthened motives for land titling and registration because of the suggestion that security of tenure will enhance the environmentally responsible stewardship of land by farmers, and because they are less likely to exploit the land and other supportive resources. Chambers [15] (p.3) argues,

> Secure tenure and rights to resources and adequate livelihoods are prerequisites for good husbandry and sustainable management. Moreover, sustainable livelihood

> security is a precondition for a stable human population in the long term; for only when livelihoods are secure does it become rational for poor people to limit family size. Enabling poor people to gain secure and sustainable livelihoods in resource-poor and forest areas is, thus, the surest protection for the environment. The poor are not the problem they are the solution.

Showing the rural population of countries in transition that property rights to land are protected and can be held against claims by others will stimulate the feeling of land tenure security. It is not the institutional arrangement that creates land tenure security; only a government showing a long and continuous commitment to protection of ownership of private rights to land can achieve it. When this policy succeeds, most researchers predict – although also doubted by some other researchers – that a better, more efficient and more environmentally responsible type of farming can be expected in return.

Thiesenhusen advocates land reform. In his review: 'Land Reform Lives!' [86], he stresses that the success of land reform depends – inter alia – upon supportive additional measures like non-land inputs, creation of markets, technical assistance, etc. (p. 199/200). He also argues (p. 207/208): 'It is quite possible that land reforms in the future will not look much like land reforms of the past; at least their rationales will be different. Rather than pitting landlords against *campesinos* in traditional agrarian conflict, the two groups have probably reached a stand-off; market-oriented measures with fewer government 'levers' will doubtless be employed more in the future than in the past. While the pressures will most assuredly be related to the mitigation of poverty and the creation of jobs, new arguments will be added.'

In many cases the non-spoken aims are at least as important as the mentioned ones. Non-spoken aims include strengthening capitalism, neutralizing peasant opposition, winning votes, fending off extremist ideologies, providing counter insurgency and fostering social stability needed for a secure investment environment. There is almost general agreement that gross inequalities in land distribution have been a highly destabilizing force in rural areas, associated with rural rebellion. An effective land tenure program must be crafted in response to the complex factors that define the agrarian structure of each country. No single formula will work for all countries at all times and knowledge of the existing land tenure structure is a sine qua non for any intervention in this area (Lambert, 1997) [45] (p. 3).

Although the hopes and expectations raised by land reform programs were not always realized, no one claims that one would be better off without reform. Lack of commitment, effective political will, and insufficient resources, play a major role in discouraging outcomes. Today there is a greater professional consciousness of the implications of land tenure diversities and the impact of improvement of the land tenure situation on both economic performance and environmental protection, although mainly focused on rural areas and the rural population. (See also Thiesenhusen [87] and Dorner [25] on this).

4.2.4 EXPECTATIONS OF CHANGE TOWARD A MARKET ECONOMY

After the failure of central economic planning to bring about general prosperity development, there is now a strong expectation in former communist countries in Europe that a market economy will bring the long awaited national economic development. This general belief is associated with the perception that all goods and services must be ready and suitable for trade in a market. Markets should evolve, not only for products and services, but also for land and real property. Individualized, clearly distinct, privately owned land plots and real property, with reliable proof of ownership are necessary for the development of a land market. Hernando DeSoto argues that only 25 of the almost 200 countries in the world have a free market economy. The most prosperous countries are among those 25 which have a free market economy. A free market economy is a capitalistic economy. It is the free market that establishes the best value of land by increasing efficient use and stimulating land markets. 'To be exchanged in expanded markets, property rights must be 'formalized', in other words, embodied in universally obtainable, standardized instruments of exchange that are registered in a central system governed by legal rules. This affords holders indisputable proof of ownership and protection from uncertainty and fraud. To be prosperous, property rights must enter the marketplace in a form adapted to massive and frequent exchange which facilitates the transfer of resources to their highest-valued use. Modern market economies generate growth because widespread, formal property rights permit massive, low-cost exchange, thus fostering specialization and greater productivity. Without formal property, a modern market economy cannot exist. When it comes to land, property rights should be embodied in formalized titles. A piece of land without such a title to specify its ownership at low cost is extremely hard to market. Any trade of this land will require enormous effort to determine the following: Does the seller own the land and have the right to transfer it? What are the boundaries? Will those who enforce property rights accept the new owner as such? What is the effective means to exclude other claimants? If finding the answers is difficult, then there will be no exchange at all, or exchange will be restricted to close circles of trading partners who trust one another.' (DeSoto [22] p. 10)

However, easy exchange of property is just one of the conditions to achieve growth of an economy under the rules of free markets. Several other conditions must be met, which we will encounter later in this book.

4.3 LAND REFORM PRACTICE

4.3.1 WHO GETS THE LAND?

As discussed earlier, at the extreme, two basic principles in land reform (and thus of tenure reform) can be distinguished in ex-communist countries; one is re-adjudication of land to former owners or their heirs. Of course, this option is only viable in countries where in Soviet times property was confiscated or where, on a large scale, individuals 'voluntarily' or forced, transferred their ownership rights to land to the State. The other principle is a distribution of land of former state farms and large collective farms among individual citizens or only to former employees of state owned farms, without taking into account the number of years they were laborers at the farm.

When there were former owners who could make claims, some countries in transition nevertheless made the choice to ignore any such claims and just distributed the land (like Albania and to a lesser degree Moldova). But, then again, this distribution of land could be done in different ways. In urban areas often the property was distributed to the people using it at the time of the declaration of independence although it also could lead to recognition of (some) former ownership rights. For rural land the decision was even more complicated. Should a government give land to all citizens irrespective of their attitude toward farming? Should the distribution of land be limited too inhabitants of rural areas only, or should land be distributed among former workers of the state and collective farms taking into account their contribution to the operation of the farms?

Re-adjudication – together with some distribution – of land occurred in most Central and Eastern European countries (except for Albania, Belarus, Russia, and the Ukraine). These countries practiced a mix of re-adjudication and distribution of land in a manner that avoided loss to some people of their possibilities to make a living from the land or of becoming homeless. But also here complications occurred. Rural areas changed during Soviet agricultural use and sometimes new farm buildings or villages were built, roads and irrigation works were constructed therefore some land simply could not be re-adjudicated in a simple way because it was not farm land anymore. Here compensation seems a possibility although sometimes re-adjudication is also practiced. Some of the countries favored a system of compensation rather than re-adjudication. Former owners of land or buildings (or their heirs) were compensated with vouchers instead of actual land. These vouchers could later be used to purchase parcels or apartments. But, also, former agricultural employees could receive vouchers on the bases of their contribution to the state or collective farm in various countries. In Central Asian countries and the countries without re-adjudication, as mentioned above, the process of land reform involved distribution of land, sometimes actual distribution, sometimes by giving out shares in land or vouchers backed by the state that could be exchanged, or sold and purchased. The political choice is an important issue because property rights in land represent a large portion of people's wealth. The importance of the decision is reflected in the additional measures that often accompany the land distribution, like a moratorium on sale of land, production criteria to be met by new individual farmers, zoning regulations and other forms that limited the freedom to use and exploit the agricultural land.

It should be noted here that the possession of rights to land is decisive for much of the future possibilities of many of the citizens. In particular in less developed countries, people do not have easy access to banking facilities and other means to acquire funds for investment. The capital they own is in their right to property. For example in the USA over 40 per cent of family assets consist of rights to land and in developing countries this figure can be well over 90 per cent.

4.3.2 RURAL LAND REFORM ACTIVITIES

Land reform in rural areas is a complex and challenging process. For agricultural land several factors must be addressed that are of no importance for urban areas. Agricultural land generally is all land suited for intensive agricultural use excluding the urban areas, the forestland, all national park land, most mountainous areas, and all other lands where only a marginal agricultural use is possible. These marginal lands can play a role in agriculture for collecting hay and fodder or for herding cattle, but they are not regarded as primary agricultural land because they provide only a minor contribution to the national food supply. To illustrate the complexity of the (re-)distribution of agricultural land, a more or less detailed description will be given of a specific land reform project in a country where both re-adjudication and distribution occurred (mostly to benefit agricultural laborers without land owning ancestors that would otherwise be deprived of their traditional way to make a living).

One of the first concerns of the government after the declaration of independence and the decision to re-adjudicate or distribute the land was to safeguard agricultural production during the time of dismantling of the large collective and state farms. In many countries some form of liquidation council or committee was established to make an inventory of the assets (including the possible debts) of farms and to determine the immediate future of these farms. The liquidation committee consists of the former management of the farm and often one or more representatives of the Ministry of Agriculture with possibly some local experts added. Most farms eventually had to close down completely with their assets distributed or sold and their land re-adjudicated and/or distributed. This process of closing could best be done gradually, in order not to disrupt the agricultural production process. Formerly employed farmhands had to get used to the idea of becoming owner-operators as self-employed farmers. As mentioned already many former farm managers were reluctant to give up their positions and tried to manipulate and slow down the process of de-collectivization as much as possible. I personally witnessed several meetings with farm managers and ministerial officials in which the latter reprimanded the farm managers for not acting according to the new instructions in due time. An often-encountered problem was the debts of a farm for which nobody wanted to take the burden. Many collective farms continued their existence because of those debts hoping to pay them off before they could be privatized.

To better implement the land reform process, the national territory is often divided into smaller areas generally following the borders of settlements or municipalities to employ local knowledge and experience in the process. In some countries the distinction has been made between three categories of land to be re-adjudicated (and distributed). Most villages have these three categories of land: Areas of land with still existing old boundaries (as before the Soviet rule) like terraced fields for vineyards and irrigated intensive agriculture; areas where old boundaries could relatively easily be restored like the fields that were between still existing roads, rivers and other topographical features not changed by any adaptation to large scale farming; and areas where re-allocation projects should be set up for the restitution, as well as possible, of the ancestral land parcels.

For the re-adjudication Municipal Land Commissions are established consisting of local experts and one or more representatives of the (regional) government. Most of the necessary legal, surveying, mapping, and land recording expertise are generally represented. These commissions (I will refer to them as local commissions) are authorized to make judicial decisions on claims and applications submitted to them in a pre-announced period of time. Claims and applications for re-adjudication of land must be supported by documents like old (notarial) deeds, (cadastral) maps, documents showing the submission of land to collective farms, affidavits, and, if no better proof is available, oral declarations of former neighbors, local authorities and all other means that are recognized as suitable for submission as supportive proof of a claim by the local commission. If actual restitution is impossible because of physical changes to the land (buildings, roads, waterways etc.) or for other reasons, the commission can propose suitable compensation either in alternative parcels of land or in vouchers or monetary form.

Often the sizes of land parcels to be restituted are restricted to a maximum size, which might vary from municipality to municipality according to the number of claims and the amount of land available for restitution. This restriction of size comes in useful because generally a certain amount of land is retained by the commission in areas of re-adjudication, often in a so-called Land Fund, to be distributed among landless people – people without heritage claims to land – in the region.

The reluctance of former managers of large farms to privatize is obvious. They lost their position by this process. When farmers got only small amounts of land there was reason for them to postpone privatizing of the large farms. In this case farm managers could persuade new landowners to form new cooperatives in which they brought in their land ownership to be managed by the former farm managers while they became employee co-owners on the new cooperative farm. Such actions can even be beneficial for all parties involved when the land parcels are too small to enable sustainable farming. The old farm managers know how to manage farms and are also well connected with most of the officials that still are needed for farming necessities as fertilizer and transport, while they also can provide assistance for marketing of products. Some farm managers deliberately gave farming families on the new cooperative their 'own' part of the land by staking out the rows of cotton or corn that were supposed to be theirs to attend to. Such division of the cooperative farm did not provide new farmers with their own land – that was 'hidden' in the total amount of land of the cooperative – but it gave them an incentive to work their part of the crop.

A complicating factor can be the national laws that might prescribe that land should be restituted in the form as it was before collectivization. This is sometimes extended with the requirement to distribute land of various categories –

vineyard/orchard lands, prime agricultural lands, and prime meadow and grazing lands – to each new farming household in order to safeguard the variety of agricultural production.

When land had to be (re-)distributed as it was before collectivization, some local commissions were challenged to make reasonable adjustments to this rule as in the case of land located near a popular vacation resort that had been converted in communist times into a vacation camp for Red scouts. Although many buildings provided only the basic amenities and needed upgrading, they nevertheless could be much more profitable to new landowners as they were now, rather than when brought back to their original farmland purposes.

Technical complications are also quite common with submission of claims and the necessary surveying and mapping activities to ensure fair and well-documented re-adjudication. During the growing and harvesting seasons most of these activities can hardly be carried out and must be postponed until after the harvest. In the first years after independence an often-met problem was the secrecy about coordinates as this information was classified and publicity would possibly be damaging for the nation's security. In later years the restrictions on classification of this type of data was mostly lifted.

A specific problem in some countries is that some claimants used the insider knowledge that land had shrunk on paper (See 2.4.3 and Verdery [96]). They tried to claim more land than they ever lost by making fraudulent claims for the commissions. My team sometimes came across documents of submission of land and farm assets to collective farms made up (in the late 1940s and early 1950s) in black ink but corrected (showing new larger amounts) in blue ballpoint ink – a writing device that was hardly available in those countries in the 1950s. It demanded a lot of wise judgment from the local commissions to make a fair re-adjudication of land and although they often did a good job, some claimants appealed decisions for which procedures and regulations must be in place.

Another often-met problem is the competition between various ministries. Initially the Ministry of Agriculture is heavily connected with the land reform project, but as the project progresses other ministries often become involved, like the Ministry of Justice, a Ministry for Planning, a Ministry of Housing and Building, and other governmental institutions and agencies. Because many of the land reform projects are funded with international donor support, there is often much more money involved in these projects than in normal national projects. Providing younger, promising government officials with an opportunity to be challenged and exposed to working with expatriate experts can be one reason for such competition, but often it is also the expectation that new activities and more international funding may come up as a spin-off of the donor assisted projects. In this respect I remember one EU representative complaining that every Ministry has the tendency to listen only to the total amount of money available for projects and seeing that amount as the (minimum) level of their own growth possibilities without realizing that other ministries have also a share in the total sum of available funding. Western land registration is often integrated into one national system, but in most of the post communist countries several agencies collect and maintain data on land that is often similar and could easily be exchanged using modern computer technology. Thereby, Western advisors recommended reduction in the number of agencies (related to one or another ministry) for the recording of property-related data and the centralization of issuance of permits is an additional source of competition and conflict.

A typical problem in land reform projects is the lack of experience of local staff with western style management, both in terms of human resources and of technical activities. There is little knowledge of methodology use for contracts and instructions; often there are no clear lines of delegated responsibility. I met a Minister of Agriculture who had a very popular weekly Tuesday-afternoon consulting hour for farmers from all over the country. Without any further consultation with local commissions, he sometimes overturned their decisions to satisfy just this one farmer resulting in a lot of problems for the local commission and with other farmers in the area afterwards.

Getting the legal framework in place is of course an important element in the required measures for a successful land reform project. This aspect has been discussed for the situation in the Kyrgyz Republic in paragraph 3.3.1. One of the problems is that most of the legal framework is copied from existing legal regulations elsewhere and this leads to frequent amendments and adaptations to make them more suitable and typical for the country at hand. For the short term, interpretation is often necessary to make the new regulations operational in concrete circumstances. Interpretation of the law is another issue causing differences between the local commissions and disputes between a commission and various ministries. The urgency of speed to complete the land reform requires interpretation by local commissions of regulations and rules for which they often use their local knowledge and experience. This could result in clashes with representatives of the central government later with, as a possible consequence non-payment by the central government – generally funding all land reform project activities – for already completed activities or delays in payment causing great problems for local commissions.

4.3.3 AGRICULTURAL LABOR

In most countries in transition in Central Asia, including the Kyrgyz Republic, agricultural land of the state and large collective farms were distributed among farm workers (in a wide sense, they did not have to be employed in specific agricultural jobs, but they also could have been, for example, staff of farm schools, canteens, and medical units). Most of the farm assets were also distributed while some assets were put up for sale. Arrangements were also established for leasing of agricultural land. There are significant differences between the countries in transition in this respect; in some countries there is disapproval for agricultural work. This is often found in more 'westernized' countries in Europe.

Among the former communist countries there are some where farming is seen as the best option to make a living and when the agricultural workforce is relatively young; which is the case in Central Asia, many young farmers seek to make a decent living in farming on their own when they can acquire sufficient land.

Research on productivity of land and labor in less developed countries has been carried out by Dorner and Kanel (1970) [24], and Barraclough (1990) [2]. Looking at the results of this cross sectional research, almost all research indicates that with slight variations output per unit of land declines systematically with the rise in farm size. There is also consensus among the studies that labor utilization per unit of land is considerably lower in large estates than in smallholdings. Labor input per unit is positively correlated with land use intensity and negatively correlated with farm size. The studies also show that small farms are at least as innovative as large estates in their response to technological change. The only difference was in introducing mechanization, which was clearly higher on large farms. The hypothesis that small farms are more productive than large farms in less developed countries has been most extensively tested by Berry and Cline [6]. Further support can be found in Sen (1981) [73], Carter (1984) [14], Feder [30], and Thiesenhusen and Melmed-Sanjak (1990) [84].

4.3.4 AGRICULTURAL PRODUCTION

Agricultural production forms the basic protection against food insecurity. Measured by accepted standards, many former communist countries are not yet 'food secure,' due to the complex economic situation most of these countries faced after the break-up of the USSR when traditional trade patterns changed, existing markets for products vanished, and imports became difficult to acquire. To stabilize food security domestic growth of certain crops was encouraged. Domestically grown produce contributes highly to national food security. It also supports economic development by increasing income possibilities for the rural population.

Because of the growing awareness of poverty and the growing gap between 'haves' and 'have-nots', the latest development is a new focus on the link between improvement of land tenure by land reform and the resulting changes in (rural) income. Agricultural development should be the motor of a developing rural economy. Too little resources are available to get a continuous agricultural development off the ground. The average farmer has little access to credit, has hardly a chance to get extended education in new agro-technology and has no way of applying mechanization for smaller scale farming by the sheer absence of assets and machinery fit for smaller scale farming. There are signs of a persistent and lingering national economic decline, a stagnating real property market both urban and rural, and little development in rural areas of specific support and training for farmers, establishment of market information and widening access to markets for farmers and their products. When land is relatively abundant to labor power and the country is technologically advanced, there is a high level of per capita productivity possible due partly to efficient management and partly to the high rate of capital and agricultural knowledge (El-Ghonemy [37] Part 2, Chapter 4). But it seems to be rational to farm with a hoe, hand sickle and buffalo, when credit markets are constrained, land is scarce and labor is abundantly available.

Farming with simple tools and intensive labor input could be easily observed in many Eastern-European countries like Albania, Bulgaria, Moldova, Romania, the Ukraine and Poland, and in most Central Asian republics after the distribution of the land of state and collective farms. Several private farms were relatively small – on average less than 5 ha – and did not have access to agricultural assets other than the hand tools and the donkey or an occasional horse to pull the cart or a pair of oxen to haul the plow through the field. The available mechanization is too costly to operate, hard to maintain due to lack of spare-parts and wear and tear while it is generally not well suited for small-scale farming for which relatively low cost agricultural labor is mostly at hand in these countries.

Many of the state and collective farms specialized in one or a few commodities and made widespread use of technology although some of the assets were old and badly maintained. Considering the proportionally high resources allocated by the State, their performance is below expectations when compared with Western farms. That is why a break-up of these large-scale farms forms one of the tools to improve agricultural production.

4.3.5 THE THREE ELEMENTS IN (AGRICULTURAL) LAND REFORM

When looking at it from the point of agricultural land, land reform programs in newly independent republics of the former Soviet block in Europe and Asia show three different elements within the land reform activities. Firstly there is the structural change of the farming enterprises. The land in use by large state and collective farms is redistributed among individual private farmers (smallholders) or smaller farming enterprises in which several farming families will share the land and will work together. Secondly, a legal change has been carried out providing private property rights for individuals and legal entities. A new property regime evolving after independence provides individual and exclusive rights to land. Thirdly, a land registration institution is established to register the new rights to land with the aim of providing legal protection and enabling relatively easy conformation of claimed rights to land by an appropriate authority. Thus the three main elements of a land reform are:

- (Re-) Distribution of the land,
- Establishment of a new property regime to formalize the new relationship between land and the holders of rights to land, and
- Registration of those rights, including protection of the rights to land and publicity of the registered data.

The approach toward the new land tenure regime differs among countries. Most of the new republics in transition in Asia do not have a tradition of widespread ownership of rights to land. After independence, land was distributed among prospective farming households under a land tenure system of exclusive use rights.

Providing farming households with use rights to land is a logical continuation of the existing land tenure situation of the Soviet era where household plots were provided to farmers with (exclusive) land use rights for subsistence farming. However, from the very start of the reform the issue of private and individual ownership rights to land was considered and debated among politicians, and often – in copying the western model – private ownership of rights to land became the final result of the land reform process. However to establish ownership rights to land, it is necessary to import a new 'Western style' legal system, to translate the legal concept as much as possible in the local language and social context, and to train local legal specialists. Importing Western style property regimes to facilitate rapid development in countries in West and Central Asia, with a population not accustomed to and possibly not yet fully understanding such property regimes, might cause future disappointment and dissatisfaction. Many farmers have mixed perceptions of land tenure security as described in the social assessment report [82]. And the course of events might strengthen them in their perception.

The newly acquired ownership rights to land will become subject to several limitations imposed by the state in order to achieve a balance between exploitation and sustainable preservation of valuable natural resources of the country.

It is likely that the state, when retaking some of the full extent of private ownership of rights to land, will fuel insecurity of tenure in the minds of the new farmers, which in turn will result in hesitation about investments in agricultural land. The question does arise whether a land reform leading to full private ownership of rights to land forms the best starting point of land reform projects or could the revolutionary tenure change perhaps better be replaced by an incremental tenure change that can evolve over the years. Some authors (like Platteau [66]) predict the evolutionary development of land rights as an autonomous process.

4.4 LAND REFORM IN CHINA

4.4.1 FROM FOOD PRODUCTION TO ECONOMIC DEVELOPMENT

China has a different position among the countries where land reform has been practiced first to adapt land tenure to the communist views and later to adapt to an agricultural policy that reflects influences of an evolving market economy albeit in an almost completely government controlled way. During the last two decades China has practiced a land reform process that can be characterized as using 're-adjustable land use contracts.'

Originally the reform attempts in China did not deliver. Already in the 1930s the urban oriented Communist Central Committee was urged by Mao Tse-Tung to initiate a moderate land reform. After coming to power, Mao initially followed the Soviet model of land reform to boost agricultural production, but later he developed a Chinese Communist alternative more reflecting China's different demography. His alternative was largely based on his own experience with peasants and most likely also on his hostile attitude to bureaucracy. In 1958 he initiated 'The Great Leap Forward' in which labor-intensive and local community initiatives should substitute centralistic bureaucracy by a cellular system of autonomous local communes and projects. The Leap Forward failed. It shattered China's economy with economic depression and enormous food shortages – some refer to it as a largely man made famine in which tens of millions of people perished (Frederick Crook [18] p. 59) – and Mao retired in 1959, for the time being. With the Great Proletarian Cultural Revolution in 1966 – 1969, Mao returned to full power to fight against the returned East European practices of communism in China (He also condemned the Russian advances toward the West because he believed that a war with the capitalist world would be inevitable). The Cultural Revolution signaled the victory of the radicals within the Chinese Communist Party who wanted to strive for a classless society in which everyone would selflessly work for the common good. One of the effects of this Cultural Revolution was the establishment of the paramilitary Red Guards which did demolish the existing political system and caused turmoil. Mao had to use the Chinese Army in 1967 to restore order.

But the economic recovery that started in 1962 survived and slowly the rural areas of China started to develop as well. Although Mao himself, in his later years, seemed to have abandoned the idea of the village autonomy, the cellular system of local initiatives started to deliver and during the last two decades of the twentieth century there was substantial positive progress in rural development that stimulated Lin et al. to publish 'The China Miracle' (Lin, Cai and Li [50]). Tuan and Ke underline in [91] (p. 16) that in China's Agricultural Policy the general goal of agricultural and food policy was to develop the country's economy. Before reform the goal was to produce ample and cheap food for urban residents and to export farm products to earn hard currency for import of technology. According to Lin et al. [50] (p.290) 'Economic reform began with the delegation of autonomy and the sharing of profit with micro-management units' (the so-called household responsibility system, later complemented with the town and village enterprises HD). It is their conclusion that (p.295): 'China opted for an incremental reform strategy with low costs and risks, but with yields timely returns. In contrast, the Eastern European countries and the former Soviet Union opted for the opposite, which caused tremendous friction and social shock and which, up to now, has not brought about growth.' The authors propagate non radical or incremental reform (p.276) that 'does not center around privatization' so it can 'avoid inequality which arises from the re-allocation of the stock of state assets and the conflicts arising therefrom, making it possible for every group to share in the economic property.' In this way the reforms are accepted by all, and become irreversible. China chooses to continue the system of distributing only the right to (exclusive) use of agricultural land in a very special way. In 'Land tenure policy in rural China: development and prospects a re-evaluation of the institutional reform of rural land use,' Zhang Hongyu [42] (p. 76 and 77) distinguishes three stages in land reform in China's recent history. The first major institutional reform involving land tenure occurred in 1952 (the agrarian reform) when land was taken from landlords and put under private ownership of peasants. The result was greater land productivity. The second land reform occurred as the people's commune movement in 1957, when peasants' private land ownership was changed into collective ownership. This change to public ownership did not produce a notable rise in land productivity. The third reform, the family contract responsibility system, did not change the foundation of collective land ownership, but it restored family based agricultural operations, which turned out to be optimal for the agricultural sector.

4.4.2 FAMILY SIZE DETERMINES FARM SIZE

The basic form of the family contract responsibility system is equal allocation of land according to the number of people or number of able-bodied laborers in the family. Until the Land Management Law of 1998, one of the special characteristics of the Chinese land reform was the continuous linking of the area of land contracted with the household size during the fifteen-year land use contract. The so-called system of re-adjustment changed the area of land contracted even during the contract term. Although, with slight variations among the provinces in China, in its application the general rule is that a change in the household members results in a change in the amount of land contracted to the household. If a household member dies the area will be decreased – in some provinces by half the amount that was originally given under contract for that member and of a piece of land at the discretion of the farming household – and similarly when a household grows in number, the area will most likely increase. For this purpose the land contracting body had a certain amount of land available. Sometimes large adjustments were implemented during the contract term and farmers received totally different land in return. The land tenure system employed land use contracts re-adjustable in size of the land contracted during the term of the contract. It is interesting to observe that this practice, although providing a certain degree of tenure insecurity, did not result in a substantial disincentive for farming households. Research [51] (p. 293) shows that agricultural output grew 56 per cent during the 1978 – 1984 period. About 60 per cent of the land in China is distributed under this rule. Constraints are uncertainty about the term of contract and no clear definition about the right of use making it impossible to transfer. In the 1980s the term was set at 15 years and in the 1990s any extension was for 30 years.

4.4.3 RULE OF LAW VERSUS RULE OF POLICY

Lack of a practiced rule of law for land tenure issues in China is a matter of concern. Bledsoe and Prosterman point out in 'Policy, The Rule of Law and Rural Land Reform in China' [7] that in China the rule of policy is often stronger than the rule of law. The relationship between the Chinese Communist Party policy statements and directives and China's developing legal and statutory infrastructure has not been entirely resolved. The policy has been used (rather than the rule of law) as an implementation mechanism. The uncertainty about the current land tenure regime among farmers is described by Liu Jianwen in 'Utilization of Land and Water Resources in China' in [43] (p. 115). 'At present, the core of the land tenure system is based on two inseparable institutional arrangements: (a) The land is owned by the farmers' collectives; (b) Land is contracted and managed by the individual farmer household. In reality, the collectives as well as the farmer households both have the right to own, use, dispose of and benefit from the land. In addition, the State can buy and use the land on a payable basis or take over the land without any payment according to certain legal regulations and procedures. Therefore, the land is not simply owned by the farmers' economic collectives as it is stipulated in the policies and regulations, but is co-owned by the State, the collectives and farmers in reality. Needless to say, there are many defects and loopholes in the present land ownership system. They are related to the ambiguous definition of the rights of the State, collective and individual farmer's household to own the land. To a large extent, this is an operational and design problem in the practical application of the collective land ownership. For example, there is no clear definition on the farmers' economic collectives, as the owner of the land; there is a lack of legal regulation and institutional guarantee for the collective ownership. Besides the right of contract, the collectives should also exert and ensure the ownership, right of disposal and right of benefit. There is no clear definition of who is eligible to contract the land and there is only a rough definition for the structure of rights, which is far from complete. There are no clear definitions on what role the government should play and how to eliminate the external problems related to land institutional arrangements (such as the co-ordination among the state, collectives and farmers). There is a lack of clear regulation on the formulation, pricing and resource allocation functions of the market for the transfer of right of use of the land, etc.'... 'The rural economic reform including land ownership reform is far from being completed. There are still formidable tasks ahead.'

4.4.4 THE RE-ADJUSTABLE LAND RIGHTS POLICY

So far research shows that the Chinese reform delivered. Justin Lin demonstrates together with others in [50] and in [51], that the results are (very) positive. It can be shown that the issuing of 're-adjustable' land use contracts instead of ownership documents, at least in China, had no noticeable drawbacks on the incentive to farmers for increased agricultural production. In this respect it is interesting to note that in the Central Asian republics agricultural production after independence also showed a general growth pattern.

Some researchers argue that the real start of China's land reform program was only very recently at the moment of the adoption of the revised 1998 People's Republic of China Land Management Law by the Standing Committee of the National People's Congress on 29 August 1998. (See Prosterman et al. [68] p. 1). They argue that with this law the nearly 200 million farming households can be provided with land tenure security necessary for long term productivity-enhancing investments in their land. They point in particular to Article 14 of the law restricting the practice of land re-adjustments. This practice of re-adjustment is called by them (p. 1): 'The single greatest threat to land tenure security since collectively owned agricultural land was allocated to farm households under the Household Responsibility System.' It should also be noted that Article 14 only prohibits the conduct of large land re-adjustments (the practice to take back all land in the village and reallocate different land to the households) and limits the conduct of small re-adjustments (to change the size of land allocated to one household) to 'isolated cases.'

The adoption of the Land Management Law is a step on the way toward a more commodified property regime and it must be expected that the debate on small land readjustments and the calling for implementation of 'long-term, protected rural land rights' continues among China's politicians and farmers. Platteau's observations in Sub-Saharan Africa of the evolution of land tenure toward individual private land rights obviously also can be observed in China. The future will tell not whether the long term use rights to land in China will be maintained or not, but for how long it will remain a characteristic of China's land tenure regime.

CHAPTER 5

BUILDING A MODEL

5.1 LINKING LAND TENURE AND FOOD SECURITY

5.1.1 THE FOOD SECURITY PARADIGM

In this chapter a tool for rapid assessment of effectiveness of land reform projects will be developed. It aims to assist in assessing the effectiveness of a project; to provide early warning signs of undesired or non-sustainable project effects, and to draw attention to failing supportive measures to ensure sustainable future benefits of a project. Land reform can have two distinctive goals, alleviating food insecurity or improving of economic development. First we will investigate a model for the food security paradigm and in the following paragraphs, a model describing the link between land reform and economic development – the prosperity paradigm – will be developed.

So, this paragraph concentrates on a model linking land tenure with food security. A simple caricature is given in Figure 5.1.1 in which land tenure appears as 'access to land' and food security in the form of 'nutritional status' is based on research by Maxwell and Wiebe [55] (p. 3) by replacing 'resources' with 'access to land' (arguing that resources can only be effective when there is access to them):

Access to Land → Production → Income → Consumption → Nutritional Status

Figure 5.1.1 First model of a food security paradigm

Access to land and land tenure, cover much of the same ground but they should not be confused with one another. As defined in 2.2.3 land tenure is the institutional arrangement of rules, principles, procedures, and practices, whereby a society defines control over, access to, management of, exploitation of, and use of means of existence, and production. The definition shows that access to land is one of the (albeit the most important) elements of land tenure.

Although simple, the above scheme already generates questions; how do people gain access to land, how do farmers gain access to agricultural land? How do different forms of access to land affect access to food? Is there an inverse relationship as the one depicted in the figure; for example, does a change in income affect production? Some dynamics can be implicitly introduced in the links; farmers can invest surplus income that is not consumed. Another dynamic is the fact that some choices by farmers are forced (and not free) choices. In times of famine or civil unrest causing food shortages, the choice can be between food consumption and asset depletion (endangering the future food security of the household), but an alternative can be to decrease food consumption and jeopardize health and thus labor possibilities in the household. Maxwell and Wiebe note an additional dynamic link that comes from vulnerability. A resource-poor, food insecure household will make the choice for a trusted crop with possible low returns instead of a higher risk – but commercial – crop with higher returns, in fear of possible failure.

Improved food security can be achieved by improved access to homegrown food. Provision of household plots can be an important measure in the combat of food insecurity. While working in Moldova in 1997, I observed that all citizens were entitled to house plots encouraging, at least partly, subsistence horticulture and small-scale agriculture. It was a measure of the government to seek a higher level of food security.

Structural improvement of food security can be pursued by (state supported) enhancement of agricultural production providing more food for consumption and incentives for a positive change in nutritional status. Interesting policy questions are: will increased access to land or will increased land tenure security lead to increased access to food and increased food security? From a research perspective primarily concerned with land tenure, an increase in agricultural yields is often suggested to be a sufficient outcome to generate improved welfare, including, presumably, food security and nutrition. The most common paradigm is that change in agricultural production in the sense of an improved agricultural production results in (positive) changes in income, consumption, and nutritional status. Since this paradigm focuses on achieving improved food security, it will be referred to as the food security paradigm.

5.1.2 EXTENDING THE FOOD SECURITY SCHEME

Figure 5.1.1 given in the previous paragraph must be slightly adapted and extended to visualize the food security paradigm. In the previous paragraph I started a model with 'access to land' linked to 'production.' In a paradigm starting with institutional change, the improved production has to be triggered by the deliberate changes of the institutions to provide for improved access to land. Land reform is often chosen as the way to improve production assuming that change of existing land tenure patterns toward more private individual property are positive incentives for farmers to raise production. The change in land tenure is represented by institutional change as well as by change of access to land.

A simple scheme (in which the improved food security results from change in consumption and a (positive) change in nutritional status) for the paradigm is given in Figure 5.1.2a:

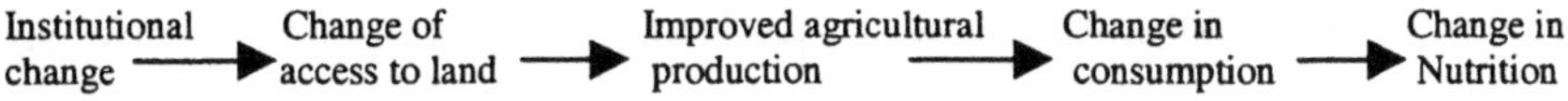

Figure 5.1.2a Extended food security paradigm

This is the basic food security paradigm. An important assumption has been made in visualizing the food security paradigm. It was argued that looking back from food security, presumably institutional changes were needed to initialize a reaction that eventually would lead to food security in the form of a change in consumption and a positive change in nutrition. But the basic feature of the scheme as presented is a casual flow from left to right. It remains to be seen if research shows whether institutional changes and changes in opportunity sets (see paragraph 5.2.4) create possibilities to change consumption and change nutritional status, two elements closely connected with a change in food security. In areas where food security is a recurrent problem (recurring droughts, famine prone places and the like) this is an important notion.

As mentioned earlier, change in institutional structures governing land tenure is commonly captured with the term 'land reform.' In paragraph 4.3.5 has been described that land reform generally consists of three elements: distribution of the land, formalizing new land rights, and land rights registration (in a cadastre). In this model land registration will be seen as part of institutional change. It could have been mentioned specifically to satisfy the often-felt need to formalize and record rights to land facilitating dealings with land as a stimulus to economic development. However to mention it separately as an element in the model will suggest that without land registration positive changes in food security and/or economic development – in the prosperity model – registration would not come about. This is contradictory to recent research findings where it was found that economic development and improved food security did occur under communal land tenure systems without formal records and documentation as commonly found in a land registration.

In summarizing the general impacts of land reform, Thiesenhusen [86] notes six goals, although, sometimes difficult to assess. Most goals also potentially affect food security. According to him (p. 199), possible land reform aims are: reductions in social polarity, increased investment, more transparent production incentives, poverty reduction, increased employment, and greater equity. With regard to food security, the presumption is that greater equity, productivity, and other outcomes resulting from changes in tenure will have beneficial impacts. (Accomplishment of these goals depends also on other measures).

The concept of Thiesenhusen in a visualized form looks is given in Figure 5.1.2b. Originally the focus in land reform projects was only on individual or household land. With new interest for environment, common lands and state property are included also. As seen before, there is evidence that livelihood strategies are not limited to individually held lands; important seasonal effects on food security can be compensated for from common or state lands and forests.

Examples can be found in Albania where peasants, in order to improve their living standard despite the small plots of land they got after privatization, increased the number of livestock grazing on common land dramatically, while at the same time intensifying agricultural production on their newly acquired plots of land. Findings and conclusions of Thiesenhusen confirm the possibility of approaching food security from the left-hand side of Figure 5.1.2b.

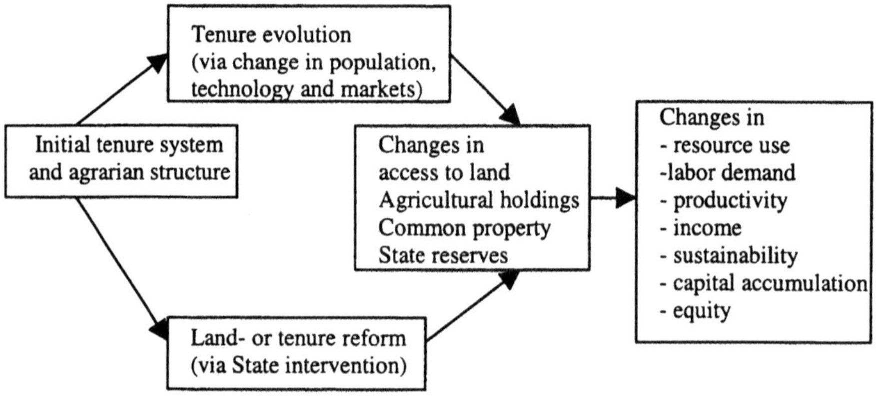

Figure 5.1.2b Land reform goals (according to Thiesenhusen)

An important confirmation of the food security paradigm is the notion that not only change in land tenure brings about an improvement (or a change) in agricultural production, but that this improvement is also the result of a change in resource use. A change in land tenure arrangements may provide farmers with the possibility to lease land (change in land use) or to buy land with credit obtained by using the land as collateral. By introduction of mechanization, labor input will change (diminish) and farmers may be able to free time to acquire knowledge of new agricultural methods and applications of biotechnology.

5.1.3 THE FOOD SECURITY PARADIGM VISUALIZED

Before visualizing the food security paradigm, I want to introduce ‘initial situation’ as a first element in the paradigm to stress that the nature of the proposed measurements aim at introduction of a new property regime. It should also be noted that the flow has been changed from left to right into top to bottom.

The model for the food security paradigm is based on the findings and considerations as presented in this paragraph. The scheme is an oversimplification of reality. By the nature of it – showing one way relations (top - down) only – it will also be clear that the scheme does not provide answers for a variety of questions that do not follow the one way pattern. Nevertheless it does raise a number of important issues for countries in transition. Do individuals gain access to land? Do individuals use the newly acquired opportunities? Does the element 'change in consumption' automatically result in change in nutritional status or do individuals make the choice to consume resources by obtaining capital goods instead of food (a situation I encountered in a project in Poland)? These questions should be asked apart from the model and the analysis of the links between land tenure and food security.

The food security paradigm with these extensions can be visualized in Figure 5.1.3 as follows:

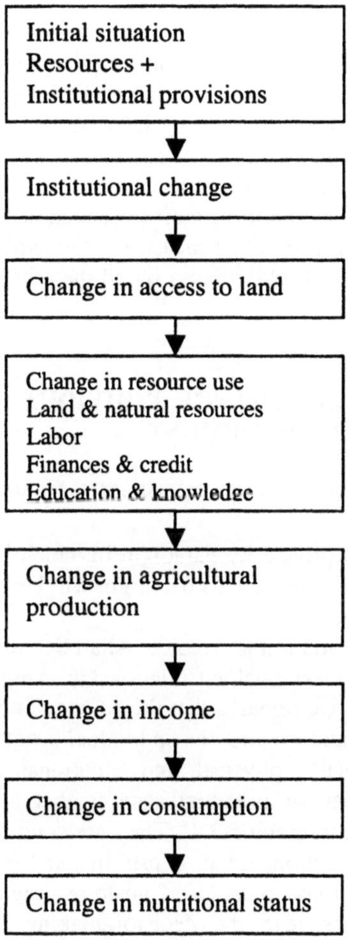

Figure 5.1.3 Food paradigm model

In most of the former communist countries in transition (recurrent) famines are extremely rare. A common concern in countries in transition is to maintain a (minimum) level of agricultural production during the period of transition in which state owned land is transferred to individual farmers. The change from a centrally planned system of agricultural production to a free market economy causes concern and political controversy at the national level among politicians. Will the government be able to continuously guarantee sufficient food for the population? Will not every new farm switch to cash crops ignoring a healthy, more reliable and balanced mix of agricultural production? Will not a minority end up with possession of the majority of land leaving most of the population without sufficient resource for subsistence?

The model developed in this research will assist in an assessment of the effectiveness of land tenure changes introduced by deliberate actions of a government whether or not supported by international donors. Although this is a limitation for a general application of the model, it enables a simplification in so far that tenure evolution via change in population, technology, and markets, can be ignored. Generally the population in most post-communist countries has to digest so many changes in a short time that measuring the evolution of land tenure under such circumstances will be highly biased by all the other impressions and changes in society.

5.2 INSTITUTIONAL CHANGE, INDIVIDUAL BEHAVIOR, AND ECONOMIC DEVELOPMENT

5.2.1 FAMILY FARMING AND ECONOMIC DEVELOPMENT

Now we will turn to the prosperity paradigm in which land reform is specifically aimed at economic development. This paradigm will be visualized in a way similar to the food security paradigm.

In Property, Power and Public Choice, Allan Schmid (1978) [71] (p. 6 and 7) indicates that institutions establishing relationships among the individuals define the rights of individuals. He remarks that the course of actions by any individual is guided by these rights and creates the individual's opportunity set (the latter is defined as an individual's physical and emotional capacities plus legal or customary understandings of potential options that are conditioned by actual choices of others – see paragraph 5.2.4). They are conditioned because individuals follow tradition and perceptions under constraints and perhaps even peer pressure of others. These conditions, plus laws, customs, regulations and materialized institutional arrangements lead the decision-making processes of individuals, which over time can be measured by economic indicators. The aggregate behavior of individuals results in (land) market activity. The institutional structure of the new land registration organization determines the available choices of potential or active participants in the agricultural land market. Partly on the analogy of Nabli and Nugent 1989 [61] (chapter 2, p. 1334), we can define that institutions as the established rules and customary relationships in a social organization form a set of constraints governing behavioral relations among individuals or groups. Institutional changes can facilitate economic development by increasing market efficiency, and market failures can also signal the need for institutional reform.

One reason for the 'Glasnosjht' (*Translation: Publicity, Openness*) was the disappointing economic result of the practiced communist doctrine. In post communist countries the assumption is that increased individual private ownership of rights to land recognized and protected by an institutional structure will lead to increased productivity, access to credit, reduced conflicts over land, permitting efficient farmers to outbid less efficient ones in the land market. The latter process will presumably lead to more efficient production, higher rural incomes and higher land values, resulting in rural economic development. The spin off will stimulate economic development as a whole. International donor organizations propagate land (re-) distribution among private individuals as a means to achieve increased economic development.

In some parts of the Soviet Union, already before 1989, experiments with more individually farmed land had begun. The then communist rulers established a number of family farms with some land from state farms. In the Baltic Republics this experiment started around 1987 (and it caused some bitter disputes at the time of de-collectivization and mass-privatization after independence). The expectation was that farms when being made a one farming family responsibility would produce more efficiently thus raising yields and agricultural production. This in turn should improve economic development. In several other parts of the world research on land tenure shows evidence that individual access to sufficient land is one of the most important factors to economic development. The link between access to land, resource use and income generation resulting in economic development is almost automatically assumed. In this paradigm improved resource use triggers income generation and economic development and prosperity. The paradigm can be put in a simple scheme (in which most of the subsequent steps are assumed to automatically result from the previous ones) in Figure 5.2.1a:

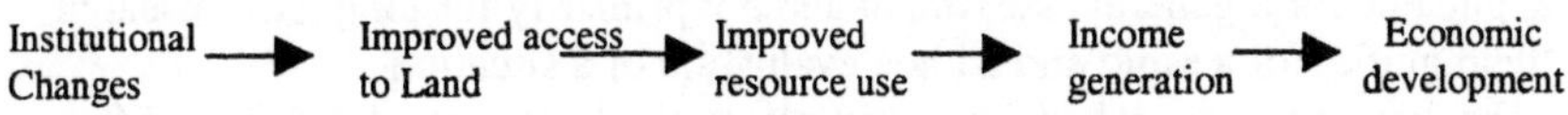

Figure 5.2.1a Simple scheme of prosperity paradigm

This paradigm describes economic development and improved prosperity as a result of institutional changes: The prosperity paradigm. It can be reformulated in substituting 'Institutional Changes' by change in access to land as a result of new institutional provisions. These new institutional provisions together with available resources aim at improved access to land. In addition to adjudication of land, farmers can buy or lease land if they have the resources to do so and this together will determine their new changed access to land see Figure 5.2.1b:

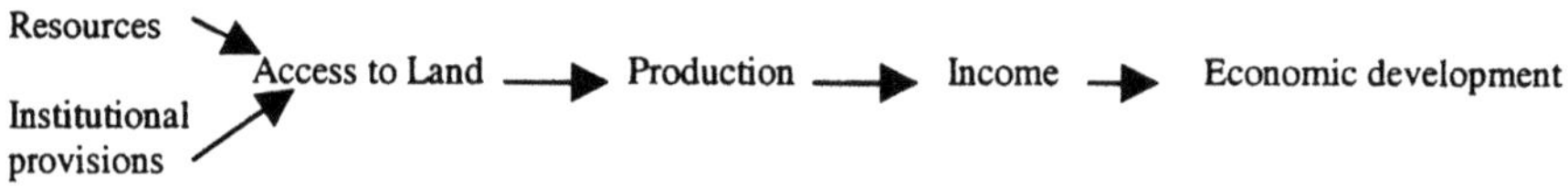

Figure 5.2.1b Reformulated prosperity paradigm

However, this is not sufficient. A dynamic model of links should also incorporate the cyclic links (to keep the scheme readable only selected cyclic links are added in dotted lines). It is given in Figure 5.2.1c:

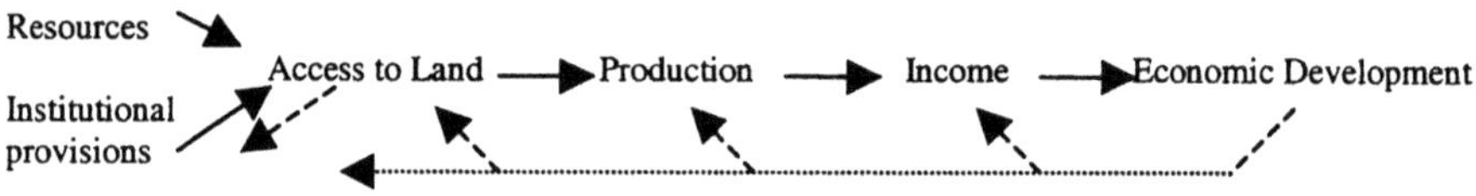

Figure 5.2.1c Dynamics in the prosperity paradigm

In most research, links are generally examined only one way to limit the complexity. In other words, most of the cyclic effects are ignored. Attention will primarily be paid to the change in production due to the change in access to land and not whether the change of production initiates changes in access to land. This research will focus on providing a simple and quick assessment of projects in which land tenure change is the aim. The model to be developed should be simple and applicable for a general assessment and not primarily for long term research. It is a 'field guide' for a rapid and ad hoc evaluation of a situation.

The 'one-way' model of links can alternatively be visualized in a different manner (using a sequence from the top downward). The start of the links is institutional change – inter alia providing a change in tenure security – and this triggers changes in resource use, the result of which is change in access to land, in production, and in income, resulting in economic development.

As stated before this is the 'one-way' approach in which cyclic links are ignored because of the fact that the model will serve primarily as ad hoc evaluation of a situation and not an assessment of events over a long period of time.

In line with expectations that improved access to land will trigger economic development, programs to improve individual tenure security were among those proposed to boost the economic development even further. One of such programs is land registration and titling.

These results are shown in Figure 5.2.1d:

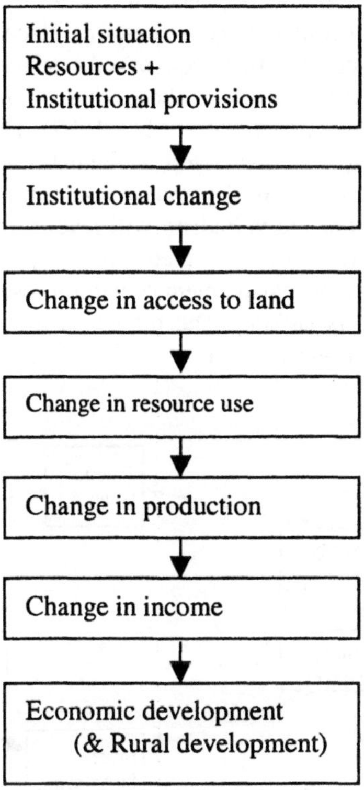

Figure 5.2.1d Prosperity paradigm model

5.2.2 LAND TITLING AND ECONOMIC DEVELOPMENT

A strong advocate of the positive impact of land registration and land titling on economic development often cited by scholars is Gershon Feder (The Economic Implications of Land Documents in rural Thailand) [31]. He presented a paper under the title 'Economic aspects of land registration and land titling,' in Warsaw (Cadastral Congress November 1998) [32]. In this paper he provided a conceptual framework (as visualized on the next page in Figure 5.2.2a) for analyzing the economic aspects of land registration and land titling. It also reviews evidence from around the world showing that land registration has led to better access to formal credit, higher investments in land, and higher output/income.

It is interesting to notice that in more recent publications Feder shows an increasing restraint in advocating a straightforward positive correlation between land registration, land titling and economic development. In the presentation in Warsaw he argues that there are several prerequisites for land registration to become economically worthwhile, and there are circumstances where the investment will not be economically successful. Place et al. [67] show similar restraints when they state that there are several reasons why the effect of the traditional assumptions may not come about. Dubois questions the usefulness of land titling in: 'Does title really matter?' [27] (1997). There is no indication that a growing awareness of private ownership by land titling will result in economic development and in conservation of resources. International development players assume that gradually more individualism will lead to more formalization of land rights, giving more security, access to credit, higher prices for land, social peace, economic stability and better management of natural resources, but systematic data to support this rationale is lacking. The model used by Feder in Warsaw stems from 1987 it is shown in Figure 5.2.2a.

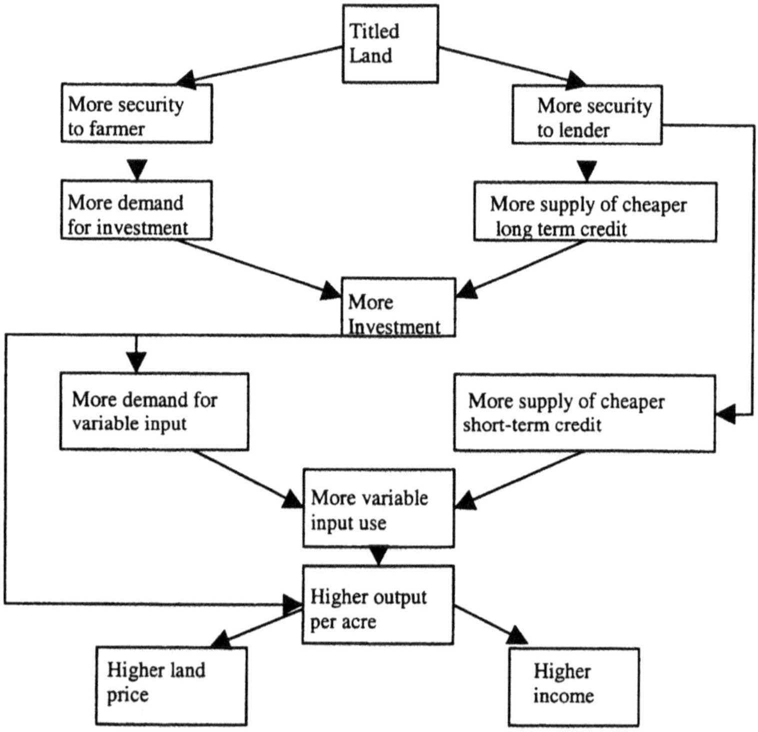

Figure 5.2.2a Effects of land titling (developed by Gershon Feder)

Feder notes that demand for land registration and titling has emerged in various societies as population growth, advances in land use technology, and increased trade made it necessary for property rights on land to be better documented, and to be reliably enforced. He distinguishes two types of effect of registration:

- Improved resource use by enhanced land tenure security (necessary to invest in land, clear it of stones, drain it, cut trees, make access, etc.) because the cost is borne up-front.
- Better position to obtain credit because a credit transaction carries the risk for the lender, hence the emergence of collateral arrangements with immovable property to be used as guarantee for repayment.

Both effects lead to higher productivity, increase of land values etc. In addition to these effects, greater clarity of land ownership, through registration and titling, facilitates a smoother and more efficient operation of the land market. This increases overall productivity of the economy, as land transactions transfer land from less efficient to more efficient producers.

A similar approach as developed by Feder in the prosperity paradigm to conceptualize links, can be found in Place et al. [67]. They note (p. 15): 'There is widespread belief that for economic development tenure security is an important condition.' Compared with weak or insufficient property rights, secure rights based on economic theory are believed to:

- increase credit use by greater incentives for investment in land;
- increase land transfers by increasing the certainty of contracts;
- reduce land disputes;
- raise productivity through increased agricultural investment.

Place et al. present in Figure 5.2.2b, a conceptual model linking title and tenure security with agricultural performance (narrowing economic development to only the agricultural effects).

In Figure 5.2.2b the demand side represents the incentives to farmers and the supply-side the incentives to lenders. Increase in demand is derived from two sources. First, greater tenure security increases the likelihood that the operator will receive the returns on the investment. Second, increased tenure security will most likely diminish the occurrence of disputes freeing the resources otherwise used for litigation. Demand for complementary inputs (farm chemicals, labor) will enhance as well, assuming the existence of viable technologies, extension services, access to input, and the availability of financial resources. Subsequently enhanced tenure security will lead to higher investment and yields.

Although tenure security in their approach is seen as a condition for economic development, in the model economic development has been replaced with specific agricultural effects like the use of land improvements and higher yields. Obviously there was reason for them to concentrate on farmer's behavior, but it should be mentioned here that economic development is not limited to only the agricultural sector of the society in which institutional arrangements aiming at an improvement of land tenure security take place.

Because of supply side effects, higher yields are possible even if households lack sufficient financial resources. The collateral value of land will be higher with title thereby raising lenders' expected returns. Increased tenure security is also assumed to have a positive effect on land markets. Security of title makes transfers easier and land leases more secure. Efficiency gains would arise if more productive farmers can outbid less efficient users of land. Increased tenure security will also positively affect land values as long as the expected yield response to investment is positive and the output price in the aggregate is sufficiently elastic.

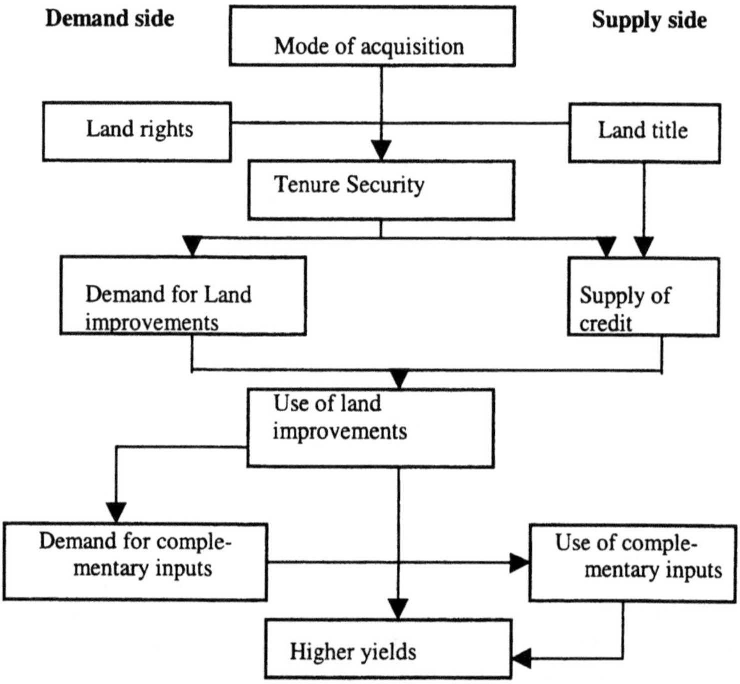

Figure 5.2.2b Prosperity paradigm by Place et al.

According to Place et al. there are several reasons why the effects as described above do not come about: Farmer's investment demand may be weak for reasons other than security of tenure. Farmers may perceive returns less risky, may avoid technologies unknown or farmers may be unfamiliar with technological options and investments may be unprofitable. Poorly developed input distribution may fail to supply enough complementary input or may result in unaffordable input prices. Even if demand for investment is enhanced, financial constraints may prevent farmers from exercising demand. Usury laws may prevent lenders from raising interest rates to mobilize capital. Poorly developed institutional systems may result in exorbitant administrative charges. Also land improvements will not always increase yields. Instead of more labor, farmers may pursue more leisure; it may be used to more variance in yield rather than enhancing yield.

Place et al make the remark ([67] p.18):

> Instead of undermining the importance of tenure security, the foregoing reasons simply suggest that secure tenure is necessary but not sufficient for agricultural development, and that the expected benefits would be strongest in situations of dynamic technology and well functioning markets. Whether registration would stimulate output response under these conditions would depend on whether tenure security is significantly higher than under the indigenous (*or original - HD*) system and on whether credit use is enhanced.

In a recent study in Indonesia, Herman Slaats [76] (p. 106) concludes that registration of land did not protect the population. He states (p. 102) that the shift from communal rights to individual rights removed the control of the community and replaced it by the legal, economic, and political system of the State, in none of which villagers have much participation. 'Under the system of individual ownership, the land becomes more sensitive to market forces. Whereas previously buying and selling of land was carried on within the community, now outsiders can buy village land ... These factors contribute to increased land prices and stimulate villagers to sell land rather than improve its productivity.'

Outsiders approach a purchase of village land primarily as long-term investment and not to increase agricultural production. Yet another example where the assumption that land titling automatically improves yields does not hold while the momentary and not sustained change of income has unpredictable effects on economic development of the rural region.

5.2.3 COMPARING PROSPERITY PARADIGMS

What is the result of the model as presented by Place et al. for the prosperity paradigm as developed in paragraph 5.2.1? First of all it should be noted that the two models do not address the same questions. The model of Place et al. (further referred to as Place) focuses on the links between use of resources, production, and income, it focuses on demand side and supply side factors that in the prosperity paradigm (for the time being) are ignored. The prosperity paradigm covers resource use, production, and income plus economic development in which rural development has an important part.

We have to examine what similarities with or potential additions to the prosperity paradigm can be found in the Place model. To assist in finding the similarities in both schemes I have added numbers at each of the elements in Figure 5.2.3. The institutional changes and the changing access to land (1) in the prosperity paradigm, are represented in the Place model by the provision of (new) land rights and land title(s) (1).

It is assumed that a land title is the written proof of a land right and that there are no land rights without land titles. With this assumption land rights and land titles can be seen as components of new possibilities opened up by institutional changes providing new possibilities of access to land. The institutional changes result in changes in resource use (2) to changes in production (3) and changes in income (4) in the prosperity paradigm, represented in the Place model by (changes in) tenure security (2) → (3 and 4).

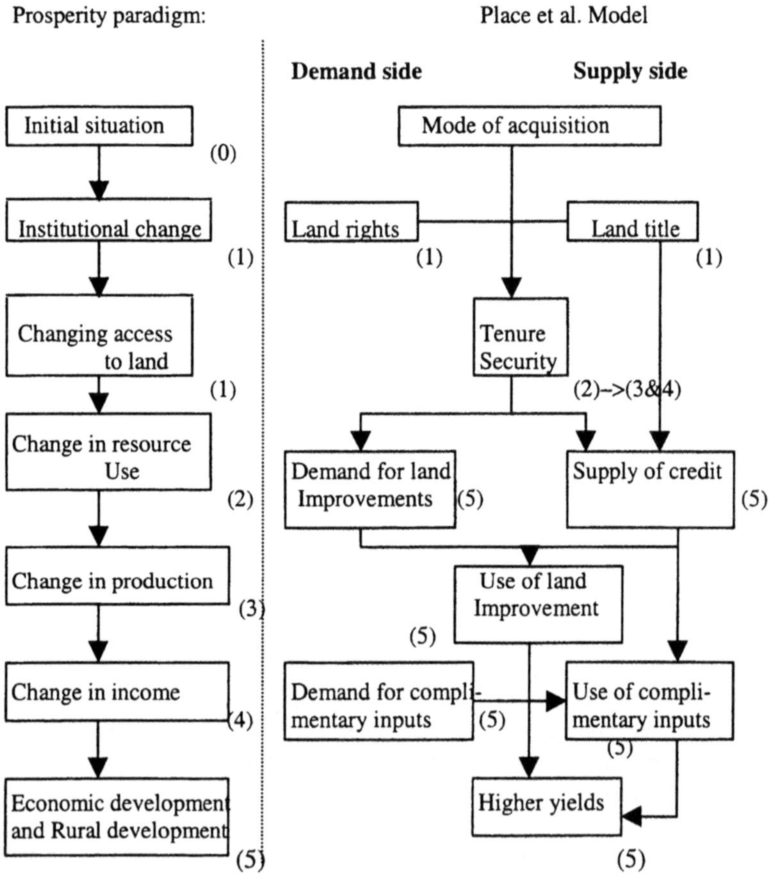

Figure 5.2.3 Two prosperity paradigms compared

The effect of economic development (5) in the prosperity paradigm is much more specified in the Place model by all the elements of change indicated by (5). All elements marked (5), in one way or another, will contribute to measurable effects. The Place model gives reason to make some additions in the prosperity paradigm. A complication in the 'streamlining' of both models is the fact that in the prosperity paradigm 'economic development' (5) is – inter alia – the result of higher income, which in rural areas will usually be generated by higher yields. The choice can be made to incorporate 'higher yields' as a byproduct of change of production. Because of the dependability of the price of agricultural products, I make a different choice. The higher (agricultural) yields used by Place et al, will be incorporated in my model as an indicator of economic development, on the quite safe presumption that statistical data on agricultural yields are available. The Feder model explicitly covers also the land market development by adding the element 'higher land price.' In my paradigm the land market has not been explicitly mentioned, it is included in the broader context of economic development.

5.2.4 OPPORTUNITY SETS AND ECONOMIC DEVELOPMENT

In this book land tenure security and food security are core issues. They determine the success of land reform projects. People interact in social life within their opportunity sets. An individual's opportunity set is composed of physical and emotional capacities plus legal or customary understandings of potential options that are conditioned by the actual choice of others. The opportunity sets of individuals interact and condition the outcome of human transactions. Although the following text mainly focuses on rural real property, it is similarly applicable on urban real property. On the analogy of Allan Schmid [71] we can argue that the opportunity sets of potential land registrants are determined in part by the rules established by the institutions as well as the expectations by the registrant of the behavior of other land owners, other registrants, and the bureaucrats in the land registration offices. The behavior of these individuals influences economic outcomes and conditions the land market. In Figure 5.2.4a the starting point is the initial land tenure structure, (peasant) income, land distribution, agricultural production and (peasant) nutrition. Note that parentheses are used to indicate that the theory also can be applied to urban areas. Any existing institutional structure will provide for a certain type of land tenure, which in turn will determine the perceived land tenure security. The (new) institutional structure will change the existing perception of land tenure security and thus influences behavior of individuals (changing their opportunity set), which results in changes in access to land, (peasant) income, land distribution and (agricultural) production. Those changes are measurable in the changing land market and economic indicators that show economic development. Following this line of thinking, an addition can be introduced in the prosperity paradigm. It should be called changes in 'the opportunity sets' of individuals. The institutions determine these sets and it will be clear that a change in institutions could spur changes in opportunity sets of individuals. The complexity of inter-human relations can result in changes both as a personal reaction on the institutional changes or as an indirect reaction because of actions by other individuals as a result of the change in their opportunity sets.

Allan Schmid [71] (p. 205) states: 'It is not argued that a change in opportunity set and advantage automatically leads to changed behavior. The persons involved may not perceive the change or may forbear. They may not take advantage of the change because of benevolence, ...' In some countries in transition it was easily observed that many peasants used their opportunity sets and took advantage in the form of a change in access to land. Moreover, with proper institutional arrangements in place some farmers will try to lease land to expand production, some farmers will lease their surplus land to others, farmers will use their land as collateral to obtain credit for improvement of land or fertilizers and quality seed, or livestock purchases.

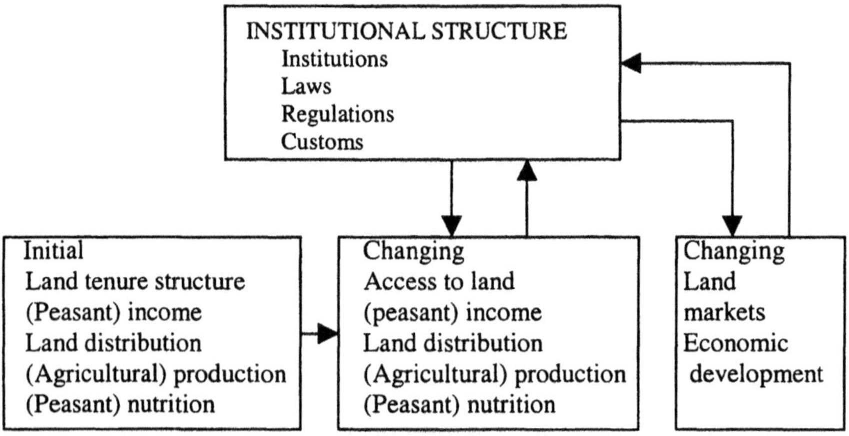

Figure 5.2.4a Determinants of opportunity sets (by Allan Schmid)

This, relatively easy to monitor, change in access to land has partly to do with a change in land tenure security, but land tenure security is a state of mind rather than a directly measurable element. A new model for the prosperity paradigm can be visualized on the next page in Figure 5.2.4b.

The change in access to land gives way to a changing use of resources and the element 'change in access' to land should thus be situated between change in opportunity sets and change in resource use. Another addition should also be made in the prosperity paradigm. In the last box of the prosperity paradigm the two indicators for economic development should be mentioned; the higher yields and the higher land value (I prefer the use of the term value to price) as used by Feder.

The growing complexity of the scheme gives way to more possibilities than can be visualized in the simple caricature of such a scheme. The simplified scheme is given in Figure 5.2.4b. One of the deliberate choices I make is to see the change in resource use as a result of several other changes (access to land, change in tenure and change in credit access). But I like to indicate that a change in the opportunity set will also create a possible direct change in resource use (labor, knowledge, education etc.) and not as a result of the other changes mentioned.

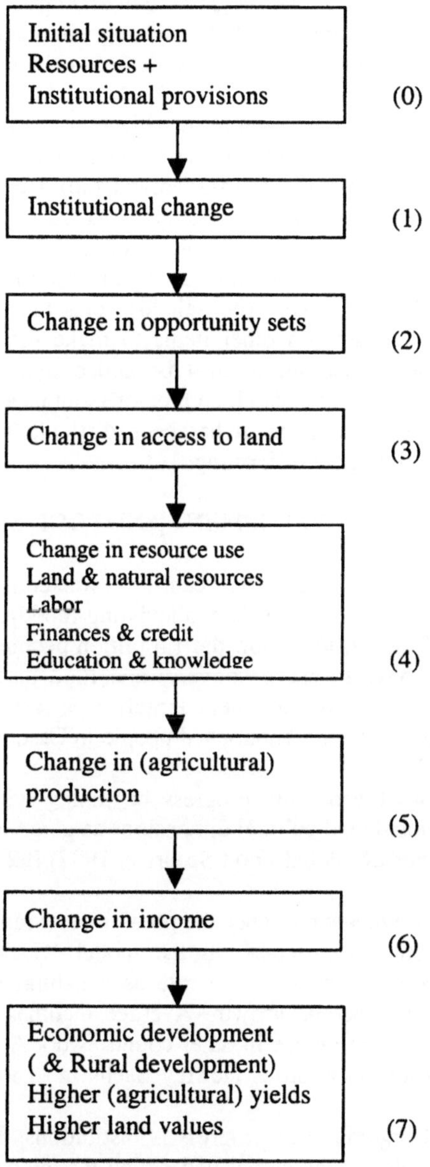

Figure 5.2.4b Completed prosperity paradigm

The model of Place et al. is based on improved land tenure security. In the model for the prosperity paradigm, change in land tenure security is an implicit element in the institutional changes. It does change farmers' behavior in both models, which is made explicit by adding (2) the changes in opportunity sets. Changed access to land (3) will lead to a different approach to land leases and land transfers, eventually stimulated by more access to credit and resulting in changes in resource use (4). Higher yields are reflected in change in income (6). Effects on land markets will be measurable by statistical data on economic development if all the conditions are met.

But it has to be borne in mind that Place et al also notes that there can be several reasons why the effects as described above do not come about. In an assignment in Poland (in the Lomza voivodship) I could observe that farmers initially were not inclined to give priority to increasing yields after their income increased. Instead of investing the surplus income in agricultural improvement, as was expected by the foreign and national experts, the first impulse was to use most of it for the purchase of luxury (household) items like color TVs, video players, new 'western style' cars and other items to make life on the sometimes rather isolated farms more pleasant. It must be added that the Lomza voivodship is located in the north east of Poland, an area of swamps and peat land. Many farms do not have running water and it has been difficult for many of the people to squeeze a meagre living out of farming.

5.2.5 ECONOMIC DEVELOPMENT AND FOOD SECURITY

In 'The Economics of Global Food Security' Tweeten [94] (p. 4) states: 'Because it is the poor who lack access to food, alleviating food insecurity means alleviating poverty. Most of the world's poor, the 1.3 billion people with income of less than $1 per day, will have to escape poverty and food insecurity through economic development. Economic development largely was responsible for a 158 million reduction in numbers of undernourished people in East, South, and Southeast Asia from 1979-1992.'

A paradigm of economic progress beginning with the underlying natural resource, institutional, and cultural dimensions as given by Tweeten and Brinkman (in 'The Economics of Global Food Security' 1997) [92] (p. 6) & [94] and shown in Figure 5.2.5.

Natural endowments influence the possibility of rapid or slow growth. This is the first ingredient for progress. In the model 'Geography' has been shown between parentheses. It does play a role as a natural resource in so far that it relatively influences income growth. Average incomes in land locked countries tend to grow slower than those in other countries do. A similar lower growth rate was found for tropical countries (Jeffrey Sachs in 'The Limits of Convergence' 1997 [70]).

The second ingredient of progress is institutions. They formulate, prescribe and impose 'the rules of the game' underlying the allocation of resources to meet the wants of the people. A well instituted educational system influences growth, as growth, as does a well functioning banking system, but also legally enforceable property rights. A problem with institutionalizing is that it introduces for example transaction costs of land. They are unavoidable, but sometimes procedures surrounding land registration are expensive, slow, and bureaucratic leading to higher transaction costs and loosing their bearing on potential users of the system. They will stay away from the system and use informal ways, negatively influencing the development of markets and the economic development.

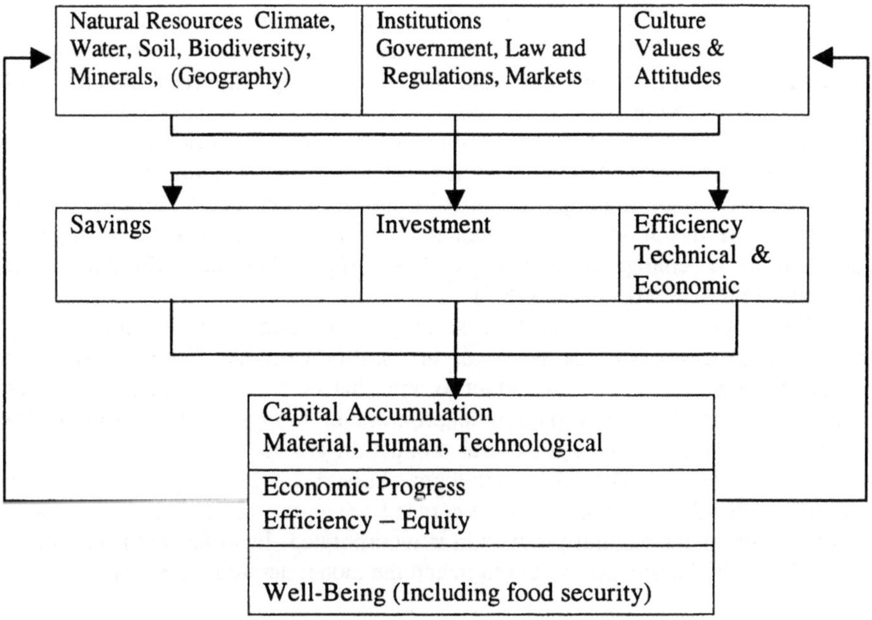

Figure 5.2.5 Tweeten/Brinkman paradigm

The third dimension is the most dynamic. It can be argued that as a result of change in the second ingredient, culture could change. But for the model, culture must also be seen as a separate ingredient. Work ethic, morality, thrift, acquisitiveness, entrepreneurship and national community are important factors for the rate of progress.

What are the consequences of the principles laid down in the paradigm of Tweeten and Brinkman for the food security model as developed for the food security paradigm? The paradigm of Tweeten and Brinkman is based on economic progress beginning with the underlying natural resource, institutional, and cultural dimensions. Via savings, investment and improved efficiency it is presumed that capital accumulation will be achieved resulting in economic development and improved well being (and implicitly improved food security).

In the food security model natural resources are the start and via change of institutional arrangements, resulting in changing opportunity sets and changes in access to land there is a change in resource use. It is certainly true that opportunity sets as used in the food security model are affected by cultural and social dimensions. Allan Schmid argues that the opportunity sets of potential land registrants are determined in part by the rules established by the institutions as well as the expectations by the registrant of the behavior of other land owners, other registrants, and the bureaucrats in the land registration offices. Cultural and social circumstances or 'rules' will undoubtedly influence the expectations someone might have. Designed for a relationship between land tenure and food security, the food security model does not pay much attention to the way capital will be accumulated. But it implicitly presumes that improved agricultural production will be the result of a change in resource use of which accumulated capital is one of the causes. In this respect the food security model does not contradict the findings of Tweeten and Brinkman. Neither does it contradict the conclusion drawn in their paradigm that economic progress results in improved well being, although this is 'translated' in the food security model as change in income -> change in consumption -> change in nutritional status. (For additional information see paragraph 15.2 'The Standard Model').

The conclusion is that the food security model aims more at food security than at well being, but that it is not in conflict with the Tweeten/Brinkman paradigm. Nevertheless it is important to note that in the food security model as based on the food security paradigm, progress in food security is supposedly accomplished emphasizing agricultural production growth resulting in increasing income. The Tweeten/Brinkman paradigm chooses a wider approach with the assumption that the increase in income comes from a general economic progress in which growth in agricultural production is incorporated. In so far that paradigm is also reflected in the prosperity paradigm and the model derived there from.

5.3 COMBINING THE PROSPERITY AND FOOD SECURITY PARADIGMS

5.3.1 ONE MODEL

Maxwell and Wiebe [55] look at food security while focusing on income generation and nutritional status. Looking at food security they promote access to sufficient productive land as one of the most important factors to determine food security. According to their view, conventional land tenure literature links access to land with resource use and income generation. While starting from land tenure the conclusion is that improved land tenure results in better access to land and income generation. Improved access to land appears in both views whether one starts at food security and looks back at a search for the conditions under which food security can be achieved, or whether one starts at income generation and looks back to where this comes from. The challenge is to combine the prosperity paradigm and the food security paradigm in possibly one model in which the differences in final aim are covered and a linkage is provided between the two domains. The first part of the two models to visualize the paradigms is similar.

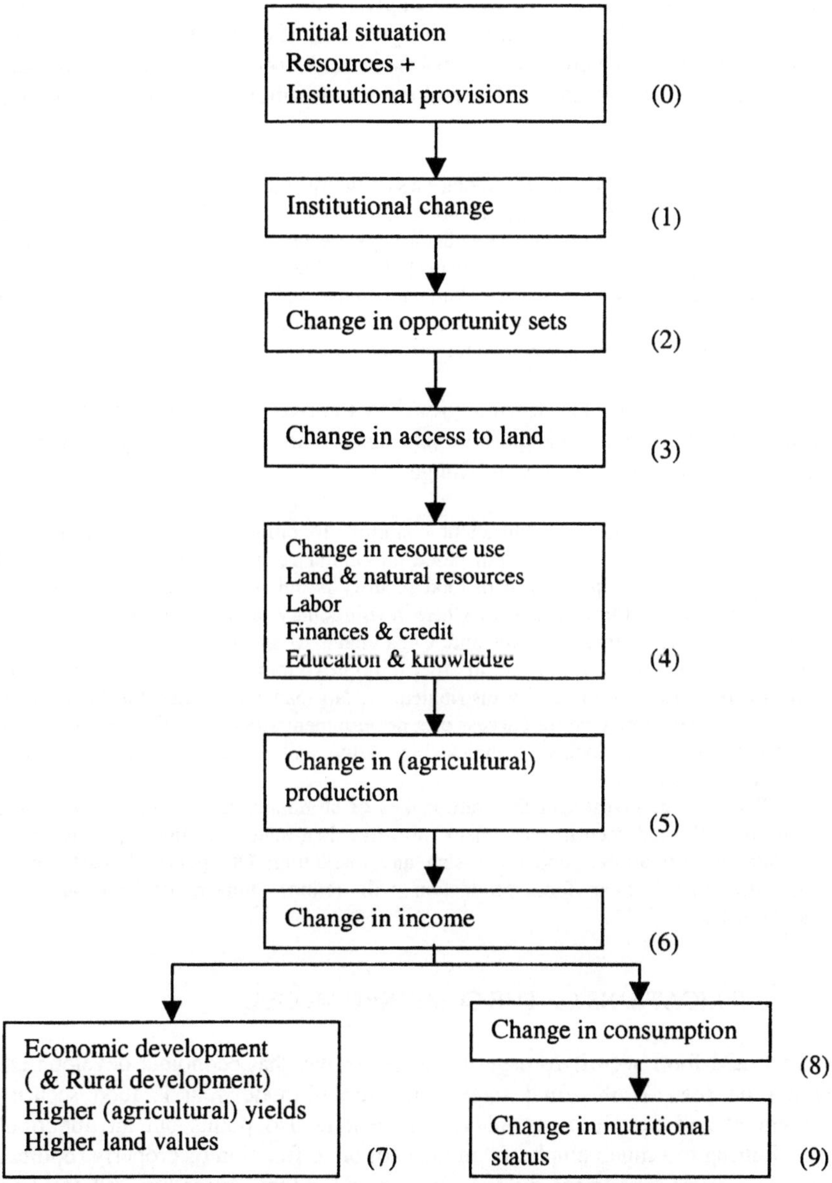

Figure 5.3.1 Combined model of prosperity and food paradigms

With some 'translation' – note that element (5) is now 'change in (*agricultural*) production – it is thus possible to combine the two models and paradigms. One simply has to substitute 'economic development' in the prosperity paradigm with 'improved food security' (change in consumption and change in nutritional status) to change it into the food security model. The significance of this 'translation' must not be underestimated. Why otherwise would Solon Barraclough [2] warn food security researchers and policy makers so unambiguously in the following way (p. 237):

> The different approaches to alleviating mass poverty and world hunger tend to cluster around several rather contradictory poles. The dominant one in the 1980s has been simply to stimulate economic growth through greater reliance on free markets and exports. The benefits of growth are expected to trickle down to the poor. A rising tide lifts all boats. This was also the dominant theme before the 1980s, but in earlier decades there was less emphasis on market forces alone and more on the positive role of state interventions to promote rapid growth.

The problem with the trickle down approach is the overwhelming evidence that a rising tide of growth may sink more human boats than it lifts in many situations.' And elsewhere (p. 72) in 'An End to Hunger?':

> Economic growth is not a sufficient condition to eliminate or even significantly reduce hunger ... Without growth based on capital accumulation and technological change, sustained improvement in food security is out of the question. This is true even with land reform. Countries where revolutionary agrarian reforms have taken place, such as China, Vietnam and Cuba, have to be as much concerned with sustained economic development in order to improve food security as do those where wealth remains very unequally distributed. ... No matter how essential institutional and social issues may be for success of a development strategy, and their importance has often been overlooked, technical innovation and capital accumulation remain crucial components.
>
> The kind of investment the state makes or stimulates tells much about its real priorities. If food security is a major priority, then state investment policies must emphasize agriculture, food processing and marketing. Of course, it must not be assumed that greater food production will reduce hunger, or necessarily be sustainable.

5.3.2 IMPLICATIONS OF THE COMBINED MODEL

The combined food security/prosperity model shows that economic development must not be seen as the final stage when the ultimate goal is food security improvement and rural poverty alleviation. But it also points out an important danger. Putting too much emphasis on the economic function of property (optimal productive use of resources) by focusing on individual ownership and the free market as dominant goals of projects can damage the social function of property. Property should serve a common good or be justly distributed among society's members. Economic development is a tool to battle the danger of food insecurity, but that battle cannot be won by reliance on economic growth as an automatism to reduce food insecurity alone.

Governmental guidance and vigilance is needed here in two ways. First, it should focus on agricultural production with sufficient resources to apply new technology and introduce more efficient farming. Second it should put emphasis on the social function of property to secure long-term effects of the land reform by ensuring a continuing (re-) distribution of resources in such a way that a minimum safety net can be guaranteed for all citizens. There are many ways to do this, of which I will briefly mention only a few. From the start of the land reform program the government should be aware of the vulnerability of land as cultural and national heritage. Programs to re-distribute the effect of newly distributed rights to land must be prepared, should it become clear that an economic development leads to undesired inequities. This can be done, for example, by income- or real property taxes. The long-term sustainability of natural resources must be protected by legal measures to curb individual exploitation beyond the long-term carrying capacity of the resources. By new legislation generally the gainers of the land reform are protected, similarly much attention should be given to protect the losers of the effects of the new land tenure system like women, elderly, sick, and landless people. Attention must be paid to effects of re-emerging customary habits excluding groups in society of the benefits of the new land tenure system. But, most of all, governments must be made aware that it is often not a matter of an economic paradigm or a food security paradigm. Putting political emphasis on both paradigms can result in an economic development model while simultaneously attention is paid to (or ensuring that the benefits of economic development result with priority in) improved agricultural production.

CHAPTER 6

INSTITUTIONAL CHANGE

6.1 IMPLEMENTATION OF A NEW PROPERTY REGIME

6.1.1 INTRODUCTION

In the following chapters (6-13), a method for rapid assessment for the situation about land reform in the Kyrgyz Republic will be elaborated. The choice for only one country to be used in the practical assessment of the model has been made to avoid confusion and complications as a result of a mixture of countries. Statistical methods used in one country will differ (slightly) from those in use in other republics in transition, and that will negatively influence the readability of the next chapters. The Kyrgyz Republic has been chosen because of its' comparatively advanced political climate and the relatively large number of international agencies that operate within the Kyrgyz Republic. It is one of the most progressive republics in Central Asia.

A description of the situation in the Kyrgyz Republic has been given in chapter three. This will serve as general background information for the following chapters. In the next chapters a description will be given to show how changes of elements in the model can be initiated, carried out and observed in the Kyrgyz Republic. Although each one of the chapters will focus on one specific element, generally each indicator or signal can be used to see the effect of more than one element. This will cause some overlap between the chapters. For example institutional changes will affect several elements; changing opportunity sets, changing access to land, and changing resource use. It should be noted that the indicators used in the following chapters are far from being exclusive. Other indicators are very well possible depending on the circumstances and data available. In discussions with researchers of the Land Tenure Center, I was assured (again) that personal observations are useful sources of information and what better way than being on an assignment in country to make those observations. Together with indicators and statistical information they form the backbone of the method as described in these chapters.

Neither land tenure security nor food security appears as element in the model. This is to underline that both are perceptions and are not suitable for direct measurement. It is through the elements of the model and the related indicators and observations that we can develop a proxy of what the perception could be. Improvement of land tenure security is influenced by institutional changes for land tenure and can be observed by changes in opportunity sets, changes in access to land, and changes in resource use. Change of food security is the effect of changing resource use, change in income and changes in consumption. In that way governments take concrete actions to change land tenure and improve food security.

One of the most used measures to do so is land reform. Land reform aims at a change of the existing patterns of land tenure. It usually starts with new legislation. The new legislation must be an incentive for individuals to make use of (new) opportunity sets. To prevent the change from being felt as a threat, institutional arrangements and regulations in which the individual right holder can find protection of rights must be put in place. Especially for land, institutionalization must support in providing security of tenure for the owners of the rights to land, legislation must provide long-term rights and protection for the exclusive use of land. Land reform requires the commitment of the government and can only be successful with sufficient supportive residual policies.

6.1.2 THE KYRGYZ CONSTITUTION, THE CIVIL CODE, AND THE LAND CODE

The Constitution, the Civil Code and the Land Code of the Kyrgyz Republic indicate a possibility of private ownership of land (and not only of use rights to land).

Article 4 of the Constitution of the Kyrgyz Republic [44] clearly states that although private ownership is recognized all land belongs to the State. It reads (in the provided English translation):

> Property in the Kyrgyz Republic may belong to the state or may be private.
> The Kyrgyz Republic guarantees the diversity of forms of ownership and their equal legal protection.
> In the Kyrgyz Republic the land, its underground resources, water, air space, forests, flora and fauna, and all natural wealth is the property of the State.
> Under the circumstances and within the limits established by law of the Kyrgyz Republic, the use of land parcels may be transferred to individual citizens and their associations. The purchase and sale of land is not permitted.
> The Kyrgyz Republic shall protect the rights of ownership of its citizens and juridical persons to property, and also their property and ownership located within territories of other governments.

In November 1998 a Law on Amendments to the Constitution of the Kyrgyz Republic was presented to Parliament. It contained the following amendments and changes (as provided in English translation):

> To set out in Article 4 the following Subparagraphs 1, 2, 3 in the following wording:
> 1. In the Kyrgyz Republic the state, communal, private and other forms of ownership shall be accepted and protected. The Kyrgyz Republic guarantees the diversity of forms of ownership and their equal legal protection.

2. In the Kyrgyz Republic the land, its underground resources, water, air space, forests, flora and fauna, and all natural wealth shall be used as vital elements for life and activity of the nations of The Kyrgyz Republic and be specially protected by the state.
3. Land may be state, communal, private and other forms of ownership
Limits and procedure of implementation of landowner's rights and protection guarantees are determined by the law.

It is to be understood that this is a change toward private ownership of all types of real property in the Kyrgyz Republic. Furthermore, it was declared that all land shares and government land grants–the documents issued for land designated for agriculture ('Ugodia') – were transformed into documents showing ownership rights to land. Apart from ownership there is possible confusion about transfers of use rights in rural land. Is it free or should an 'initial cost' be paid (25 times the tax rate) for the right to exclusively use the land. The Civil code of the Kyrgyz Republic does not clarify this issue further, but the preamble of the Land Code reads:

> This Land Code regulates land relationships in the Kyrgyz Republic, the grounds for emergence and procedure of exercising and termination of the rights to land and their registration. This Code also aims at development of land market relationships in the conditions of state, communal and private ownership to land and of rational use and protection of land.

This implies that private ownership of agricultural land is clearly an option.

6.1.3 MORATORIUM ON 'UGODIA'

Another confusion remains about the moratorium. What does it cover? The Land Code of 1999 states in article 35:

> The owner of a land plot or a land user may transfer the rights he holds to a land plot fully or partially to other individual or legal entity without any permission of state agencies subject to limitations established in paragraph 2 of this point, unless otherwise provided by this Code, other legislative acts of the Kyrgyz Republic, conditions of allocation of a land plot.
> The owner of the land plot of agricultural designation may not perform purchase and sale of the land plot of agricultural designation for 5 years from the moment of acquiring the right of ownership.

The moratorium expectedly is limited to the 'Ugodia.' But article 73 of the Land Code states (again in the provided English translation) reads:

> Land plot of agricultural designation shall be used by individuals and legal entities for running of seed-growing, pedigree cattle breeding, and commodity agricultural production, protective forest planting, gardening, vegetable raising, dacha

> construction, carrying out scientific research and experimental works and for other purposes associated with agricultural production

This seems to imply that the moratorium on land sales, as stated in article 35, also includes sales and purchases of house plots and dacha plots. Local authorities were flexible in the application of this moratorium on house plots. I observed that in urban areas it is not applied, in rural villages it depends on the size of the house plot. There has been a tendency to increase the size of house plots with land available from 'shrinkages' of state farmland. My suspicion that house plots 'grew' in size over time after independence is indirectly confirmed by a table I found in WB paper # 394 [100] p. 113. Derived from that table the market surplus for example for potatoes grown on house plots increased from just over 23,000 tons in 1992, to 94,500 tons in 1996. In the same time the market surplus of milk from house plots increased from 36,000 ton to 169,000 ton. And apart from considerable market surplus quantities in other products, this increase was achieved at approximately 600,000 rural households in total.

During the assignment in the Kyrgyz Republic I was told that, with consent of family members, a holder could sell the certificate to other members of the same farm or to citizens and entities of the Kyrgyz Republic (no foreigners!) for purposes of agricultural production. Former members of the farm are given priority. When certified by a notary in agreement with the rules set by the appropriate rural committee and the rayon land management office, certificates may be transferred or used as security.

In June 2000, a presidential decree 'On pilot projects on land market and registration of rights for agricultural lands' enabled experiments in land markets including the registration of purchase and sale transactions, effectively suspending the moratorium in three rayons where new style land registration offices had been opened.

6.1.4 NEW REGULATIONS

During the land and agrarian reform, more than 15 legislative Acts, 12 Decrees and over a hundred Governmental Resolutions have been adopted and became effective. Most of the new legislation on property issues in the Kyrgyz Republic is the result of cooperation between local legal experts and (US) foreign legal consultants. Some of the new legislation is copied from similarly compiled laws in Kazakhstan where US experts and local experts had been active earlier to design new legislation on land related matters. Like the Kazak government, the Kyrgyz government strives at providing a higher level of tenure security by adopting a series of laws, decrees and regulations in relation to land tenure. In 1998 and 1999, the following documents were developed and were soon adopted by the Jogorku Kenesh (the Kyrgyz parliament):

- A Law to Amend the Constitution of the Kyrgyz Republic (introducing ownership rights to all land),

- The Land Code of the Kyrgyz Republic,
- The Law on State Registration of Rights to Immovable Property,
- On mortgage – for ensuring execution of all sorts of financial obligations, using real property rights as collateral,
- On cooperation – regulating the operation of cooperations in the Kyrgyz Republic,
- On Peasant farm(s) – determining the legal basis for establishment and operations of peasant farms.

Resolutions were drafted on 'Allocation of land shares and property in kind,' and on 'Utilization of State agricultural land.'

A confusing matter is the fact that staff of new registration offices in the Kyrgyz Republic will be recruited mainly from the existing offices of BTI and Land Engineering. So the same staff will assist Kyrgyz citizens with registration of their rights that previously exercised (and still exercises) control over the proper use of immovable property. The same staff that had, and still has, the authority to expropriate farmers from farmland and others from real property when it is not properly used (for farm land meaning its production level is below that of the cadastral estimates).

6.1.5 IMPROVING LAND TENURE SECURITY

Will farmers in the Kyrgyz Republic generally feel more secure in their land tenure than urban residents, after the recent change of land certificates into ownership documents? In the draft social assessment report [82] some interesting remarks about land tenure security can be found.

- No one has such security as we all depend on society. For example, if communists will be in power again, they can take away our property. (Uzbek male, business man in Uzgen)
- I don't feel secure myself. I don't recognize myself as the owner of my shop. (Russian female, shop owner, Sokuluk)
- Not any guarantee, No one from Architectura, the BTI or the akaimat (local authority) knows where the mill is situated. I hope to register it. If necessary I will pay bribe. (Kyrgyz male, business man/farmer, Naryn)
- Of course I am sure of my rights. Many people are involved in this process (of privatization). Therefore our agreements give guarantee and confidence. (Kyrgyz male, farmer, Naryn)
- I am sure of guarantee for 100 per cent because there is a lot of land. Only people have no resources to make the best of it.[1] (Kyrgyz farmer and leaseholder, Naryn)

---

[1] Most likely this respondent refers to the general lack of access to supportive financial resources for citizens assisting them to invest in land.

- It does not depend on me; it depends on the type of authority of the state.
- Stability should be reached in everything – economy, policy, etc. Not only develop a legal system but also make it work. There is no benefit if the law is only on paper, a dead law. (Kyrgyz male, farmer Sokuluk rayon)

No institutional provision by just this government, although trying to be the most democratic in the region, will add much to the perception of land tenure security. For most farmers private ownership of rights to land and registration of their newly acquired rights will not considerably contribute to their feeling of having secure tenure of land. The registration process of the newly acquired rights has not yet changed in many areas (only three new style registration offices were operational by the end of 1999) and systematic registration of rights did not start before almost the end of 2000 with little or no public awareness campaign. It must be expected that only a long term proven commitment of successive governments to protect private ownership of land will provide a solid base for land tenure security. The conclusion is that the government of the Kyrgyz Republic has provided institutional arrangements for a development of improved land tenure security but that sustainability of land tenure security can only be perceived after a period of time.

6.2 LAND REFORM IN THE KYRGYZ REPUBLIC

6.2.1 IMITATING THE 'WEST'

The land and agrarian reform in the Kyrgyz Republic is one of the most obvious changes carried out after independence. The Kyrgyz Republic tries to establish itself as the most democratic and advanced country in Central Asia. It definitely succeeded in becoming the region's most preferred country among donor organizations. Sometimes it is even referred to as the 'pet of international donors.' And although democracy at Kyrgyz standards is not exactly the same as it is in Western countries, the current government seems to be the most liberal and democratic in the area. Recent reports about the political situation suggest that the government is leaning toward a more dictatorial course, but this political correction of the policy is mild compared to the political measures in neighboring Republics.[2]

[2] Elections for the Kyrgyz Parliament in early 2000 were followed by oppression of the opposition. Most likely because of his outspokenness an opposition leader was jailed causing supporters to set up a picket line in Bishkek for several weeks. Although this is a serious denouncement of democracy, the fact that picket lines could be maintained for several weeks and that the press could freely report about it shows the ambivalent attitude of the government. In neighboring countries Uzbekistan and Kazakstan the current presidents have made themselves president for life and act like dictators, almost similar to Soviet leaders during the pre-democratic times.

After independence the newly elected government followed a 'western pattern' by introducing private property, individual taxation, and taxes paid in money rather than in food (quota). This requires them to make institutional arrangements and establish agencies that identify boundaries, register property descriptions and identify the taxpayers. So one of the motives for the Kyrgyz land reform program could well have been the wish to show the world – once more – the rapidly evolving democracy in this country in Central-Asia.

6.2.2 WHAT MOTIVE?

The land and agrarian reform in the Kyrgyz Republic aimed at replacement of the existing approximately 450 (the number varies depending on the source but about 450 is a good proxy) large-scale state and collective farms, which counted for virtually all agricultural production in the Kyrgyz Republic. These large-scale farms had to be replaced by smaller-scale farms managed by individuals, families, groups of families, and corporate farm enterprises. In urban areas most of the state owned housing in use by individual households were privatized as well.

There is no clear political statement or written reasoning at hand for such a drastic maneuver as land privatization is in the Kyrgyz Republic. What can be found is scattered among written intentions in governmental regulations, in project documentation of international donors, and in the terms of reference of projects. Undoubtedly there has been a certain automatism following an international trend with a genuine intent to distribute the land of state and collective farms among families living on the farms. This is reflected in the distribution of land shares, because the size of the family determined the area of land to be transferred. Each spouse received a certain amount and every child in the family also received an amount of agricultural land. Local committees determined the size of the land shares but that was done in accordance with the total land available for distribution. This resulted in fewer land per capita in the more densely populated south of the country than in the north. A typical distribution, for example, was 1,5 ha (± 3.75 acres) for the head of the family, 1 ha (± 2.5 acres) for the spouse, and 0,75 ha (± 1.9 acres) for each child in the family. As far as urban property is concerned, the size of living quarters generally reflected the family size and no specific program had to be developed in this respect for privatization.

A certainly never freely expressed motive for land reform in rural areas might have been a backlash against the agrarian elite in the form of the management of the state and collective farms. This motive is one of the findings in research as carried out by the Land Tenure Center and this type of envy plays a role in almost all land reform projects in transition countries.

6.2.3 REVITALIZATION OF KYRGYZ LAND REFORM

The privatization of the housing stock did not result in complex regulations or situations. But progress of the agricultural restructuring was fitful until 1994. As described in chapter 3, it is difficult to precisely monitor the progress of the privatization plan because of many ambiguities and shifts in the definition of concepts (peasant farm, private farm, cooperative farm, and reorganized enterprise) causing confusion and difficulties in interpreting statistics. After struggling with restructuring of agricultural production in the first years of independence, the President of the Kyrgyz Republic took the initiative to re-vitalize the agrarian reform in 1994. The result of this 1994 initiative for speeding up restructuring was both a continuation of previous measures and methods, and also a frontal assault on collective and state farms that had ignored previous restructuring edicts. The Ministry of Agriculture declared its intent to transfer nearly all of the country's 1.5 million ha of agricultural land to small holders by 1995. From 1995 onward the Kyrgyz Republic experienced a progressive land reform program.

A 22 February 1994, Presidential Decree (titled: 'Measures on Promoting Land and Agrarian Reforms in the Kyrgyz Republic') underscores government priorities to improve agricultural production. All people living and working on the territories of collective and state farms got a use right to a share of land designated for agriculture with the right to sell, exchange, bequeath, mortgage and lease (art 1 & 2). They are granted rights for 49 years (later this was extended to 99 years) of tenure with preferential rights of extension upon termination (art 3). Arable land plots must be used for agricultural production (art 10). There are restrictions set on the maximum size for one family (art 11) in correspondence with the composition of the family, and the location and soil quality of the land. If a family was already holding more land than allowed under the new regulations, the surplus should be returned for redistribution with cash compensation as set by the government (art 12). State authorities are prohibited from interfering with individual use rights (art 14). The Ministry of Agriculture is given power to control the whole reform and cadastral taxing. The MAF was instructed to physically identify land for the National Land Fund (NLF) together with rayon administrations. With oblast administrations the MAF should submit orders to ascertain land shares to citizens etc and implement the NLF. Heads of rayon administrations had to develop regional programs for implementation of all this with proposals on the minimum size of plots taking into account climate, and natural conditions. That State authorities cannot interfere with individual use rights as stated in art 14 is limited by the Land Code – as still practiced in 1999. The 'State Inspectorate on Land Engineering' maintains records on the use of arable land and can also expropriate owners of rights because of insufficient use, improper use, or illegal use of the real property.

6.2.4 ECONOMIC STAGNATION

Unfortunately the economic recovery that seemed to start in 1995 did not continue as expected. The following short anthology of the current situation in the Kyrgyz Republic can illustrate this. The Kyrgyz national currency (the som) showed a devaluation of 55 per cent in 1999. The first half of 1999 was the most difficult period ever for the Kyrgyz national currency, the som.

Prime Minister Amangeldi Muraliev reported on 28 January 2000, that inflation in the country over 1999 had been as high as 39.9 per cent. Annual inflation in 1993 was 1209 per cent and came down from 35 per cent in 1996 to 14.7 per cent in 1997, but the recent figures over 1998 – 20 per cent – and almost 40 per cent over 1999 indicate a worsening trend. In 1999 treasury bills for a three months period had a yield between 28 per cent and 71 per cent, the six-month treasury bills had an average yield of 52 per cent. Mortgages with real property as collateral for a maximum period of six months (!) had an annual interest rate of more than 70 per cent.

The number of transactions in real estate in the capital Bishkek over the period 1 January-1 June 2000, was reported as 5,865 or an average of 1173 per month. Monthly numbers reported over January and February 2000 were 886 and 1123. This indicates a persistent stagnation and still a significant lower monthly average than reported over 1998 (1527) and 1999 (1338) the year the decline became obvious. I do however realize that this observation covers only a short period of time. It is possible that the real estate market in Bishkek went through a specific (negative) situation at the time the data were collected. It is difficult to give an indication of a 'normal' level of transactions in a city like Bishkek, because there hardly has been a 'normal' situation in the few years of independence to set such a standard.

Table 6.2.4 shows data of Bishkek with data of Osh and data of the suburban areas of Bishkek and Osh. The table shows no notable increase in transactions between 1997/1998 and now, except for the number of transactions in and around Osh, the unofficial capital of the densely populated Ferghana valley. It indicates that there is not yet the expected developing property market.

Table 6.2.4 Real property transactions in three (sub) urban areas

Yearly level of transactions in	1997	1998	2000-2001
Suburban areas of Bishkek:			
Kant	1600	1500	1622
Sokuluk	1858	1912	1922
Further away from Bishkek:			
Chui-Tokmok (Eastwards)	2225	2160	1065
Moscow (Westwards)	–	1231	1411
In the South of the country:			
Osh	3608	2534	4500
Djallal-Abad	1070	1118	1315
Kara-Suu	1200	1640	1436

Source: GosRegister (see also Table 14.2.1)

The newspaper 'Vecherni Bishkek' reported in October 1999 that so far only 146 'brave people' started their own business in Bishkek in 1999, compared with 583 in the whole year 1998. A few weeks earlier the same newspaper reported that for the majority of schoolteachers in Bishkek living conditions continue to worsen. The wages are minimal (some basic rates amount to 280 som – or approx. 70 US dollar – per month). Not capable of paying for fares of public transport, many teachers go to work on foot sometimes almost across the city, a daily walk of over an hour one way. 'Voluntary' non-paid vacations have become more common in the education sector.

Economic stagnation is noticeable everywhere in the country. The Times of Central Asia [88] reports: 'Kyrgyzstani Agriculture Requires Equipment and Technical Servicing,' on 9 December 1999; 'The fleet of agricultural equipment has greatly reduced and deliveries of farming equipment have almost stopped. Compared with 1991, in 1998 the number of tractors reduced 12.7 per cent, trucks by 14 per cent, grain harvesters by seven per cent, corn harvesters by 81.8 per cent, plows by 14 per cent, and sowing machines by 28.5 per cent. To boost agricultural production in the Kyrgyz Republic, the Government issued a decree establishing technical servicing stations in the country. To date their number has reached 300. However, these service stations still lack the necessary repair facilities and funds.'

6.2.5 LAND ACQUISITION

LTC report # 128 [52] states that nearly one-third of the new farm enterprises have acquired exclusive use of land during the transition. Because of the moratorium on arable land most acquisitions of land happened through rental arrangements, through (new) shareholders joining the enterprise and through leasing or purchasing from the National Land Fund. Although certainly not sufficient for proof of a vivid land market, it is a sign of transfers of land and activity on a land market, all happening without the new land registration system established.

LTC researchers found in the Kyrgyz Republic that few households see themselves selling land in the future. Many individuals (within the enterprises) in the case studies declared that they intend to hold on to their land at all costs; no household interviewed appeared to want to sell its land shares or engage in land speculation. Statistics show that few enterprises have disposed of land since the restructuring of agriculture began. This confirms a research finding that most transactions of land take place shortly after implementation of the land reform process and slows down after a while. Given the poor economic situation and the relatively high costs of formal land transfers it is also possible that people are avoiding formal transactions and instead make the choice for the informal transfer. This certainly is a non-desired development because of the possibilities of cheating, fraud, and corruption that might occur at informal transactions.

It is interesting to note that the situation in the Kyrgyz Republic obviously is different from Albania and some other European countries in transition, where the willingness to sell land among the population is substantially higher (See Stanfield [80]). It could be that this is caused by a higher degree of familiarity with private individual ownership of property in these more westerly located countries where communist ideology did exist for a shorter period of time.

6.3 LAND REGISTRATION IN THE KYRGYZ REPUBLIC

6.3.1 LAND REGISTRATION AND LAND REFORM

The 'Times of Central Asia' [88] of 11 November 1999 reports on a Real Estate Registration Seminar in Bishkek organized on 1 November 1999. In the article the project on registration of rights to real estate and land is described as being a proposal of the World Bank stemming from 1995, in the form of a reform of the real estate sector in the Kyrgyz Republic and the unification of the registration of real estate rights. A unification of registration of real estate rights is a reasonable description of the project of which the preparatory phase started in 1999, but a reform of the real estate sector in the Kyrgyz Republic initiated not in 1995 but already in 1991. The Kyrgyz Republic embarked on a course to change the tenure of its state owned property after the declaration of independence in 1991.

The less dramatic project for land registration has been discussed almost since the start of the land reform in the Kyrgyz Republic as an additional method to support the restructuring of the agriculture. Thus as a sideline of restructuring of agriculture, investigations for the land registration project started in 1995, and in 1997 a pilot project by US-AID was completed. The approval of the Law on State Registration of Rights to Immovable Property in 1998 and the approval of the Land Code in 1999 provide the legal basis for a land and real estate registration project. The World Bank could allocate specific funding and schedule a preparation phase in 1999, that will provide the foundation for the land registration project for which two other expatriates and I were assigned.

As explained earlier, a new land registration system operational at the moment the first land certificates were issued would have been the most effective and efficient measure. Now data recorded in the registers is more or less 'second-hand' and will most likely contain some errors and misinterpretation.

The current land registration improvement project in the Kyrgyz Republic is not going to provide much surveying of boundaries and hardly any additional mapping. And although land registration and land titling as being institutionally arranged in the Kyrgyz Republic will enhance land tenure security, it is still doubtful that it will make much of a difference for the Kyrgyz citizens. The long period of dependence on the USSR also contributes to a hesitant reaction on privatization among the Kyrgyz citizens. The many experiments and forms of privatization underline the struggle of those willing to (re-)introduce private ownership in the Kyrgyz Republic. Conflicts about lands between the State and villagers have been rare in the Kyrgyz Republic but there have been some arguments about boundaries between villagers, although there is little evidence of real conflicts.

6.3.2 LAND MARKET DEVELOPMENT

The World Bank's land registration project documentation and, in particular, the terms of reference for the project that effectively started in 1999, put as much emphasis on land market development as on protection of individual property rights. The terms of reference for the land registration project indicate the intention of the Kyrgyz Government. It says: 'The Government of the Kyrgyz Republic has requested assistance from the World Bank in the preparation of a land and real estate registration project. The objective of the project will be to secure rights in real estate, and to facilitate the exercise of those rights through the efficient functioning of markets for sales, lease, mortgage and other transactions. A critical aspect of the transition to a market economy in the Kyrgyz Republic is clarification and protection of rights in land and other real property. The traditional approach to collecting and maintaining information on land and other forms of real property cannot serve the needs of a modern market economy. There is a need to develop a unified system of registration, which will incorporate all relevant information on a given piece of property and provide clear guarantee and security of property rights. This requires determination by the Government of how any existing activity in the collection and management of information on real property will fit into a new unified registration system.'

Markets for sales, leases, mortgages and other transactions currently function without the new land registration system. However it is only a small market and it is not likely that this will soon change. For the few transactions now taking place there is obviously little concern or uncertainty about the rights to land among Kyrgyz citizens. It can be questioned whether the current 'system' is reasonably efficient, but then, what should be the urgency to improve efficiency? Looking at the data provided by the Kyrgyz authorities on the number of transactions currently effected, efficiency improvement could hardly be used as an argument to change the current system. The number of transactions registered in the whole country in the relevant offices (BTI or Land Management) reported for 1998 was between 40,000 and 45,000 (the number varies depending on the source). The Bishkek BTI office had the most transactions: 18,329. Some of the more rural regions in the country report a number lower than 10 transactions of real property for the whole year 1998. Even in Bishkek the activity comes down to an average number of less than 80 transactions per working day in 1998. (For an overview of transactions on real estate in the whole country see Table 14.2.1).

6.3.3 FOCUS ON URBAN PROPERTY?

The reference made to a 'modern market economy' without any indications on how to stimulate the rural (agricultural) economy, reveals that the focus is on the urban real property market. Initially the project was linked with the restructuring of the agriculture and with rural poverty alleviation. Now the emphasis seems more on economic development by stimulating the real property market. The original aim could be captured in the food security model, now it seems more appropriate to follow the prosperity model aimed at economic development. However, given the persistent economic decline in the Kyrgyz Republic and the absence of any emphasis on land market development in the project, the change in goal for the Land and Real Estate Registration Project seems to be a rather opportunistic one.

In a project information document explaining the objectives of the Land and Real Estate Registration Project in the Kyrgyz Republic (World Bank document by E. Cook [101]), the emphasis of the project is clearly on market development. It reads in paragraph 2 'Objectives': 'The primary objective of this project is to encourage and support development of markets for and investments in land and real estate.' For the Kyrgyz Republic this goal is only possible in the long run. The project information document seems to be based on the often-assumed link between increasing security of land tenure and a developing land market. There is mounting evidence that this link is not an automatic one. The development of a land market depends on several factors of which increasing land tenure security is just one (and most likely not the most relevant). As shown earlier, for a land market to evolve, economic circumstances are dominant; such circumstances will include factors like demand for real property, control over inflation, a well functioning banking system, and land market expertise.

6.3.4 A MORE PUBLIC-FRIENDLY SYSTEM

The director of the newly established organization for land and real estate registration in the Kyrgyz Republic stresses as major accomplishment of 'his' project the concept of a 'one-stop-shop' for registration of land. Instead of the various offices and windows to visit in order to formally transfer real property as described in 2.3, his new organization envisages one window in the one office that registers real property in the area where the property is situated. The new office will take care of all the aspects of registration. In this way he wins public support for the new system for land registration because most people are aware of the fact that transactions with real property are currently cumbersome and time consuming.

Furthermore, it is a well-known fact in the Kyrgyz Republic that in order to speed up the procedure at each window, some extra cash will assist thus increasing the cost of a formal transaction. An account of this practice can be found in the report [82] containing a social assessment of the land registration project among Kyrgyz citizens. The (draft) report states (p. 32): 'Many clients during Focus Group – a specifically selected response group for the social assessment project – discussions noticed a practice of official and unofficial prices for provided service. Many clients don't know and have no opportunity to get information about official cost, except at Bishkek's BTI, where available stands explain prices for service provided. Clients accept an amount of official fee for service offered, no claims from their side, they also agree with additional payment to fasten document procedures.' (For the Social Assessment, five focus groups with clients have been organized in Bishkek City, Osh, Uzgen and Naryn cities. Groups of clients consisted of various people: lease holders, private farmers and agricultural employees, social servants, owners of houses and apartments, businessmen such as owners of shops, mini-markets, mills and private companies registering real estate, insurance and building firms, private legal advice offices). (Report on Social Assessment of the Land Registration Project of November 1999 [82]).

Proposed institutional arrangements of the 1999 preparatory project in the Kyrgyz Republic focus on land registration in such a way that it is simple, affordable and easy to understand for a population that is getting used to private ownership of real property. The establishment of a land registration system in the Kyrgyz Republic is not a goal in itself. It is a tool to improve the security of land tenure. Land registration is a modern tool, but it is not the only means to achieve land tenure security and certainly not the only condition to be fulfilled to accomplish economic development and or food security. To be really effective in alleviating food security and economic development, land reform and land registration activities must be supported by society. A stable government, protection and security for all citizens, and an institutional framework in which the forces of a market economy can flourish are necessary. It includes a land registration system designed according to the social and cultural circumstances under which the system will function.

6.3.5 CURRENT SITUATION ON LAND REGISTRATION

All three elements of a land reform project have been initiated and implemented in the Kyrgyz Republic. These elements are; restructuring agricultural production by re-distribution of land and assets, a change in property regime, and a land registration project.

The usual de-synchronization, as observed elsewhere, is also present in the Kyrgyz Republic and this time difference between the actual land distribution and the start of land registration activities (to implement in the new form of land registration) provides some complexity. Restructuring of the agricultural production was in its final stage of completion at the start of the land registration project. Much land had been distributed already even before the preparatory activities specifically aimed at improvement of registration began. Private farmers and new farming enterprises had taken possession of the land and some of them used the existing old institutionalized structure for registration of their rights to land. The result is that at the beginning of the new millennium, only about 20 per cent of the land in private hands was officially registered in one or another governmental office. Many holders of land shares or land certificates did not yet spend time and money on registration. In January 2000 the new registration system had been established in only four offices. In urban areas the de-synchronization caused even more problems in those cases showing discrepancies between official documents and claimed rights. Most of the current urban property users are bona-fide in this respect and the compulsory registration confronts them all of a sudden with evidence of encroachment or improper use, because of mistakes with approval applications or intentional encroachments of former occupants of the real property. A proposal to give registration officials the authority to resolve minor discrepancies so far resulted only in the possibility to issue a provisional title, but not to actually solve the problem on the ground. New owners must go through a long and sometimes costly bureaucratic process to eliminate the discrepancies.

The expatriate advisors proposed to start a detailed outlined process of systematic registration in each new registration office directly after opening and to provide them before opening, with maps showing the parcels in the territory of the office. Systematic registration includes the allocation of owners of rights to each parcel basically paid for by the State (or by foreign donor organizations), in order to set up a complete and accurate registration. Specially trained teams of registration specialists, not part of the normal operational staff but specifically hired for the job at hand, will carry out this temporary task, moving from one newly opened office to the next one. Owners of rights to land who want to transfer their rights before systematic registration has been completed on their parcels, will have to apply for sporadic registration (at their own expense) to comply with the new rules. At their request a procedure for sporadic (meaning just one investigation to check the data) registration was carried out. Systematic conversion of existing rights to land (free of charge for the owners of rights to land) is scheduled for each of the new offices directly after their opening to provide them with correct data in the new registration system. So owners transferring rights to land in areas of new land registration offices where systematic registration is completed can benefit from the completed and available land registration data and have a relatively quick and simple transfer at reasonable cost. It has been estimated that even in the largest offices the process of systematic registration could be completed within two years after opening of the new registration office. The ambitious program for systematic registration of all land in the territory of newly opened offices started on a small scale in 2000.

The urgent need of the project at this moment remains doubtful looking at some umbers used by the new organization for land registration (GosRegister). In the Bishkek (BTI) office the number of transactions decreased from 1466 in January 1999 to a little under 1000 in December 1999 or less than 50 on average per working day in December. During personal observations in this office – where all information has been computerized since April 1998 – one would never see long lines of people waiting for a window and, if customers became impatient, this was mostly because of the long processing times.

The second largest office with respect to number of transactions is the Osh BTI office with 2534 transactions in 1998 or a daily average of around 10 transactions. The newly created and relatively large Kant office announced 145 transactions in October 2000 (both urban and rural) in this first of the new type of registration offices which comes down to less than an average 8 transactions for each working day. Offices in dominantly rural areas reported figures that come down to an average of less than one transaction per working day or even a month in 1998. But this can change after lifting the moratorium on farm land transfers, although it is not expected that in rural offices transactions will increase to a level of more than several per working day.

Researchers of the Land Tenure Center claimed several years ago that a land registration system is not urgent for the continuation of the farm-restructuring program, but they stated that it would be essential to have such a system in place soon (they indicated 1997) to facilitate transfers of land or development of a land market. The reasoning behind this is:

> Every landholder wants to be assured that his or her claim on the land is secure, be it rent or ownership. Likewise, banks will require clear title for lending purposes. Furthermore, legally secure tenure increases the likelihood that the owner will be willing to make long-term investments in the land. The lack of a single land registration system suited to market transactions is not an obstacle to land reform and farm reorganization, but such a system, which protects the rights of buyers, sellers, owners, renters, and mortgage holders will be necessary for the full development of a land market ... At present, land parcels are registered in several different places within the rayon administration. Parties to a transaction involving land shares would have to go through several channels to complete the transaction. Moreover, information contained in the registration records does not include information on mortgages, easements, court decisions, and other restrictions on the parcel. In addition, there are two separate systems for rural and urban land. A single system for all immovable property would greatly simplify the process required to perform transactions in land.

With the continuous stagnation in the economy the necessity of implementation of a new registration system now can easily be doubted, unless it must be expected that the constraints on the development of a land market to evolve will be actively attacked by (yet unrevealed) specific project activities.

6.3.6 PERSPECTIVE OF THE NEW LAND REGISTRATION SYSTEM

Over three million Kyrgyz citizens in rural areas got their land shares and half a million land certificates had been issued in June 2000 on the basis of the combined land shares. A farming family generally combines the shares of the members and will receive one land certificate, which in turn can be brought into a cooperation or a collective, or just remain in the hands of that one family starting a single family farm. Many farmers are not yet registering the certificates perhaps because of the complexity of the registration system but most likely because of the cost involved in registration. Since they have no obvious uncertainty or doubt about the formal value of the certificate, why should they hurry with registration? Moreover, the moratorium on transfers of land designated for agriculture is still in force – although very recently it seems that there might be a discussion in parliament to lift it, or at least to diminish the length of the term (as in June 2000 still 5 years).

The 1999 World Bank project was scheduled to have at least fourteen new registration offices operational in June 2000, but in June 2000 only four out of a projected 48 offices were operational under the new unified and single registration system and so far only for sporadic registration. A maximum of only a few hundred transactions had been registered under the rules of the new single registration system as of June 2000. All the other owners of rights to land are still holding certificates under the old system without obviously serious problems. Although transactions with real property do happen, a real land market has not yet materialized. What is more remarkable, even with specific reference to the development of a land market in the terms of reference and other project documents, no specific actions to stimulate the development of such a market are part of the project.

The World Bank Land and Real Estate Registration Project in the Kyrgyz Republic, as initiated in 1999, started both too early and too late. It is too early to support the establishment of a rural land market because of the already mentioned moratorium on sales of land designated for agriculture. Without additional supportive projects it will hardly assist an urban real property market because of the continuing economic stagnation. It is too late to ensure continuous protection of rights to land as established with the land certificates of which more than half a million have been registered already. Besides, it could be challenged whether this project is one of the most urgent projects to be carried out in the Kyrgyz Republic where still so many other factors are hampering the economic development and thus the alleviation of poverty.

Supported by Gershon Feder [32], I conclude that careful investigation of the situation in the Kyrgyz Republic would most likely have offered more urgent projects to be funded than this land registration project. In his report in Warsaw in 1998, Feder warns that (p. 58): 'If it is not clear as to whether the key factors for economic viability of land registration systems are present, it may not be an opportune time for the government to invest in land registration. The society would benefit more from other types of investment, which address more binding constraints of its economic development.'

It is interesting to notice the tendency among Kyrgyz registrars to continue the custom of physically inspecting the real property before registering it in the land registration. The expatriate advisors attempted to explain that, under the new situation, state inspection of a property to be sold, that is assessing the condition before it can be transferred, is not necessary and certainly not usual in 'the West.' The Kyrgyz registrars do not want to be responsible for registration of facts that have not been verified on the ground. Explaining that a prospective buyer will inspect the property and that the offered price thus will reflect the condition of the real property in a market economy does not convince them either. They defend these ongoing inspections – for which the individuals have to pay and have to provide transport for the official physical inspection – by indicating the responsibility of only registering true facts for which the physical inspection is necessary. Heated debates between expatriate advisors and national experts did not resolve this matter. I have been informed recently that the officials still insist on inspection of the real property before registration.

6.4 ASSESSMENT OF CHANGE IN THE KYRGYZ REPUBLIC

6.4.1 INDICATORS FOR INSTITUTIONAL CHANGE

The elements of my model will generally be evaluated with macro indicators. Indicators based on availability of data in the Kyrgyz Republic. The land reform project started some nine years ago, now providing several data sets to assess some of the progress and the possible effects of initiated changes. The further back the start of the changes in institutional arrangements, the more elements will be measurable with indicators and observable phenomena. As far as relevant some of the indicators will be given the adjective proposed, because it is sometimes possible to assess proposed measures although these measures did not yet materialize. All the first elements in the model can be evaluated with indicators of change in land tenure. At macro level these indicators also measure changes in land tenure security. The first part of my model is shown in Figure 6.4.1:

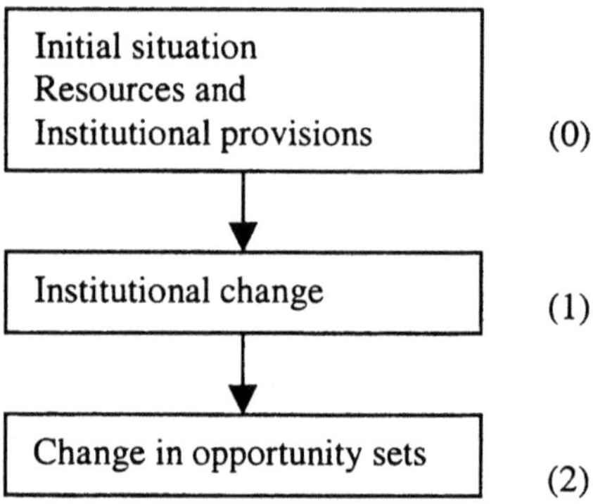

Figure 6.4.1 Indicators of land tenure change

Improvement of agricultural land resulting from enhanced tenure security can lead to changing short term inputs measurable by demand for farm chemicals and labor, but also demand for medium- and long term land improvements (irrigation, farm buildings, road access etc.) and – to a lesser degree – demand for mobile farm equipment. Another indication of changing land tenure security is a change in land lease contracts and other ways to utilize land more efficiently. Land leases are often without any form of written contract. Even with a written contract, registration is not always pursued because of costs and time involved in registration. The more informal the system of land leases the more trust there obviously is in tenure security. Measuring of the ideological side of land tenure security is more difficult. Getting accustomed to land tenure security will take time for a population that has no experience with the concept of private ownership of real property. The perception of land tenure security among a population has to be earned by a government by showing a long-term commitment to the protection of private rights to real property.

For the first element 'institutional change' (marked (1) in the model) relatively easily accessible indicators for change are:

- the number of (proposed) new or renewed laws and regulations,
- process descriptions and instructions for implementing the new systems,
- (proposed) organizational changes by the government,
- schedule for implementation of the new institutional arrangements,
- training and education of officials and others involved in the application of the new system.

The above list of indicators is not about real changes, one might remark in truth, it only reflects the various steps taken in the direction of change in institutions.

M.Riad El-Ghonemy (1990) [37] estimates that a period of fifteen to twenty years is required for the stabilization of the relative economic position of losers and gainers from restructuring of agriculture. At least the same period of time will be needed for beneficiaries to experience their new responsibilities in production, marketing, capital formation and participation in the development of their communities. The same goes for the manifestation of improved abilities in beneficiaries as a consequence of new motivations, better nutritional standards and developed skills. To show results of land and agrarian reform programs as initiated in Eastern Europe and Central Asia after the political changes in 1989, a period of about twenty-five years is needed. This implies that little can yet actually be measured about the effects of restructuring of the agriculture in those areas. A fundamental problem while trying to show the outcome of land reform (or restructuring of the agriculture) is to separate or to isolate the consequences of reform from the totality of dynamic forces driving change and development. So indicators should not be regarded as absolute or as final, rather they are signals of change and should be used as such. The scope of indicators will be wider in the prosperity model than in the food security model. In the food security model, specific institutional arrangements (implying a narrower approach) for the alleviation of food insecurity will appear and they will, in general, focus primarily on agricultural issues. For food security improvement the Ministry of Agriculture will play a dominant role in the organizational arrangements.

6.4.2 ASSESSMENT OF INSTITUTIONAL CHANGE

It is obvious from the list of new legal regulations and institutional arrangements that the foundation has been laid for institutional changes. Fifteen laws, 12 decrees and more than 100 governmental resolutions have been adopted and became effective between 1991 and 2000. A July 1997 survey of large farm managers (30), private farmers (60) and household plot owners (90) across all regions of the Kyrgyz Republic provides some insight into the perception of various groups of farmers about the agricultural reforms. Nearly two-thirds of the large farm managers and private farmers support the reforms. In the Kyrgyz Republic many of these managers expect to play an important role in managing new but smaller cooperatives formed by the new small farmers with the joined individually-owned parcels of land. Cooperatives will now be free of government intervention giving them more personal freedom than even before; but, the household plot owners are equally divided among 'satisfied,' 'not satisfied' and 'no opinion.' (Source: WB discussion paper # 394) [100]. The report on social assessment does not provide much additional information on the perception of the institutional renewal because there is no specific questioning aimed at an assessment of the renewal of institutional arrangements. A few conclusions can be found throughout the report. The main problem is that the average Kyrgyz farmer has insufficient knowledge to formally establish an agricultural enterprise. Officials, because of (supposed) little understanding of formal procedures by peasants, carry out most of the formal activities required from new heads of a small farm. Former management members of the state and collective farms can also take care of formal procedures. In most rural areas the latter do still have the contacts and the (informal) authority to get things done. The general knowledge about the new possibilities of starting private firms and private farms is limited among the people by lack of proper information and instruction. Education and information of individual citizens about the legal aspects of restructured farms and land registration is crucial to improve the trust that people will have in the government, but so far little attention has been paid to this aspect. More than 70 per cent of 'Ugodia' (land) is privately owned nowadays and farmed by single-family farms, associations of peasant farms, cooperatives or new (smaller) collective farms. More than a half million land certificates have been issued. The institutions of the centrally-planned economy that dominated the old Soviet system are gradually being dismantled, privatized, or transformed into institutions that primarily serve private agriculture in a market economy. The legal and regulatory framework required for private ownership and a functioning market economy is being put in place. The Ministry of Agriculture is shifting from owner operator to regulator, service agency, and policymaker.

CHAPTER 7

OPPORTUNITY SETS

7.1 IMPLICATIONS OF OPPORTUNITY SETS

7.1.1 WHY OPPORTUNITY SETS?

An individual's opportunity set is composed of physical and emotional capacities plus legal or customary understandings of potential options that are conditioned by the actual choice of others. In paragraph 5.2 opportunity sets were introduced in the model to be able to pay attention to perceptions while at the same time remaining aware of the shaky character of the indirect measurability of emotions and the feeling of security or trust provided by formal or informal institutions. Institutional change is one of the factors determining change in land tenure security because change in land tenure security is only measurable by observing the effects of it. Thus the logical next step in the method is to examine a change in opportunity sets. Schmid [71] argues that opportunity sets of potential actors are determined in part by the rules established by the institutions. The institutional infrastructure has a large influence on the behavior of individuals, and as far as farmers are concerned, it is also determined by expectations of the behavior of other land claimants, other farm workers, and the bureaucrats both in the decision making agencies and the supporting agencies.

Abraham Maslow presents in 'Towards a Psychology of Being' [54], his hierarchy of needs of mankind. His theory builds a pyramid of needs. Basic physiological requirements at the base of the pyramid are food and shelter, followed by security on the next level, above that the requirement to love, esteem and finally at the top self actualization. Maslow developed self-actualization as a goal to all men. Men – humans – have unique levels of potential development, unique in relation to observable life because the human's individual potential is open-ended. This is in particular what Maslow is calling attention to. People, once satisfying more basic needs, tend to develop higher needs which drive them to attain more of their own potential.

I presume that the statement, without saying it explicitly, in the National Food Security Policy report of the Kyrgyz Republic of 27 July 1999, was inspired by Maslow's thoughts:

> First of all, man is a biological being. It is only after his basic needs are satisfied that he can develop into a full-fledged social, cultural, economic, or public being. An

> adequate daily food intake is the first among man's basic needs. The state, with its form and course of food policy in society, can play a key role in promoting the level of this development. An appropriate food security policy, therefore, is vital for the nation's future

7.1.2 INFORMAL MARKETS

It can be assumed that people will investigate all possible ways to obtain a reasonable daily food intake. In rural areas where income from agricultural employment is not sufficient, ways of supplementing this income are limited. It is possible to find some non-farm labor, but in many countries the poor rural regions do not have much to offer in this respect. Migration to urban areas can be considered, or the less drastic solution of commuting to urban areas. Families living not too far from urban areas often practice the latter. In many post communist countries 'semi non-farm' income in nearby urban areas comes from the informal sector. Unofficial 'table-shops' (setting up a table along the side walk or the street) along main urban routes for sale of farm produce not through official markets, and also work in sweatshops unrelated to farms is a well-known example. Hernando DeSoto describes in his book, 'The Other Path' [23], aspects of this informal sector. He concludes that it is a safety valve created by the poor themselves. But an informal sector competes with the formal sector and deprives the government of tax income while it generally creates poor working circumstances and sometimes-unhealthy conditions for workers. It dodges the official statistics and so masks evidence and insight in the real situation in the country.

Field observations in the Kyrgyz Republic reveal that there is a widely spread informal economy. Farmers can be seen along major routes in towns and villages selling some of their produce. Along the walkways in the capital, Bishkek, many farmers are selling farm produce, others are setting up a table and sell candy, cigarettes (by the piece and lighting is free!), and – a very popular item – sunflower seeds. Near official markets, where people pay rent for a stall, various vendors are active trying to sell freshly baked bread (out of old prams, bags, buckets, or baskets), homemade pasta products, home made artistically decorated cakes, and in season, berries picked in the fields and sold in jars. Occasionally the police (militia) does organize a raid to chase these informal vendors away from near official markets, but generally they return to their places the next day.

Another example contributing to the informal sector is the custom to obtain priority treatment by winning the mood of officials with some favors. Among officials it is common to accept favors to smoothen difficult procedures or to shorten periods of time to complete requests and give official approval. It goes too far to qualify this attitude as corrupt. In most of the former communist countries it was rather normal to use relations and 'political capital' or to establish relations with favors and it is not felt as corrupt. Like a saying that goes in Surinam, 'Kennis is minder belangrijk dan kennissen' (Knowledge is less important than knowing whom to address). Using your relations, knowledge of the system, or some extra cash to your advantage was part of the culture in Soviet times.

People use opportunity sets to pressure for individual private property rights as revealed in a study by Platteau. He shows that there is an evolutionary development toward a more individual property regime without formal institutional arrangement changes. Platteau argues that 'The evolutionary theory of Land Rights (ETLR) can be considered the dominant framework of analysis used by mainstream economists to assess the land tenure situation in developing countries and to make predictions about its evolution. A central theme of this theory is that under the joint impact of increasing population pressure and market integration, land rights spontaneously evolve toward rising individualization and that this evolution eventually leads right-holders to press for the creation of duly formalized private property rights.' (Jean-Phillippe Platteau [66] in the 'Abstract').

7.1.3 RE-EMERGING CUSTOMS

Traditionally the Kyrgyz Republic was a society dominated by the male population in representing the family or the community. Paternalism was common in family matters especially when the Kyrgyz people lived as roaming families in their yurts on the common mountain pastures of the country. Under Soviet rule women gained (almost) equality in matters of citizenship and individual decision-making, education became obligatory for boys and girls. It is easy to observe that communism is one of most 'liberating' concepts of society for women. And although formally much of these improvements in the status of women are still in effect, there is a tendency to return to the former male dominance in matters of family decision-making and in representing the family. Family farms are registered in the name of the male head of the family and women leave property matters mostly to men. Women are the first to let go if the labor force is shrinking. With the cutback in social services and social provisions (especially on the large farms) women are shunted into (part-time) lower level jobs and they take up more of their traditional role of homemaker and child raiser. Tendencies in the region, and particularly in the south of the country, will most likely underline this development. The registration system could be of assistance in preserving rights of women by insisting that they are registered as co-owners of rights. Specific attention during training of staff for registration office and their vigilance can avoid that women are easily left without claims on property rights when it comes to a break up of the family.

Apart from these re-emerging customs there are evolutionary developments that should be monitored to avoid rapid growing inequalities. Platteau's [66] research in Sub-Saharan Africa has implications for the situation in the Kyrgyz Republic as he warns of some evolutionary developments. He draws attention to three points in this respect.

Firstly, there are winners and losers at land tenure changes and land titling programs. He states that losers are most likely women, pastoralists, hunter-gatherers, and outcast people. Most often these groups benefit from a form of (in)formal usufruct, which likely will become difficult to continue. The land is generally registered in the name of the compound head and what is going to happen next depends on him. Increasing land sales tend to exclude women, and even when they acquire title to land, it might be difficult to get it sanctioned or protected and their customary access to land (and that of other minority people) may be limited. In June 2000 I had a lengthy discussion with Suzanna Lastarria [47] a senior-researcher at the LTC who did extensive research on the changing position of women in former communist countries. We concluded that women are generally inclined to leave it to men when it comes to land tenure. The situation in the Kyrgyz Republic confirms this assumption. There are 3,481,800 individuals or more than 510,500 families residing in rural areas and they all have been allocated their land shares. In single-family farms those land shares have been registered as land certificates by combining them to one certificate per farm. In June 2000 it is reported that 510,500 land certificates of the proper format were distributed. Mostly these certificates are registered in the name of the head of the household – commonly the oldest male. In this way females are subordinated to males according to previous customs and are facing difficulties of obtaining their share of land in case of falling apart of the family. This is also reflected in the political arena. In times when the parliament's power is limited – like in communist times – striving to gender equity is often present. It certainly was not unusual to meet women in parliament and women in other high-ranking political positions in Soviet times. However, the political role of women is quickly downsized after independence and the return to increasing power of politicians and political bodies. Men show an eagerness to regain their dominant position. For many researchers it is not surprising that women return to housekeeping after the change in a transition economy. The responsibility of women for running the household did only marginally change under Soviet rule and they had to attend to both career and household, while commonly men hardly bothered about household chores. Among women nowadays there is often a feeling of being able to again assume responsibility for childcare and household chores, forced also by decreasing possibilities to have childcare in government supported child nurseries, and by lack of sufficient full-time job opportunities. However many women have to work because of the otherwise insufficient household income.

As mentioned before, it is important that staff of new registration offices is vigilant (and educated in this respect) to register married women as (co)-owners of property rights.

The second point raised by Platteau is that in a social context dominated by considerable differences in education levels and by differential access to the state administration and governing bodies, there is the often met likelihood that the adjudication/registration process will be manipulated by the agricultural elite to its own advantage. Original occupants may have difficulties defining their (customary) rights to land under such circumstances. Bureaucrats, insiders, and land surveyors dominate land allocation procedures while most of the peasants are still unaware of the new provisions. Therefore, land tenure changes and land titling procedures can have a negative effect on vulnerable sections of the population at a time when their survival depends on access to land. A solution for this problem might be complete openness of registration and drawing attention to 'suspicious' or remarkable accumulation of land ownership by certain individuals or groups in the population.

A third point by Platteau is that it is often difficult to diligently keep record of changes in land ownership after completion of a land reform and land registration project, making 'cadastral' records rapidly incomplete and outdated. The failure to maintain a valid record of successions and the absence of updated records constitutes some of the major disappointments of any land-titling program. Titling is cumbersome and weighs heavily on a government with limited resources, and it is almost unrealistic to expect overall valid record keeping. It is not sufficient, however, to conclude that discrepancies between records and reality come from administrative failures. It is also demand factors that contribute to it. If the new laws fail to gain popular understanding or acceptance, individuals continue to transfer land according to local customs. If the title shown on the record is increasingly at variance with actual use and possession, considerable confusion is the result. Conflicts cannot be solved by cheaper procedures with local authorities, but require litigation of official courts costing so much money that only the well-to-do can afford litigation. Incompleteness or out of datedness of records is a serious matter because it undermines trust and the perception of security of tenure. Once the decision is made to set up a (new) land registration the government is committed to do an excellent job to avoid such a negative development.

7.1.4 FIELD OBSERVATIONS

In many former communist countries institutional arrangements for land registration will only address the last element of Platteau's points. The general attitude toward 'following the official rules to secure any obtained formal rights' is positive in former communist countries. Many years of an almost all-encompassing bureaucratic regime have left their mark in this respect. When asked why they register, people show a kind of utterly surprised reaction. The answer was generally something like: 'Of course we register, because it is our only proof of security and safeguarding of our assets.' However, there are also several contradictory observations. Formal rights and formal documentation are carefully monitored and rules are arduously followed, but as soon as it is possible to achieve anything outside the formal circuit it is also almost a 'formalized' rule that one should not hesitate to jump at such a chance.

It is my experience that the effect of the first two points by Platteau can be observed almost everywhere in former communist countries where land reform programs have been implemented. I did observe a number of occasions where a state or collective farm manager took care of the interest of elderly widows by manipulating the land reform to his/her own benefit while assuring: 'I will do it for you "Babushka" (grandmother).' I also noticed managers assisting nearly illiterate peasants with the filling out of forms for land claims and registration at a 'small' fee or favor for themselves. In a society where, for many years, people publicly and blatantly used political capital and other relations to acquire favors for themselves such behavior comes almost naturally.

7.2 USE OF OPPORTUNITY SETS

7.2.1 INTERACTING OPPORTUNITY SETS

In most of the ex-communist countries part of the donor aid will always first benefit those who are well organized and have acquired political capital. In this respect one has to realize that in many former communist countries – as in the Kyrgyz Republic – the communist rulers often changed their political color from 'communist' into 'social democrat' but continued being politically (very) active. So political capital gained under the previous regime might well pay off under a new social democratic regime. The management of former collective and state farms and the upper echelon of farm workers know how to use land and agrarian reform for their own benefit, and they can coordinate (and sometimes manipulate) political action and support.

Furthermore, it is almost impossible for the Western observer to fully understand the impact of the change in opportunity sets presented to the Kyrgyz agricultural laborers. Being an employee on the large state or collective farm without any concept of possibilities, other than to provide labor for the benefit of the communist ideal, following orders without questioning most of them, then suddenly an opportunity was offered to become a private farmer. No wonder it took some time before it dawned on the majority of those workers and they were able to react and start to explore the new opportunity sets.

It is interesting to note the effect of the measures as issued in the presidential decree of February 1994. In the newly organized collective farms, in particular when they are registered now as (new restructured) collective farms, the management is largely the same as in the former (old style) collective or state farms. However, decision-making is not any longer centrally planned, but is made by the management, whether or not with active participation of members of the cooperative. (Some of the former farms also may have been re-organized into associations of peasant farms or cooperative farms, and in many of the statistics, these types are combined with private farms, presumably indicating that the management here has been largely replaced). Unfortunately the distinction between peasant and private farms and associations of peasant farms in one category and the agricultural cooperatives and smaller collective farms in the other category has been lost due to changes in definitions and in terminology. The distinction is not very reliable since 2000, and so it is more correct to use the combined figure of 84 per cent.

According to documentation received in June 2000 from the Ministry of Agriculture, 493 large farms have been restructured into 63,288 smaller farms. Nine years after the start of the land and agrarian reform program in the Kyrgyz Republic, over half a million families or 3,481,800 individuals residing in rural areas now have their documents proving ownership of rights to land which is more than 72 per cent of the population of the Kyrgyz Republic. Statistics show that about 70 per cent of the population lives in rural areas. It can be presumed that in urban areas most of the real property is also privatized. Both in urban and rural areas it is easy to make daily observations of private owners registering their right to real property, not because they just achieved that right, but because they postponed registration although they had the official documents showing their right for some years. In part, this is also the result of considerable confusion about where to register. Most people will certainly follow official rules, but since independence it has been unclear – to say the least – if and where rights to real property should be registered. One of the motives for the Land and Real Estate Registration Project in the Kyrgyz Republic is to improve this situation with a new registration system.

The fact that in January 2000 over sixty thousand agricultural enterprises are registered does not imply that almost every Kyrgyz farmer has got the farm structure of his (or as an exception her) choice. Observation shows that it was not always possible to acquire the most wanted form of farm. In the south of the Kyrgyz Republic land shares were often too small to start operating a sustainable single-family farm. And in some areas of the country the influence of former land managers – sometimes combined with the occurrence of small land share areas – simply allowed only slight changes in the organization of former large farms. As mentioned before, most of the new collective farms are re-organized large state or collective farms but smaller in size (former farms split in parts) with often part of the same management running the new collective farm. Here the opportunity sets opened only theoretically to farmers while social context dictated a practical way to follow. Whether the land shares were too small or where peer pressures limited the opportunity sets, time will tell how farmers cope with that situation. For the small shareholders it might be in the form of evolving land markets for lease of land that can make a difference. For the members of new collectives having sufficient land in their shares fading influence of the old agricultural elite might create new opportunities after a certain period of time. Nevertheless as far as the conditions allowed them, the peasants in the Kyrgyz Republic have taken advantage of the change.

In urban areas, it was reported that almost everyone entitled to real property became owner since independence. The privatization program with its generous[1] payment schedule for acquiring real property was an enormous incentive to pursue private ownership. So the main conclusion is that Kyrgyz citizens have taken advantage of the change in their opportunity sets to become private individual owners of rights to land.

[1] Law 'On privatization of housing stock in the Republic of Kyrgyzstan' of 20 December 1991 Article 4 (See Annex A)

7.2.2 CHANGING OPPORTUNITY SETS

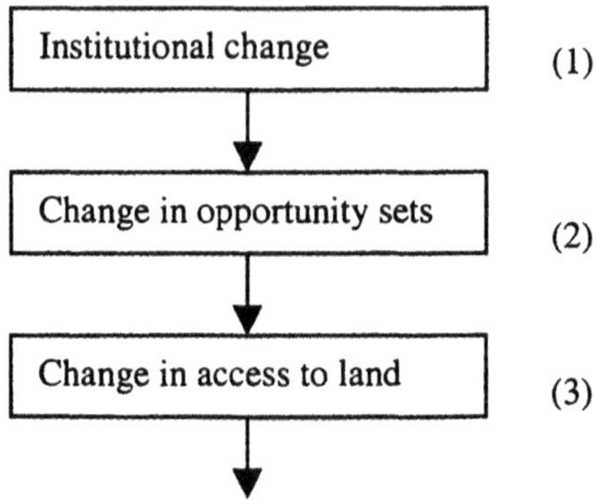

Figure 7.2.2 Change in opportunity sets

Element (2) in the model depicted in Figure 7.2.2, 'change in opportunity sets' will have a slightly different contents whether the model is derived from the prosperity paradigm or from the food security paradigm. Most of the indicators in this element will only be observable after some time has passed from the start of the implementation of institutional change.

In a dominant agricultural society like the Kyrgyz Republic, improvement of food security is primarily a matter of domestic food production and improvement of efficiency in agricultural production. The emphasis will thus differ between the prosperity and the food security paradigm in creation of opportunity sets. In the food security paradigm it is important that farmers will use new opportunities to enhance agricultural production and effective use of farmland. Their experience of the changes should result in an incentive to make the most of their farm in sustainable productivity terms. Although eventually everyone will benefit from this change in opportunities the focus is mainly on the rural population. Macro level indicators are listed:

- (proposed) change in the size of farms;
- initiatives to start new agricultural enterprises;
- start of new farms and changes in the farm management;
- change in labor relations on farms (for example more family oriented).

In the prosperity paradigm it is important that from the start the whole population will take advantage of and will benefit from the changes and thus the scope has to be on creating opportunities for all citizens. Macro level indicators apart from the ones mentioned for agriculture are listed:

- change in numbers of formal and informal transactions by citizens with real property;
- development of institutions assisting with transfers of real property (realtors);
- initiatives to start new farming enterprises.

Changing opportunity sets are an important indicator for re-emerging customs and customary rules but also early warning signals of less-desired developments. Some general indicators of this type of change for specific property related issues are listed:

- decreasing female representation among property right holders;
- changing property inheritance gender (in)equity;
- changing number of females registered as co-owners of rights in cooperative properties;
- changing use of common pasture lands (livestock expansion, hay and fodder gathering);
- increasing evidences of squatting (outcast people and ignored (ethnic) minorities);
- increasing occurrence of fallow land (because of growing emphasis on capital investment in property and decreasing interest in farming).

Some of these indicators can also be used for other elements of my model. The last indicator for example will also be an indicator for increased food security.
Imported legal regulations will not always have a clear-cut solution to counter non desired developments. As mentioned before, willingness both by local lawmakers and authorities is required to adapt imported rules and design additional regulations to further guide the land reform.

7.3 RESULTS OF CHANGE IN OPPORTUNITY SETS

7.3.1 INVENTORY OF CHANGE IN OPPORTUNITY SETS

The effect of a change in opportunity sets (element 2 of the model) for the rural population in the Kyrgyz Republic is measurable in the increasing number of single-family and associations of peasant farms during the transition period. Starting from almost zero before independence, now more than 62,000 farms of such kind have been registered and are operational in the Kyrgyz Republic in June 2000. Almost 3,500,000 individuals living in more than 500,000 families in rural areas received land shares. However, the change to private ownership of farmland has not yet delivered in terms of economic development. Initially the private ownership of land designated for agriculture was excluded from the reforms. Farmers received use rights of this land first for a 49-year term that was later conversed to 99-year term use rights. Farmers were pleased with those rights but they preferred and pressured for outright private ownership, which was achieved by an amendment on the Kyrgyz Constitution in November 1998. The new farmer entrepreneur left his mark on the development of agricultural production. The typical growing pains – seen also elsewhere in former communist countries – of inexperienced farmers, inappropriate farm machinery, and lack of agricultural support, resulted in a drop in agricultural production that lasted until 1996 – 1997. The agricultural gross domestic product experienced a negative annual growth for the first five years of independence but it started to recover in 1996. However, reports on the development of rural areas in the Kyrgyz Republic reveal a persistent lack of progress in battling rural poverty. There are signs that the opportunity sets of the rural population altered only with respect to the way of managing farms and planning agricultural production.

Many of the necessary additional institutional arrangements to assist farmers in the development of their farms still are in an initial stage, having recently been planned, or are still part of rhetorical political statements. These issues must be solved – in other words these are still persisting problems – according to the June 2000 report of the Director General of the Ministry of Agriculture are (in the original 'English' translation provided to the WB) [44]:

- 'Execution and protection of peasants' and villagers rights for industrial inputs, including land shares;
- Development and improvement of legislative and legal basis promoting rehabilitation of economic situation in the agrarian sector;
- Enhanced responsibility for the status of national agriculture born by the executors at each level; support of rural manufacturers independent of property form;
- Introduction of effective tools for accumulation of food resources based on economic stimulation of the domestic producers and introduction of market relations and development of the appropriate infrastructure;
- Stimulation of integration and cooperation between private business entities involved into production, processing, supply and procurement of agricultural products;
- Training and development of human resources in conformity with requirements of the market economy;
- Strengthening of bodies involved into the implementation of privatization processes, and solving issues of reorganization and realization of citizens' rights;
- Finalization of issue and distribution of titles for land ownership and other types of property;
- Amplification of agriculturally suitable lands, their quality and quantity;
- Introduction of market relations in the area of utilization of agriculturally suitable lands and pasture lands, especially with regards to the new land assimilation;
- Improvement of irrigation and melioration networks, and operation of those;
- Improvement of the taxation system and customs policy;

- Development of local agricultural processing industries, taking into account foreign and domestic demand;
- Switch to the market system for introduction of new varieties, production of seeds, breeding work and pedigree animals' production;
- Timely provide villagers, farmers and peasants with necessary information, advice and practices at the local level;
- Improve functional capabilities of the bodies, responsible for the reform processes;
- Equip peasants and their cooperatives with necessary infrastructure;
- Development of competition among agricultural support services and transfer of management by those services under the charge of private peasants' associations;
- Activate investment processes and ensure effective usage of those;
- Improve legal basis of the state authorities and create stimulating conditions for the work of civil servants;
- Timely and efficient resolution of disputes and conflicts in the agricultural sector; act a guarantor of rights and agreements.

Above set of objectives differ from the previous years,

> and call for revising ministerial functions and its approaches in solving issues. Therefore, significant changes defining policy in the main national sector have taken place and continue to happen in the Ministry of Agriculture and Water Resources. Currently, deviation of function and role of the Ministry of Water Resources is in process.

This quote from the report of the Ministry of Agriculture to the World Bank shows that the restructuring process is not yet over. It also shows the intentions of the responsible politicians. Unfortunately – but not unusual – the report does neither give a time schedule of when, nor any specifics on how, the Ministry plans to act on the issues mentioned. Opportunity sets have changed in the transition period, but the full advantage of changes – in so far as there will ever be such a thing – could not yet be delivered to the majority of the (rural) population.

7.3.2 ASSESSMENT OF CHANGING OPPORTUNITY SETS

Table 7.3.2 (derived from various sources) gives the combined effect of changing opportunity sets and the changing access to land by showing the distribution of farmland among different categories of farms (the subject of the next chapter). The area of land held by private farms has increased to 84 per cent of total farm land, showing that many peasants took advantage of the change in opportunity sets by applying for privately held land. It is also interesting to note that the total area of arable land increased during the transition period as a result of private farms turning the best of pasturelands into agricultural land. In the table the amount of 1,496,000 ha (± 3,740,000 acres) has been used, because of its correspondence with a figure of 1,500,000 ha of arable land in the Kyrgyz Republic in 2000 used by other sources.

Observations in the country imply that the number of peasants starting single-family farms is higher in the north (particularly in the Chui oblast) than in the south.

Table 7.3.2 Effect of changing opportunity sets and changing access to land

	1991	1992	1993	1995	2000	
Total area of farming land held By all agricultural enterprises (in 1,000 ha)	1,289	1,284	1,298	1,302	1,496	
Percentage of land held by Peasant and private farms, and associations of peasant farms	1%	8%	13%	24%	49%	together 84%
Agricultural cooperatives (Partly a number of newly organized smaller collective farms)	1%	13%	9%	11%	35%	
State and Collective farms	98%	79%	78%	65%	16%	

World Bank sponsored research shows that the size of land shares in the densely populated areas of the southern Djallal-Abad and Osh oblasts is generally too small to start a single-family farm. Taking advantage of one's opportunity set here does most likely imply that a form of peasant farming enterprise, cooperative farming, or the construction of (new) collective farming had to be chosen. While driving through the countryside in the south in spring, summer and fall, one can see the single families working their own rows of crop allocated to them in their location in the large fields of cooperatives or new collectives. Often marked by small wooden pegs in the field, it is clear to all families where their part of the crop is located and so which part of the field is theirs to maintain.

CHAPTER 8

ACCESS TO LAND

8.1 ISSUES CONCERNING ACCESS TO LAND

8.1.1 STEWARDSHIP FOR RESOURCES

Access to land can change as a result of evolutionary changes as well as a result of state intervention. The latter takes effect through changes in institutional arrangements (including legal changes) and is a deliberate action commonly referred to as land reform. In doing so, formal and physical 'access to land' will change almost overnight. Also the other form of 'access to land,' the perceived one, will change but most likely this will take more time (see also 8.2.1).

The psychological effect of rights to land should not be underestimated. The emotions a farmer feels about farmland are well depicted by Hector de Crevecoeur [16] in his 1999 book 'The Land was Everything; Letters from an American Farmer;' (1999) As a follow-up Victor Davis Hanson [39] engages himself in a renewed attempt to describe the bond of the (American) farmer with the natural world. Maslow assumes that humans find satisfaction in higher levels of the emotional hierarchy, once lower levels are satisfied. When a family grows its own food and produces for its own living, the work they put into the production brings personal rewards higher than the basic emotional level of food and shelter. It takes them to a new level of security and it will give a desire to reach beyond that.

Responsible stewardship of land and environment can be expected only if the peasant has been made responsible himself. Responsibility cannot be asked from peasants who themselves have no responsibilities. This is an important rationale for land and agrarian reform. Restructuring of agricultural programs must continue because they provide small farmers with a possibility to sustain themselves and their families while making them responsible for their environment. Restructuring of the agriculture presents people living in rural areas a chance to improve their life, decreasing the attraction of cities; it makes small farmers responsible and challenges them to use the land efficiently. A small farmer/landowner – perceiving sufficient land tenure security – will protect the land from over-exploitation and over-grazing in his own interest, and he will in general pursue more responsible stewardship for the land.

8.1.2 LAND TITLING

As mentioned before the link between improved access to land and economic development is often made. Improved access to land is then related to improved access to credit and evolving real property markets in which land tends to achieve the highest potential economic value. This is also mentioned in the terms of reference for the project in the Kyrgyz Republic to establish a system of land and real estate registration. After referring to a real property market development that is expected, the terms of reference read: 'In order to achieve this, a number of issues have to be resolved. Privatization of land and immovable property; access to credit; a group of professional experts involved in real estate agency, management and administration; appraisal expertise; public awareness and understanding of the principles and practice of private ownership; and support from local authorities. The basis upon which all this works is secure tenure provided by a competent and efficient registration system, and simple, secure procedures for conducting transactions.'

The terms of reference for the real property registration project that started in 1999 refer to 'privatization of land and real property' a process that, at the time these terms of reference were written, was almost completed in the Kyrgyz Republic. Much of the agricultural land of former state and collective farms in the Kyrgyz Republic that was made available for distribution was actually privatized by the end of 1999. Three new registration offices were operational (covering only a fraction of the total land area of the Republic) providing a model for more offices to be opened. But the reference made to accessibility of credit and the professional assistance by developing a land market was almost lost in the actual land registration project.

Dubois [27] (1997) questions the usefulness of land titling. There is no indication that a growing awareness of private ownership by land titling will result in economic development and in conservation of resources. It is often assumed that gradually more individualism will lead to more formalization of land rights, giving more security, access to credit, higher prices for land, social peace, economic stability and better management of natural resources. However, systematic data to support this assumption is lacking. The World Bank admits that nearly all its titling schemes have achieved poor results. Some authors even prove that in places were swidden agriculture prevails registration may bring more insecurity and inequity (Bruce and Fortman) [9].

8.1.3 LAND REGISTRATION

The misfit in synchronization between land reform projects and land registration projects is almost usual. There are different incentives for starting such diverse, although related, projects. A land reform project is highly politically motivated, while land registration is mostly donor fund driven. International donor organizations do link improved access to land with the establishment of a titling program and land registration. However, there is often a different experience in the recipient country. Many people having acquired their certificates of land ownership postpone registration because of the relatively high costs and, the presumed, very little benefits of registration as such. The certificates are seen as proof of ownership of rights to land because they are generally issued by government agencies and bear all the characteristics of title certificates. How will a person growing up under communist rule, without even a sense of land ownership, and now rapidly adjusting to new circumstances in a country in transition, be able to understand the full meaning of private land ownership? Why register when officially appointed authorities in an official nationwide program issue documents? Moreover, the existing registration procedures are sometimes confusing and it can be rather unclear where to register.

The acclaimed urgent need for a land registration project to be executed is contradictory to the noticeable lack of interest among the Kyrgyz to register. However, this situation is not of much concern – economic laws dictate the need for an effective land registration to assist in the development of the national economy – unless of course, the money spent now on land registration could have been used more efficiently for other purposes. The real property market in the Kyrgyz Republic has not really evolved because of the moratorium on transfers of land designated for agriculture, and also, the urban land market has barely started to evolve because of the stagnation in the national economy. However, because the Kyrgyz Republic likes to follow a European model where title always matters, land registration and titling are seen as issues requiring attention before the real property market will start to develop. The project for registration could have contributed by carrying out the scheduled public awareness campaigns. With lack of ministerial approval of the regulations for the opening of the new registration offices by GosRegister, opening ceremonies of new offices had to be held low profile and a scheduled nationwide public awareness campaign was postponed.

For measuring the change in access to land, a change in the number of transactions of real property in rural areas as registered in the registration offices does not seem a good indicator in the Kyrgyz Republic. It can be assumed that there is little understanding of the benefits of registration yet among the population.

8.2 ASSESSMENT OF CHANGE IN ACCESS TO LAND

8.2.1 INDICATORS FOR CHANGE IN ACCESS TO LAND

The formal component for element (3), 'change in access to land,' depicted in Figure 8.2.1. in part of the model, can be measured by the changing number of registered transactions, although as mentioned in the previous chapter with limitations in the Kyrgyz Republic. It has to be kept in mind that a relative long period of time between the start of the distribution of real property rights and the implementation of a new registration system has a negative influence on the willingness to make an extra effort in order to register. Most people do have possession of the distributed property for several years already and there has not (yet) been a large-scale awareness campaign about the benefits of land registration.

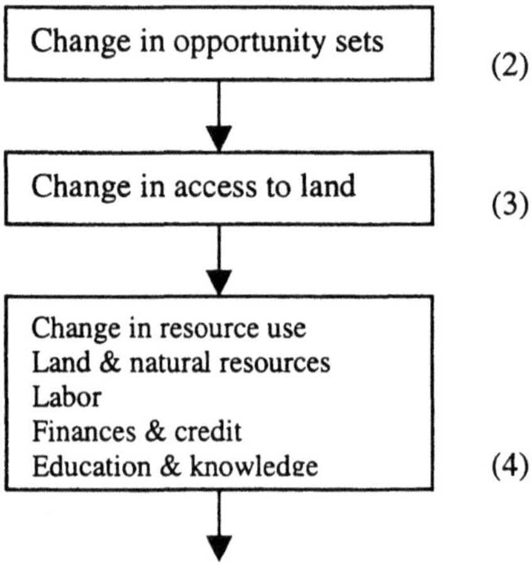

Figure 8.2.1 Change in access to land

In respect to access to land there is a slight difference between the two paradigms. In the food security paradigm, change in access to land will be of importance only as far as rural land is concerned. But when the model is primarily aimed at economic development, then land titling and registration in urban areas are important.

In a modern land registration system any distinction between rural and urban real property is strongly discouraged, because of likely changing borders between urban and rural areas in the (near) future. Experience shows that such a distinction severely hampers equity in exercising rights, provides barriers once boundaries between urban and rural areas shift – and they will shift after economic development starts – and hampers applications of governmental guidance on zoning and regulations of land use. Since the government of the Kyrgyz Republic made the choice for a national unified land registration system, the differences in the two paradigms for the element 'change in access to land' will be limited to accents put into the institutional arrangements when applied for the two different goals. Indicators for 'change in access to land' can be observed by:

- changing number of transactions of real property;
- changing numbers and terms of land leases and land rents;
- a change in use of fertilizers;
- demand for improvements of agricultural infrastructure (access roads, irrigation etc.);
- a change in use of real property and the care given to it.

Statistical data indicating changes in the latter sense are changes of the area of agricultural land, changes in crops, and home improvements (of importance for the prosperity paradigm).

Change in access to land, has two distinctive forms, as mentioned before. One is the formal and physical form, which can be measured by the change in the way people formally hold rights to land and how they gain access. In Soviet times they formally held an inheritable use right, nowadays many Kyrgyzstani have ownership rights to land and can prove this by showing registration documents, land certificates, or State Acts. But the formal form is just one element. The second form of change in access to land is a perceived one. It is not so much what is formally possible and approved that will shape the future of the Kyrgyz Republic, but the idea citizens have formed about the possibilities and the opportunities they seize. It has more to do with emotional readiness and with presumed acceptable social and customary behavior to seize opportunities, than with any formal documents 'proving' rights to land.

8.2.2 SEIZING THE OPPORTUNITY

The opportunity to change access to land has been realized in optimum by those farmers choosing to use their land shares for farming on their own, or in an association of peasant farms. Originally only a few farmers started completely on their own with single-family farms and these were either former managers of state or collective farms, or brave individual former workers on those large farms. The latter category generally got plots of land of lesser soil quality or at the very periphery of the large farms.

In 'Landed property in capitalist and socialist countries; the Russian transition' William Thiesenhusen [85], argues that increased job security was included as part of the rural social contract and work on a collective farm came not to be too demanding. In comparison with the long work hours characteristic of farming in many other countries, the Russian rural worker had predetermined hours, and at harvest it became common to mobilize workers from cities to help out (but also students and sometimes the army). For those in Russia today, individual farming is beyond the realm of their experience. Not surprisingly the situation in the Kyrgyz Republic is almost similar. During the summer months Kyrgyz students were supposed to assist with agricultural activities and were sent to summer camps for that purpose. Also teachers were temporary workers on the state and collective farms during the summer vacation.

After independence most farm workers remained agricultural employees like before, and their land shares were just administrative parts of land in the big farm types. Over time these large state and collective farms were forced by the new legislation to reorganize into new farm enterprises. But as mentioned before, the reorganization was mainly cosmetic. Most of the reorganized farms are basically a continuation of the former state and collective farms in a split up form, under new names, smaller in size, but with part of the former management firmly in control. Officially employees on those new farms had to elect the management and had to vote on operations on the farm, de facto it was the old management that made decisions and continued to run the farm, although now without state directives for the farm operation.

There is not much data available on changing agricultural credit, but an interesting table can be derived from WB data [100] about use of agricultural credit. Table 8.2.2 shows use of agricultural credit for several items for the following amounts:

Table 8.2.2 Changing use of agricultural credit

Item (Amounts in million som)	1994	1995	1996	1997(estimate)
Fuel for farm machinery	117.7	117.5	78.9	28.9
Seed	11.5	28.1	35.5	53.8
Fertilizers and chemicals	7.4	27.9	80.2	146.9

Source: WB reports

Although the data show only the use of credit, the decreasing amount for fuel seems to be the effect of smaller scale farming, and the other data indicate more intensive farming methods on the smaller farms.

8.2.3 LAND MARKET

A land market did not yet evolve. The government reports in 1998 that a land-leasing market was in the process of being established but could only evolve with substantial governmental support. The government has used some of the land out of the National Land Fund to start some experimental land leasing, but this turned out not to be very successful. Only 125,000 ha (a little over 310,000 acres) of agricultural land of the Land Fund is rented or leased out. Paying the rent and lease due for use of the agricultural land is not a real virtue in the Kyrgyz Republic. The average percentage of rents and leases paid in the whole country in 1999 is about 80 per cent, but the list shows significant differences between the oblasts. The peasants renting or leasing in Talas oblast are definitely the worst payers – an average of only 22 per cent of the total rent due has been paid in 1999 – while those in Chui oblast (around Bishkek) pay on average 90 per cent of their rent on time. Official lease has so far hardly developed as a major instrument to extend the area of agricultural land used by individual farmers; there is however evidence of informal lease. Accounts of lease of agricultural land can be found in the social assessment report [82]. Accounts of informal agreements – often without written contracts – and of feelings of uncertainty can be found throughout that report. They also come up in discussions with peasants and officials in the Kyrgyz Republic.

In 2000 a substantial area of land of the Fund has been used for experimenting with auctions of agricultural land, this resulted in transfer of 2,250 ha of land for a total of 7.6 million Kyrgyz som.

It should be mentioned here that it is difficult to determine the exact amount of land designated for agriculture in the Kyrgyz Republic. In an official June 2000 report to the World Bank from Director-General Kadyrkulov of the Ministry of Agriculture and Water Resources, two distinctive numbers can be found. Point 2 of the report refers to 1,496,300 ha of agricultural lands (excluding pasturelands) and point 3 refers to 1,573,700 ha of agricultural lands (excluding pasturelands). Whatever the exact figure, it leaves no question about the fact that Kyrgyz farmers used the opportunity and the increased accessibility of farmland to enlarge the area of it.

CHAPTER 9

RESOURCE USE

9.1 LAND AS ECONOMIC PRODUCTION FACTOR

9.1.1 ECONOMIC MOTIVES

Economic theory assumes that competition in an open and free land market under a market economy will in the end allocate land to the most efficient farmers, because they as the most efficient producers will be able to afford the (rising) prices for land.

Several researchers underline the importance of free markets. An economist strongly associated with a pledge for a free market economy is Hernando DeSoto [22]. Adam Smith [77] wrote as early as 1776 that the most important motive for people to be economically active is self-interest. People do not pursue economic goals to contribute to the wealth of the nation, but to gain their own wealth. A free market economy is a prerequisite for this.
Csaba Csaki [19] (p. iii) argues in 1994 that:

> The land reform and privatization of the land is one of the most economically important and politically sensitive issues of transition. The creation of unrestricted private land ownership is a precondition for agricultural transformation, similarly to privatization of industry and real estate assets in the rest of the economy...The establishment of transparent individual ownership rights to specific plots of land and other farm assets and the full freedom of the owners to choose the farm structure they individually wish to participate in, are the critical first steps of the land reform process. In these days, land privatization and farm restructuring is in the focus of heated political debates, practically in all lesser developed countries. The Central European countries have made substantial progress in establishing private land ownership mainly through various forms of restitution (also referred to as re-adjudication). In the republics of the former SU still some of the basic issues are being debated, namely, should a full-fledged private land ownership be acknowledged, and who should be the beneficiaries of the land reform. In general, the land reform in Central and Eastern Europe is still far from finished. Current experiences underline the difficulties of a transition from large scale agriculture to private farming and the market-based agriculture.

Agrarian reform programs and privatization of land do raise expectations. In 'Actors of the Changing European Countryside' [38], Tisenkopfs [89] reflects on the current situation in Latvia by making this remark:

> In the farmers' minds the restitution (of land) was closely knit with the thought about the state support and protection of the farm sector. Whereas farmers' market knowledge and management skills are insufficient and inadequate. Many farmers are convinced that their duty has been to create a farm and then to engage in production. In their mind, the duty of the state is to provide economic support for the (small-scale) production up to the state regulation of input prices and fixing output prices. As it is almost impossible to implement such a policy in the conditions of needy Latvia, the farmers deem the government as ignorant and indifferent to their problems and needs. This feeling is only intensified by the conditions of the governments' open market policy.

9.1.2 LITTLE SUPPORT FOR FARMERS

The remark of Tisenkopfs, quoted above, holds for many farmers in other former communist countries like the Kyrgyz Republic. Agricultural workers on the large farms are expecting that all the planning and management be provided by the State via the managers. Most new private farmers expect this type of support to continue after privatization. This concept of thinking emphasizes the need for complementary policies to accompany land distribution (in Latvia there is actually re-adjudication) to assist farmers in their agricultural management during the first period of private farming.

The most important problems facing farmers in the Kyrgyz Republic as reported in 1977 (Source WB discussion paper #394) [100] were in order of severity: unfavorable prices, lack of agricultural extension services and specific education, difficulties in output marketing, lack of rural credit, shortage of fuel and machinery, lack of chemical fertilizers, shortage of agricultural land, irrigation and water supply problems, lack of quality seed, reduction in the social safety net, and high taxes and payments (land tax, pension funds and others). This illustrates that land tenure security or land titling is not an important issue among the Kyrgyz farmers. Their concern is much more about the implementation of the reform; government support in restructuring property relations on farms, creating efficient new farm production methods, use of appropriate farm machinery and financial incentives.

9.2 ASSESSMENT OF CHANGE IN RESOURCE USE

9.2.1 INDICATORS

As for the element 'change in resource use' (4), this partly overlaps the previous element 'access to land.' It is the following element in the model as shown in Figure 9.2.1.

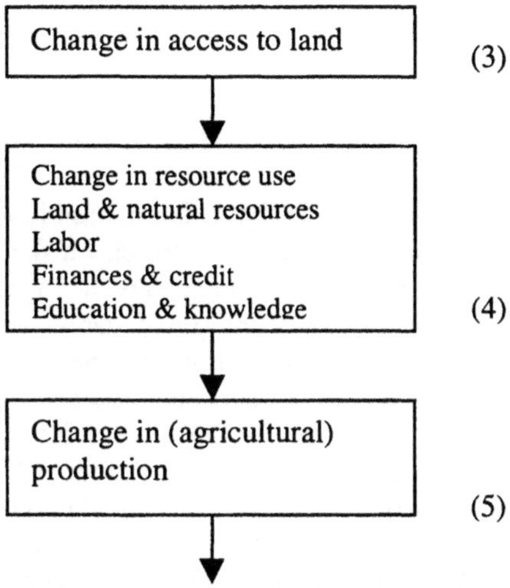

Figure 9.2.1 Change in resource use

A change in the use of land and natural resources can best be measured by changes in crops and the change in use of fertilizers, the choice for fallow land and a more conscious use of agricultural land with respect to environmental effects. The latter might be measurable by statistics on water, air, and soil quality, although providing this type of data is not popular and measured results are generally not made public in former Soviet countries. Another indicator is the demand for extension services and specific agricultural education and training.

If the emphasis is on the food security paradigm then the element of change in resource use will mainly focus on changes in agricultural production. Measurable effects are:

- changes in crops and yields;
- changes in the level of mechanization on farms;
- changes in labor input;
- changes in the efficiency of agricultural production;
- changes in credit use and changes in the number of loans using land as collateral;
- changes in agricultural extension services and use of agricultural (bio) technology.

In the prosperity paradigm the focus will be more on general changes in resource use:

- change in financial resources and credit (number of mortgage transactions);

- change in use of banks and capital investment;
- greater tendency to exploit real property either for obtaining credit or by renting it out.

9.2.2 STATISTICS ABOUT CHANGE IN RESOURCE USE

Change in resource use is so wide that it is impossible to explore such changes in depth without a lengthy and extensive research on the ground. In the prosperity paradigm partially observable phenomena are a change in use of capital and financial resources, in use of credit, and (hired) labor. Statistical data on new crops and changes in yields and mechanization are indicators, as well as changes in institutions for education and in the curricula, are also signs of change in resource use. During the preparatory phase of the project for land registration there have been attempts to add at least some aspects of modern land registration systems in existing educational curricula but it has not materialized. The bigger picture showed some changes in institutions for higher education during the transition period. The Kyrgyz Republic now has a university with a curriculum completely in the Kyrgyz language. Lack of sufficient agricultural extension services is a matter of concern. Farmers in the Kyrgyz Republic need to be informed and educated in new techniques and methods of farming.

The use of credit is limited in the Kyrgyz Republic mainly for two reasons. The Kyrgyz Republic has an unreliable banking system with rumors of possible bankruptcy and sometimes loss of resources for citizens by actual bankruptcy of a bank. Another reason is that when credit becomes available (for farmers) there are a number of channels through which the credit passes on its way to farmers and at each step a small margin is added by the lender making the interest rate unnecessary high. Western observers wonder how some people can manage to mortgage their real property with mortgages running at 70 percent or more in interest annually. For the rural population the possibilities are even more limited. Kyrgyz peasants have an almost complete lack of financial resources. The largest asset they generally have is the title to their land and real property. It is risky to mortgage that land since it is their only source of security and livelihood.

In a transition country another indicator for change in resource use is a change in efficiency in land use by farms of the various types. Kyrgyz agriculture suffered from the transition and production shrank considerably from 1990 to 1995, before picking up again in 1996. Crop production has improved more than livestock production. But the figures reported on livestock production might not reflect reality. As mentioned earlier the privatization of farming turned livestock over to individual farmers, and it is known that the reporting of numbers of livestock in private hands tends to be substantially lower than the actual number of livestock present in the country. Wheat production has grown since 1990 due to an increase in sown area of 185 per cent. However, the average yields declined by eight per cent annually. The expansion in wheat production was driven by an implicit policy of self-sufficiency in wheat, but is now becoming a concern for the government. With the limited area of arable land in the country, now more than half of it is used for production of one – not highly competitive – crop. It must be the policy of the government to abstain from directives to private farmers and use farming incentives away from wheat production. From data reported by Natskomstat the following table could be made in which the production shifts of the large state and collective farms are compared with production shifts in 'private farms.' Natskomstat makes a distinction between 'farmers' and 'household plots' in their production statistics. In the table all private farms (farmers and household plots) are taken together in one category to avoid possible errors because of changing definitions over time. The shift in production between state controlled and private farms can be easily observed. Total production of grain and potatoes (combined with sugar beets) has risen from 1849 tons in 1990 to 3107 tons in 1999. Natskomstat provides the data that are shown in Table 9.2.2a:

Table 9.2.2a Production of selected crops

Type of crop (1000 ton)	1990	1991	1992	1993	1994	1995	1996	1997	1998	1999
Grain in total	1482	1358	1493	–[1]	987	906	1322	1608	1605	1613
State Farms	1415	1285	1351	–	806	564	650	670	572	512
Private farms	67	73	142	206	181	342	672	938	1033	1101
Sugar beets and Potatoes in total	367	339	497	528	425	540	752	884	1302	1494
State Farms	178	144	234	283	154	117	177	209	266	264
Private Farms	189	195	263	245	271	423	575	675	1036	1230
Vegetables and Fruits in total	743	569	585	332	381	429	506	650	722	902
State Farms	433	306	300	131	135	98	107	105	97	135
Private Farms	310	263	285	201	246	331	399	545	625	767

Source: Natskomstat

The data shown for grain production in 1993 are obviously a mistake. The data suggest a very high harvest in wheat in that year, but comparisons with data given by the same source for yields reveals the mistake. Natskomstat reports wheat production over the years as follows, and the same source gives yields for wheat as depicted in Table 9.2.2b and this does not reflect a spectacular yield in 1993:

[1] The number persistently appearing at Natskomstat tables is 2586 which is obviously a mistake. I could not find any confirmation in other sources. It can be assumed, that 1993 was a year with a good, but not exceptional, harvest. Most likely the figure should be around 1400. For State farms only the corresponding number would be around 1200.

Table 9.2.2b Wheat production (1990-1996)

	1990	1991	1992	1993	1994	1995	1996
Wheat production in 1000 ton	482.3	434.2	627.9	2129.1	565.7	624.7	964.1
Yields of wheat in 100 kg per ha	24.9	22.4	25.5	24.6	17.0	18.3	22.2

Source: Natskomstat

It is obvious that the harvest in 1993 cannot have been three times bigger that the harvest of 1992 with yields that are almost similar in both years, without suddenly and considerably enlarging the sown area for wheat. Tripling of the area for wheat should have had dramatic effects on other crops, which cannot be found in the data. Moreover, a World Bank document (discussion paper # 394) [100] reports a total wheat production for 1993 of just over 800,000 ton, which is more in line with expectations and the data on yields. Albeit this obvious mistake, there has been more than a doubling of wheat production in the Kyrgyz Republic between 1990 and 1999 due to an almost doubling of the sown area for wheat and the introduction of spring and winter wheat varieties.

As for livestock production, Table 9.2.2c gives an insight in the decreasing need for hay and fodder because of the drop in numbers of livestock breeding in the Kyrgyz Republic.

Table 9.2.2c Hay and fodder production

In 1000 ton of product	1990	1991	1992	1993	1994	1995	1996	1997	1998	1999
hay/fodder in total	4686	4249	4318	3659	2781	1916	1690	1502	1458	1287
State farms	4597	4177	4054	3338	2373	1371	1019	819	732	555
Private farms	89	72	264	321	408	545	671	683	726	732

Source: Natskomstat

Official reports of the Ministry of Agriculture stress the point that, as far as livestock breeding is concerned, there is a need to improve the quality and productivity by transfer of technology for feeding, breeding, animal health, meat processing, and sustainable management of pastureland. Although these figures look dramatic, the national food policy report states that there seems to be sufficient livestock available to meet basic nutritional requirements. Regrets about the decreasing number of livestock are offset by advantages like less overgrazing and overfeeding (two features of Soviet husbandry). The national policy report assumes that free market forces take care of redressing the danger of livestock deficiencies and the problem of overgrazing and overfeeding with grain.

I would like to close this paragraph with Table 9.2.2d derived from Natskomstat data about the shift in marketable surplus from 1992 to 1996 for grains, potatoes and milk, which are indicators of changing resource use in the Kyrgyz Republic.

Table 9.2.2.d Marketable surplus of grains, potatoes and milk

Product	Grains		Potatoes		Milk	
Year	1992	1996	1992	1996	1992	1996
Surplus brought to market by:						
Large farming enterprises	86%	55%	77%	12%	92%	17%
Private farms	10%	39%	0%	20%	2%	25%
Household plots	4%	6%	23%	68%	6%	58%

Source: Natskomstat

The increased surplus brought to the market from house plots is remarkable. It most probably (combined with my observations) indicates an enlargement of house plots in size (from 'shrunken' land of collective and state farms?), but also a strong pursueance of people to increase their earnings by selling agricultural produce from their household plots. Combined with the data as used in chapter 11, it can be concluded that poverty among the population of the Kyrgyz Republic is, on average increasing, incentives for more intensive use of agricultural resources – including house plots – will provide them with a chance to make up for the economic decline.

CHAPTER 10

AGRICULTURAL PRODUCTION

10.1 DISMANTLEMENT OF LARGE SCALE FARMS

10.1.1 MORE PRIVATE FARMS THAN LAND; A COMPROMISE

The question in former communist countries often is 'How to manage the process of distributing land in an economically efficient way while at least maintaining or rather improving the current level of agricultural production? In other words: What type of land tenure system best serves the economic development of this particular country?'

There is no textbook, 'best tenure system,' solution for this question. The practical implementation of restructuring of agricultural production in the Kyrgyz Republic resulted in a variety of farm types as shown earlier. The slow progress of reform in terms of actual distribution of land among individuals might have been in part the result of a compromise which is specific to the Kyrgyz situation. It relates to the country's highly diverse and less favorable agro-ecological conditions; low rainfall and irrigation dependent crop agriculture (over 80 per cent of arable land is irrigated); water logging, salinity, nutrient deficiency, and erosion in soils, overgrazing and poor management of pasture land, inadequate number of all-weather roads, lack of an efficient transport network; long distances to world markets, and the legacy of the centralized system of (economic) planning, resource allocation, input distribution, and state procurement of agricultural output (WB discussion paper 394) [100].

There is not sufficient arable land to satisfy the wish of peasants to establish their own private, and preferably, single family farm. On the other hand there is the wish to abandon as much as possible the old system of large scale farming with its agricultural elite in management and other controlling positions. The problem must be solved by a compromise; combining very small household land holdings within the greater efficiency to be derived from relatively larger farms without returning to collectivism in farming.

10.1.2 INCREASED AGRICULTURAL EMPLOYMENT

Peasant and private farms (the 'privatized' farms) in the Kyrgyz Republic employ more workers per ha of arable land, or cultivate fewer hectares per worker of arable land – but presumably much more intensive – than the other types of farms.

Table 10.1.2a contains an overview on the distribution of arable land and agricultural workers among categories of farms in the Kyrgyz Republic and gives the situation of January 1995. It has been assembled using data from two sources.

Table 10.1.2a Distribution of arable land and agricultural workers

Type of farm	Total of arable land (ha)[1]	Average size(ha) of arable land	Approx. # of farms	Average # of workers	Total # of workers	Workers per ha
Peasant and Private farms	159,000	12	13,250	4.6	61,000	2.61
Associations of Peasant farms	153,000	800	191	475	90,000	1.68
State and Collective farms	625,000	1903	328	1120	367,350	1.70

Source: LTC reports and Natskomstat

A problem in collecting the data for this table is that there is not always a clear distinction between private and peasant farms so they had to be taken together. Peasant farms are enterprises owned by several farming households using larger land areas than private farms, (which explains the average area of 12 ha for the combined category of single family and multi-family peasant farms).

Associations of peasant farms also referred to as (new but smaller) collective farms (often a continuation of the former state and collective farms but under a new name and considerably smaller in size) use roughly similar labor input per hectare on arable land as the 'old' large former state and collective farms. The data are rather rough and some rounding off has been done. Because of the sometimes unspecified nature of data available, it is important to make a series of other comparisons.

It is not only arable land that is in use by the former and new farms. Apart from arable land, farms use pastures and non-arable land (land of lesser soil quality) for fodder and haymaking for their livestock. The data do not specify the nature of land, so only a rather unpolished comparison is possible. The total amount of land in use by associations of peasant farms in January 1995 was a little under 4.0 million ha (of which only 153,000 ha was arable land). It is interesting to note that the total amount of land in use by state and collective farms at the same time was around 6.7 million ha. Looking at the number of workers in both types of farms, the number of hectares per worker differs significantly. For associations of

[1] The total amount of arable land in Kyrgyzstan in 1995 is estimated to be over 1.300.000 ha (at the beginning of the transition period). During the first years of transition some 200.000 ha of the best pastureland has been converted into arable land. Apart from the farm categories mentioned here arable land is also in use by cooperatives, joint stock companies, and small enterprises.

peasant farms, this number is far more than double that for state and collective farms.

Table 10.1.2b Distribution of arable land and agricultural workers

Type of farm	Total area of Land in use Agricultural/Arable	# of farms	Total of workers	# of workers per ha (of total land area)	hectares per worker
Peasant and Private farms	457,300/ 159,000	13,250	61,000	0.13	7.5 ha
Associations of Peasant farms	3,968,000/ 153,000	191	90,850	0.02	43.7 ha
State and collective farms	6,710,000/ 625,000	328	367,350	0.05	18.3 ha

Situation of January 1995

Source: LTC reports and Natskomstat

Taken together the privatized farms (associations of peasant farms and peasant and private farms) had approximately 4.4 million ha land in use in January 1995. The total amount of land in use by state and collective farms was approx. 6.7 million ha. Given the total numbers of employees/workers on the three types (61,000, 90,850, and 367,350 respectively) the average amount of land per worker is 7.5 ha for private farms, 43.7 ha for associations of peasant farms and 18.3 ha for state and collective farms. Another important factor to bear in mind is that state and collective farms continued to own and manage pastureland as part of the farm, while pastureland for other farms has been limited, and for private farms has almost been discarded. All pastureland in 1991 was state owned and parts of it were attributed to state and collective farms for exclusive use. That situation remained pretty much the same because only land designated for agriculture ('Ugodia') was distributed among private individuals and that contained only very little pasture land.

In 1996/1997 still only 22[2] state and collective farms were operational, while the number of private farms – peasant, private and association of peasant farms – had risen to 38,218.

It is interesting to note also that according to statistics provided by Natskomstat, the share of agriculture in employment increased from 33 per cent in

[2] This number is given on page 109 of WB paper # 394 [100] on the situation 1996/1997, but note that numbers vary.

1990 (before reform) to 49 per cent in 1996/1997. This implies that employment in agriculture has risen. The share of agriculture in the GDP rose from 32 per cent to 47 per cent an almost similar relative increase. Although, as mentioned before, the data are rather coarse; the conclusion is that privatized smaller farms use more labor input per ha than the associations of (larger) peasant farms and the large state and collective farms.

It has to be taken into account that apart from people employed directly for agricultural production, the state and collective farms also employed people for social services, to serve in medical clinics, schools and nurseries in the villages on the land of the farms. For the most part the difference between associations of peasant farms and the state/collective farms seems to stem from the fact that state and collective farms have seen a major lay-off of employees because of the measures taken by the government during the transition.

Economics of scale can have some effect and should be taken into account in observing the advantages of small-scale farming above large-scale farming. Large state and collective farms do have and will use more machinery and mechanization than associations of peasant farms and private farms. With regard to food security, there is some evidence that for specific crops like wheat and barley, large-scale farming is not always less productive than smaller scale farming. For the time being however, the Kyrgyz Republic faces the harsh reality of increasing poverty during the transition, a fall in production, a breakdown of trade, loss of fiscal transfers, rising unemployment, a shrinking social safety net, and widening income disparities.

It is not an easy task to perform restructuring of the agriculture, but natural resources are finite, human skills and intelligence are not. It is a tragic waste that millions of humans have no, or so little, opportunity to be challenged to develop their human capacities. The human resource plays a double role. People are resources as well as users of resources. Making people responsible citizens gives a possibility to demand responsibility in return.

10.2 RESOURCE CONSERVATION

10.2.1 INCREASED AWARENESS

The question arises as to whether the land and agrarian reform changes the attitude of people toward resource use in a sense that there is a greater awareness of stewardship of natural resources. Although it is not an element in my model, environmental issues are of such importance nowadays that it should be mentioned. It is a known fact that in communist countries the awareness of stewardship of the population for the natural resources has decreased. This was the result of two factors; one being the establishment of collective farms where former peasants now became agricultural laborers. The other factor has been the lack of responsibility felt by the people for the environment they lived in. All decisions were made by the 'state,' represented by councils and governing bodies. Individual decision making and taking of responsibility resulted eventually in a situation were such a person was regarded as dangerous for the common – communist – case. Almost all travelers through communist countries during the 1980s must have noticed the lack of care for the environment as exercised by both the population and the government alike in these countries. In 'Agricultural Landownership in Transitional Economies,' Gene Wunderlich [102] states (p. 9): 'Do pressures of intensification on small units require exploitation of marginal qualities of land, thus causing erosion, wildlife habitat decline, and greater use of chemicals? Or does widespread ownership provide new flexibility in reassembling a greater variety of farm operations to exploit micro-differences in topography, soils, and cover? Large scale farming operations may be less sensitive to micro-environments; widespread ownership, to the extent that it encourages greater variety and management intensity in production, may induce more environmentally friendly practices.' But he also remarks (p. 6): 'Private landowners, pursuing their own objectives, may use their land in ways detrimental to others. Privatization is under suspicion for its environmental effects, because individual objectives may be shorter term or more localized than the objectives of those in a larger community. Pesticides may increase short-term production but pollute soil and water. Burning may control weeds but pollute air, destroy wildlife habitat, and expose soil to erosion. The terms of bargains struck on the environment may differ by who owns the land.'

10.2.2 GOVERNMENTAL ACTION

A higher level of stewardship for land is not explicitly mentioned in any of the reports and documents highlighting farm restructuring in the Kyrgyz Republic. There is also no clear indication about what level of government intervention should be maintained or acquired to ensure long-term sustainable growth of the agricultural sector in the country. But politicians in the Kyrgyz Republic are aware of the relationship between using the country's natural resources in a more effective and efficient way by changing the land tenure situation and the danger of environmental degradation that might come with these policies. And although there is a lot of rhetoric in documents circulating in the Kyrgyz Republic about environmental dangers and farming, it shows concern for environmental issues at government level.

In the Land Code several articles show the intent of the government to protect valuable resources and ecologically responsible use of the 'Ugodia' (Art.17, 20 and 50). In the National Food Security Report (1999), concern for the environment is the core of policy issue # 5 although in a rather idealistic way. It reads: 'Indeed, appropriate management of the rural environment by economically successful family farmers is expected to be carried out as a natural way of life since it means preserving their present and future livelihood.' It must be added however that the government of the Kyrgyz Republic shows its responsibility for ecologically sustainable agriculture in various other ways in the report.

10.3 ASSESSMENT OF CHANGE IN (AGRICULTURAL) PRODUCTION

10.3.1 INDICATORS

Change in agricultural production appears in the model as shown in Figure 10.3.1:

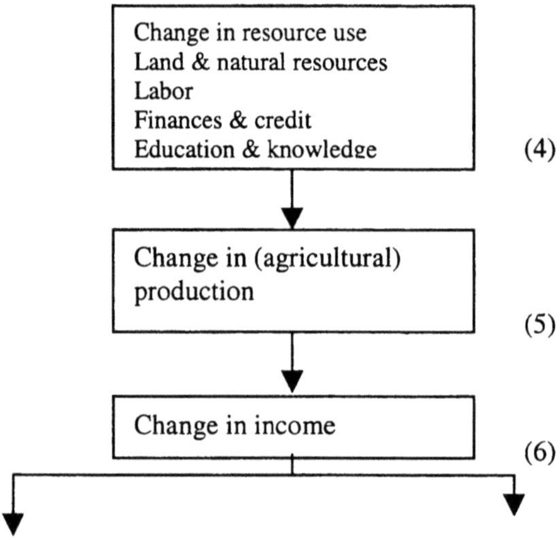

Figure 10.3.1 Changing agricultural production

For the prosperity paradigm the element change of agricultural production, or rather 'improved (agricultural) production,' (5) will be more related to general production changes, while it will be more focused on agricultural production improvement when applied to the food security paradigm. Production changes can best be found on the macro level in statistical data on production. Normally that type of statistical data is not hard to collect. Improved production can be observed in the following:

- statistical data on (agricultural) production;
- statistical data on yields;
- data on the establishment of production enterprises;
- (well interpreted) labor statistics.

When applied to the prosperity paradigm, agricultural production of cash crops, or crops that will enhance export of agricultural products (whether processed or not, but when stimulating the development of processing enterprises in the nation this may be an extra advantage) is an important indicator of a growing economy. One of the agricultural export products is sugar – although sugar beets

are imported – and production of it is significantly higher than before independence.
The data in the previous chapter are not limited as indicators of only a change in resource use. They can very well be used also as indicators for changes in agricultural production.

As far as agricultural production is concerned, it has been mentioned earlier that the government still is involved in the planning of crops and in efficient use of arable land. In its national food security policy the government of the Kyrgyz Republic promotes the development of the production of food commodities for which the country has comparative advantages and other measures in direct support of improving long-term competitiveness of the Kyrgyz agriculture both on domestic and export markets. Land and agrarian reform, crop and livestock production, rural finance, extension services, natural resources management, reform of agro-industries, institutional reform and the Ministry of Agriculture and seed development are key policy issues included in the national food security strategy. (Report on national food security policy July 1999) [44]. The publishing date of the previous policy statement suggests that agricultural reform might be well under way, but is not completed yet. Especially the marketing of input and output of agriculture is a matter of concern combined with the removing of physical barriers in transport between agricultural commodity markets and the farms.

10.3.2 IMPROVEMENT OF RURAL INFRASTRUCTURE

In September 1998 the World Bank published its earlier mentioned discussion paper (# 394) [100] on Kyrgyz agriculture. In that paper the agricultural situation in the country is summarized. The Kyrgyz Republic has made significant progress towards macroeconomic stability during the recent years. Overall, the Kyrgyz Republic is among the leaders in agricultural sector reform in Central Asia. The government has followed an agenda to privatize and transform the agricultural sector from a centrally planned economy into a market oriented rural economy.

The reforms, for which there is widespread support, are now irreversible, but the transition to a market economy is not yet complete. Some of the institutional arrangements for the rural market economy are now in place, but progress on the ground has been slow in some of the regions in particular. Because of serious budget constraints, the Government has been unable to adequately maintain or rehabilitate rural infrastructure or to develop new infrastructure where it is needed. Adequate rural infrastructure is important to the overall quality of life of people in rural areas; to improve the productivity of the land, labor, and capital; for access to domestic and world markets; and for the creation of jobs in rural areas.

Currently there is a road network connecting the towns to the major cities, but it is in disrepair. Rural feeder roads for farm-to-market access either do not exist or need major improvement. Most of the markets where farmers need to buy inputs and sell outputs do not yet exist and should be created as soon as possible.

There is no modern telecommunication system in rural areas. Smaller rural villages may have only one telephone line to be used by the whole village.
A major constraint to farm restructuring is the lack of funds at local government level to provide services like water supply, sanitation, schools, and hospitals, at an adequate standard.

10.3.3 STATISTICAL DATA

Statistical information about the development of agricultural production in the Kyrgyz Republic is not always unambiguous (as shown before), but a number of effects of restructuring of the agricultural production can clearly be noticed.

Table 10.3.3a Change in agricultural production after independence

Production data in 1000 ton	1990	1999	Change (1990 = 100)
Total production of grain	1482	1613	109
Wheat	482	1109	
Barley	592	180	
Corn	406	308	
Rice	2	15	
Total production of sugar beet + potatoes	367	1494	407
Sugar beet	2	536	
Potatoes	365	958	
Total production of vegetables, fruits and berries, grapes and melons	743	902	121
Vegetables	487	719	
Melons	71	63	
Fruits/Berries	141	101	
Grapes	43	18	
Cotton, Tobacco + Vegetable oil crop	145	175	120
Cotton	81	87	
Tobacco	54	30	
Vegetable oil crop	10	58	

Source: Natskomstat

The size of land designated for agriculture increased during the first nine years after independence, most likely due to the sowing of areas in the best pasture land by private farmers, land that was under state and collective farms only used as pasture land. An increase of around 15 per cent in the amount of arable land in the country can be observed from a reported 1,300,000 ha in 1990 to 1,500,000 ha in 1999 (some sources even suggest a larger increase). Against this increase in arable land, it is interesting to assess the increase in agricultural production.

Based on data provided by Natskomstat the Table 10.3.3a can be assembled (hay and fodder production is excluded as it is currently mainly harvested on common pasturelands and non-arable land). Note the overall increase of production as a whole when groups are taken together. However, looking at the individual crops, there are some lower figures. The total of grains has gone up, but that is because of a considerable increase in wheat production. Barley production has substantially decreased, and corn production is lower than in 1990. Crops of tobacco, melons, fruits/berries, and grapes show lower figures than before independence.

The spectacular rise in the production of sugar beets and potatoes might indicate a change in production patterns more aimed at the market. It is reported that white sugar, uncombed cotton, ethyl spirits, cattle skins, and unfermented tobacco are main export products. Livestock and unfermented tobacco are assumed to be increasingly grown on house plots escaping official statistics, because the official data for livestock breeding, and hay production show significant declining levels, while at least for tobacco the local market does not seem to shrink taken into account the continuous high number of smokers using domestically grown tobacco in the country.

Do the numbers in the Table 10.3.3a suggest that agricultural production is now more efficient than in Soviet times? To answer this question Table 10.3.3.b produced with data from Natskomstat about the development of yields of major commodities is interesting.

Table 10.3.3b Yields

	1990	1991	1992	1993	1994	1995	1996	1997	1998	1999
Wheat	24.9	22.4	25.5	24.6	17.0	18.3	22.2	23.7	24.6	24.3
Barley	22.2	19.2	22.1	20.3	13.9	13.0	16.7	18.8	21.6	19.7
Corn	61.8	58.5	51.3	45.2	35.3	37.4	43.2	45.9	49.2	53.0
Rice	17.1	14.2	14.7	9.6	13.0	15.5	17.5	19.3	22.0	24.5
Sugar-beet	169	156	213	188	116	123	152	181	200	203
Potatoes	136	137	124	108	90	99	114	121	131	150
Vegetables	196	180	154	140	115	103	113	132	143	152
Fruits/ Berries	41.2	25.9	35.4	14.2	20.1	20.9	24.1	27.1	25.4	23.9
Hay	58.2	53.1	53.1	51.3	42.8	42.6	45.3	49.1	54.0	48.0

Source: Natskomstat

Table 10.3.3b indicates that the efforts for improvement of the agricultural production after nine years of transition start to pay off. Restructuring of the agriculture in the Kyrgyz Republic has resulted in an improvement in production both by enlarging the arable land area and by increased harvests. Combined with the findings in paragraph 10.1.2 about higher labor input per ha in privatized farms, the perspective for agriculture and also for rural living is positive. Table 10.3.3b does not yet confirm clearly findings in other global research showing that privatized smaller farms are (in the long run) more efficient than large state and collective farms. Perhaps it is too early for such findings in the Kyrgyz Republic.

Yields are in general lower than before the start of the agrarian reform in 1991. For the Kyrgyz Republic there is still a long way to go, but the decline in agricultural production of 1993 – 1995 has been followed by a continuous growth with currently higher overall production levels than before independence.

10.3.4 EFFECTS ON RURAL LIVING

International research shows that results of land and agrarian reform deliver noticeable results for rural living only after fifteen to twenty-five years. A conclusion made in 'Changing land relations and farming structures in formerly socialist countries'; by Zvi Lerman [49] (p. 80), is that: 'The remarkable changes in land ownership and farm organization have not yet brought the productivity gains as expected. In part this is because of the general economic depression that took place parallel at the privatization process. A decline in use of productivity enhancing inputs, a backdrop of demand for livestock products, and reduction in returns to agricultural production were the result.' This suggests that at least a considerable period of time is needed before noticeable changes in agricultural production can be observed. Furthermore, the researcher concludes: 'To enable agriculture to reap the benefits of private ownership and individual initiative, governments must provide a stable legislative environment with clearly defined and easily transferable property rights, speed up de-monopolization of support services, and encourage the development of functioning markets in land, assets, and commodities.' This all requires resources to be spent and that is often a very limited possibility for governments of economies in transition by their general lack of sufficient resources.

There is no doubt about the drastic change in the way farms are managed nowadays when compared with management styles before independence. But the manifestation of improved abilities in peasants as a consequence of new motivations, better nutritional standards and developed skills, takes about fifteen years (as reported by Ghonemy [37]). Indeed, discussions with local experts reveal that the restructuring of agriculture is still not seen as complete in the Kyrgyz Republic. It implies that the effects of restructuring of the agriculture in the Kyrgyz Republic cannot be completely seen yet.

CHAPTER 11

ASSESSMENT OF CHANGE IN INCOME

11.1 OBSERVATIONS AND INDICATORS ON INCOME

11.1.1 OBSERVATIONS

Asking people about their changing income situation will provide data on the change in income. Daily observations during the project were mainly limited to the situation in the capital city, which is not representative for the actual situation in the country, let alone for change in income in rural areas.
Indicators of income change on the macro level must be used to make an assessment. It will be clear that data on income, as long as this is nominal, does not give the right information. Nominal income changes should be corrected for changes in the cost of living.

In Table 11.1.1 the national average wage is compared with the minimum consumption budget for the last five years (data from Natskomstat):

Table 11.1.1 National average wage and minimum consumption budget

Year	1995	1996	1997	1998	1999	2000
(Amounts in Kyrgyz som)						
Nominal average wage	368	491	680	841	1050	1177/1210[1]
(averages per month)						
Minimum consumption budget	334	534	691	799	1097	1205

Source: Natskomstat

Although there are no specific data available, it can be assumed that there is a difference in income between urban and rural residents like in almost all other countries. Expressed in monetary amounts the rural people may be worse off than urban dwellers, but this can be more than compensated for by the advantage of

[1] These two different numbers appear in two different Natskomstat statistical report sheets. The first number appears in 'Main social and economic indicators' and the second number is reported in 'Social Sector annual data'.

some subsistence agriculture, which is out of reach for the majority of urban dwellers. The table indicates that a nominal increase in average wages in the Kyrgyz Republic could not make up for an increase in costs. The situation worsened until 2000, but looking at one of the numbers perhaps for the first time in several years, the nominal average wage might be higher than the minimum consumption budget. It is too early to see this as a positive sign, because over January/February 2001, the average wage was reported to be 1218 and the minimal consumer budget was 1292 by Natskomstat. It is important to realize that apart from the figures presented here, the social safety net disintegrates more and more, leaving many citizens in the lower income group without protection against the persistent inflation. Many retired persons are dependent on the state (as their former employer) for pension payments and the state has enormous difficulties to satisfy all material needs in the country. The conclusion is that official data on income and minimum consumption in the Kyrgyz Republic show persistence of a stagnation of the economy.

It should be borne in mind also that statistical information in many countries in transition gives only 'official' data. While discussing income change with people during my assignments, it always surprises me that rural residents can survive even if there is hardly any monetary income. Close observation shows that there is a vast informal barter economy in which goods are traded for other goods. As a reminiscence of the communist times, there is also a strong sense of survival and persons related to each other by family ties or kinship will generally go very far in supporting each other during times of hardship, further than familiar to the Western observer with experience in a dominantly capitalist society. Another observation in the Kyrgyz Republic (and in other former communist countries) is that people continue coming to work even if there has been no wage payment for several months in a row. Due to some bureaucratic problems and the bankruptcy of a bank chosen by the project, we encountered this situation with our own project staff in the Land and Real Estate Registration Project in the Kyrgyz Republic. For several months payments could not be made and we, as expatriate project staff, were sometimes asked for (small) personal loans, but as a whole the project staff continued working, mostly as we were told, out of fear of losing the job.

11.1.2 INDICATORS

Because of the strong focus on rural areas, change in income in the model, given in Figure 11.1.2, is mainly the effect of changing or improved agricultural production. However, because of the nature of the land reform in countries in transition, there is also a change in property ownership in urban areas. Very little can be said about the effects of the new property regime for dominantly urban dwellers. Their possibility of an increase in income can be achieved by actively exploiting the property either by putting it up for rent (and move in with relatives – a situation encountered and observed in Bishkek where there is (foreign) demand for temporary lodgings), by selling one property and sharing another apartment with relatives or others, or by taking out a mortgage and using the extra cash for –

hopefully – lucrative dealings. The potential gainers in income by land and agrarian reform are more likely the inhabitants of the rural areas.

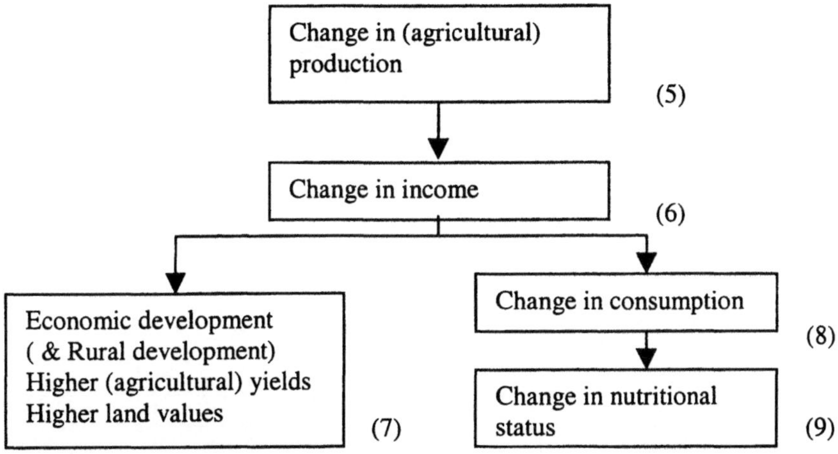

Figure 11.1.2 Change in income

Typical indicators for change in income are:

- Change in monetary income,
- Change in demand for 'luxury' goods (like TV sets and household appliances),
- Change in demand for appropriate agricultural assets (especially for smaller-scale farming),
- Change in investment for on-farm living conditions in general (for example pavement of drive ways, replacement of out-houses etc.).

Most of these changes must be collected by field observations since most data is hard to collect elsewhere. Interesting personal observations in Bishkek were the presence of video rental shops and the opening of the first Internet café in the Kyrgyz Republic in 1999.

CHAPTER 12

ASSESSMENT OF ECONOMIC DEVELOPMENT

12.1 THE PROSPERITY BRANCH OF THE MODEL

12.1.1 INDICATORS AND STATISTICS

The 'prosperity' branch in the model will be followed first. All changes discussed previously are often supposed to lead to economic development (7) in the prosperity paradigm.

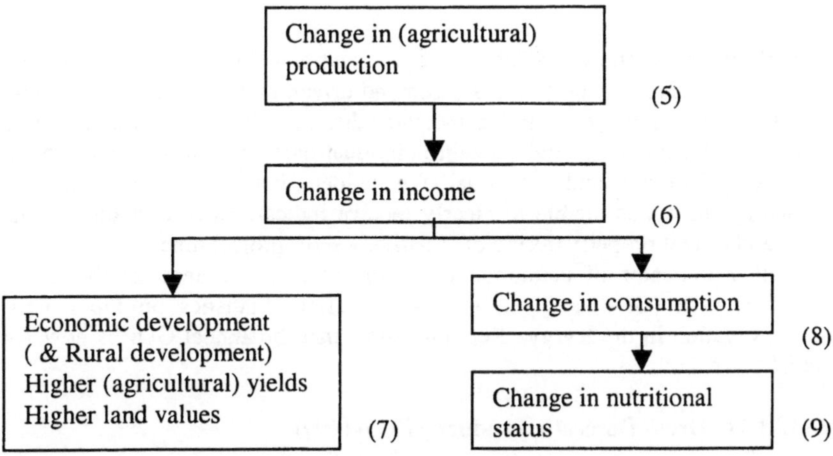

Figure 12.1.1 Economic development in the model

Two possible indicators for economic development mentioned in the model are higher yields and higher land values (or in a wider perspective higher incomes and higher values of real property) as depicted in Figure 12.1.1a. When discussing the element, change in agricultural production in chapter 10, it could be demonstrated with data from Natskomstat that agricultural production declined in the first years after independence. The production as a whole has since recovered and shows for most crop yields that are higher than the level before independence.

The full table of higher levels of agricultural production can be found in paragraph 9.2.2 as Table 9.2.2c, but it is illustrative enough to repeat it in very short form in Table 12.1.1a:

Table 12.1.1a Development of Yields (1990-1999)

Type of crop in ton x 1000	1990	1993	1996	1999
Grain in total	1482	2792* (~ 1400)	1322	1613
Sugar beets + Potatoes in total	367	528	752	1494
Vegetables, Fruits In total	743	332	506	902

The overall growth as shown in Table 12.1.1a seems a positive sign for the growth of the economy – presuming that it is a demand driven growth – , but not enough to draw any conclusions yet. Another indicator discussed in chapter 3 is the value of land and real property. I could obtain individual data about this on the ground just by asking BTI staff and individual right holders, but the answers were very contradictory and I was unable to clearly receive indications of a change in the value of land or real property during the relatively short project time.

Another indicator of economic development is the change in the Gross Domestic Product (GDP)as given in Table 12.1.1b. Statistics on the macro-economic situation in the Kyrgyz Republic show that the annual GDP is now 1.4 billion US$.

Table 12.1.1b Gross Domestic Product (1991-1999)

Variation given in per cent (each year)

1991	1992	1993	1994	1995	1996	1997	1998	1999
- 7.8	- 13.9	- 15.5	- 20.1	- 5.4	+ 7.1	+ 9.9	+ 1.8	+ 2.1

The annual variation in GDP over the past nine years is shown in the following table (source: Prime-minister's report on economic results in the Kyrgyz Republic

* As indicated earlier the number 2792 is an obvious mistake and should be given as somewhere around 1400

published in January 2000, calculation via a combination of 8 volume prices and 2 price indices).

The National Statistical Committee (Natskomstat) published the 1999 figure as reported in the Times of Central Asia [88] of March 9, 2000. A week earlier the same paper reported that the goal of the government for 2000 is a growth in the GDP with 4–5 per cent. Recent reports (mid 2001) from Natskomstat show a growth cf 5 per cent in 2000.

Also data of Natskomstat about the average wage and the minimum consumption budget shown in the previous chapter can be used to measure changes in economic development. Here the picture is less positive. There is a persistent negative gap between average wage and minimal consumer budget. For most Kyrgyzstani the transition to a market economy has not (yet) been beneficial with respect to their prosperity.

12.1.2 POVERTY ALLEVIATION

Poverty alleviation is an important development challenge facing the Kyrgyz Republic. The government states that agricultural and rural development must lead the effort to combat poverty. Poverty has increased during the transition. Poverty assessment surveys show that poverty is more severe in rural areas and in the southern oblasts. Other indicators of declining living standards are the increase of malnutrition, particularly among children, and the greater difficulty of residents in rural areas to receive pensions and other social benefits, in part because of the inadequate banking system in rural areas (Source: WB discussion paper # 394). Although at the national level food security is reasonably reached, at the household level, the situation has worsened between 1991 to 1999 especially in the two lowest quintiles of the population. Under the FSU, social benefits were guaranteed to every citizen, regardless of economic or financial costs. Under the current rules of free market economy total coverage of social services is much harder to achieve, another reason that industrial production dropped drastically after 1991 due to lack in demand and causing widespread unemployment. The share of the agricultural sector in employment has grown from 33 per cent in 1991 to 49 per cent in 1997 (Source: WB paper # 394 [100]) but it has to be born in mind that wages in rural areas are significantly lower than wages in industry. That is why poverty in general increased, poverty being more severe in the southern – mainly agricultural – oblasts (Osh and Djallal-Abad) than, for example, in the northern oblast of Chui, which is situated around the capital city Bishkek.

The conclusion is that the effects of the institutional changes introducing the restructuring of the agriculture in the Kyrgyz Republic show positive signs, but have not yet delivered (beginning of 2000) on their full expectations with respect to economic development. Average living standards in the Republic have hardly improved and living conditions in rural areas are hardly any better now than before independence. But most farmers now are independent farmers and not agricultural employees and they may make their own decisions on how to run their farm.

12.1.3 ECONOMIC PERSPECTIVE

It is difficult to give a prognosis for the development of the economy and rural living in the Kyrgyz Republic. The economic decline has still not been turned around into convincing economic development, but small signs of improvement or at least of a possibility of this about to happen can be observed. The inflation has come down and is stabilizing to an acceptable level. The government is able to control the exchange rate of the national currency. The agricultural production is back on its pre-independence levels and for some crops it is even higher than before.

The new smaller farms seem to absorb more labor per hectare than the old style farms and this will result in more employment in rural areas. There are still a number of conditions that should be fulfilled in order to achieve a sustainable economic development. The infrastructure for marketing agricultural produce needs urgent improvement, agricultural credit must be expanded and be made less cumbersome to obtain, extension services for agricultural education are needed and agro-technology should be promoted and employed. This combination of measures will make the Kyrgyz Republic more competitive in agricultural production.

CHAPTER 13

CHANGE IN CONSUMPTION AND IN NUTRITIONAL STATUS

13.1 SUSTAINABLE AGRICULTURAL PRODUCTION

13.1.1 NEW APPROACH TOWARD AGRICULTURAL PRODUCTION

In this chapter emphasis will be on improved food security as a result of changes in consumption and nutritional status. The two elements are taken together in one chapter because they are closely linked and changing consumption is the only source of change in nutritional status.

A 1987 publication of the United Nations sponsored Brundtland Commission [81] report 'Our Common Future,' draws much attention to the concept of 'Sustainable Development.' It is a term everyone seems to like, but nobody is sure exactly what it means. The report defined it as a development that meets the needs of the present without sacrificing the ability of the future to meet the needs of the global population. The question of course will be immediately 'What are 'the needs?' Such a vague definition allows a broad consensus, and it becomes a breeding ground for disagreement. Or it can be used under almost all circumstances by any government.

In LTC research paper # 129 [55] Maxwell and Wiebe conclude that improved understanding of the impact of both evolutionary and statutory changes in tenure rules governing control over and access to land and natural resources will inform food policy. Understanding of the dynamic interaction between access to land and access to food may also provide food policymakers with a wider menu of tools with which to address food-related problems.

A threat in countries in transition is overexploitation of resources in a situation of shortage followed by not enough good years with sufficient yields to restore depleted assets leading to in-sustainability in the long run. This will result in food insecurity. It will also enable wealthier farmers to gain in endowments over the poorer ones in due time, making the poorer ones more rapidly and persistently food insecure.

The call for more international donor support for agro-biological research by Serageldin might be a way to perceive long-term sustainability. In an interview in Newsweek 'Can we feed our world?' in 1998 Ismail Serageldin [75] states: 'There is no way of dealing with poverty, protection of the environment, or food without transforming agricultural production at the small holder level in developing countries. But we are, in parallel, on the cusp of a new revolution in the biological sciences. Now we are getting into the manipulation of genes, all sorts of possibilities are opening up. The application that plants are more drought-resistant, more salt tolerant, more resistant to pests without pesticides.' It is useful to recall here the example of India given by him while presenting a paper at Ohio State University [74] in 1998. In that country food production rose from 7 million tons in 1961 to 197 million tons in 1990 on almost the same area of arable land, mainly because of the application of newly developed seeds with biotechnology.

13.1.2 ENVIRONMENTAL ISSUES

In the National Food Security Policy of the Kyrgyz Republic report [44], policy issue #5 deals with 'Management of Natural Agricultural Resources.' The reported background of this issue is that the way farming's main natural resources, soil, water, and natural vegetation, are being exploited has very important consequences on the agricultural economy, on the National Food Balance, and on food security. It also has direct implications on the environment, on nature conservation, and on local biological balances. On the one hand, some farm policies such as market and price stability, security of land tenure, adequate irrigation methods, community control on access to grazing land in the mountain range, proper animal feeding principles, and availability of adequate rural services, are factors which can motivate farmers towards conservative natural resources management attitudes, without having to impose too much of a constraint. On the other hand inappropriate policies can all too easily result in improper use of soil, inconsiderate utilization of water, overgrazing of rangeland, excessive deforestation, and consequently lead to soil erosion, water logging, salinization, and severe depletion of precious natural resources. As the report states it:

> In order to maintain food stability during future years, it is the Government's policy to optimize the use of the three basic natural resources, farmland, water, and range-land, needed for a sustainable domestic food production. It means at the same time increasing the productivity of each of these resources, and to set rigid standards in order to avoid overexploitation. A policy of preservation of the nation's vast natural capital is considered to be a guarantee of a continuously stable National Food Balance.

13.2 ASSESSMENT OF CONSUMPTION AND NUTRITIONAL STATUS

13.2.1 MEASURING CONSUMPTION AND NUTRITIONAL STATUS

How can we find data for this 'branch' of the model, given in Figure 13.2.1 that concentrates on change in consumption and change in nutritional status?

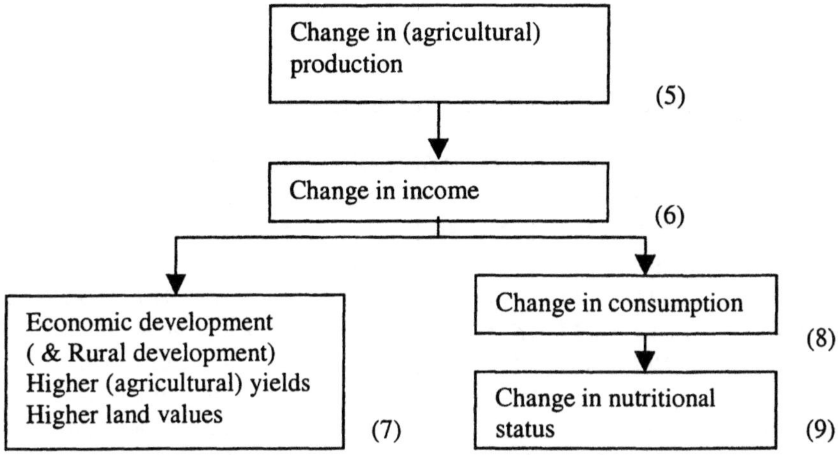

Figure 13.2.1 Change of consumption and nutritional status

Under ideal circumstances of research, counting the daily calorie intake will be done for measuring food security. The World Bank uses a diet of at least 2000 calories a day for food security. Checking the intake of a selection of a population is a time-consuming and costly activity. Another factor seriously limiting the study of caloric intake is the weak reliability of statistics in most countries in transition. There is still a kind of barter economy in the rural areas limiting reflection of the real situation in reported data. Researchers have used several measures as the basis of strategies for coping with food insufficiency. Human beings are not passive victims of food insufficiency; they will actively try to diminish the effects of food insufficiency. If these effects could be recognized and described it would most likely give a good proxy for food security, but again that takes a considerable amount of time.

13.2.2 CHANGE IN DEMAND FOR SPECIFIC FOOD

Data presented at the National Food Security Policy Seminar in July 1999, in Bishkek, provide insight into changes in consumption and changes in nutritional status. A table on agricultural production in the Kyrgyz Republic in chapter 12 indicates that there are obviously some changes in demand for specific food and so, expectedly, a change in consumption. This is of course only an indicator, because export and import of agricultural products should also be taken into account. However, all reports underline that most of the agricultural production is for domestic use (For example grain export is marginal and estimated to be around 20,000 tons annually or less than 1.25 per cent of the national production in 1999).

Agricultural production in the Kyrgyz Republic has developed according to the Table 13.2.2 derived from statistical data provided by Natskomstat.

Table 13.2.2 Agricultural production in 1000 tons

	1990	1991	1992	1993	1994	1995	1996	1997	1998	1999
Wheat	482.3	434.2	627.9	2129[1]	565.7	624.7	964.1	1273.7	1204	1109.1
Barley	591.6	556.4	582.0	477.0	288.2	158.8	166.4	151.6	161.7	179.8
Corn	406.0	364.4	280.7	183.7	129.3	116.0	182.2	170.6	227.8	308.5
Rice	2.1	2.5	2.8	2.3	4.0	6.7	9.3	11.7	11.1	15.1
Sugar beet	1.7	12.7	134.6	220.2	114.2	108.1	189.8	205.5	529.3	536.1
Cotton	80.9	62.4	52.4	49.2	53.8	74.8	73.1	62.4	77.9	86.9
Tobacco	53.9	49.3	43.1	48.6	36.4	17.6	17.9	25.8	28.1	29.9
Vegetable oil crop	10.3	4.8	6.3	7.1	14.2	25.2	34.9	37.9	43.8	58.0
Potatoes	365.5	326.3	362.3	.330.8	311.0	431.6	562.4	678.0	773.6	957.6
Vegetables	487.3	399.9	404.0	259.3	265.6	318.4	368.5	478.1	555.9	719.3
Melons	71.4	54.3	32.5	18.6	18.9	23.2	40.5	38.3	46.6	63.5
Fruits /Berries	140.9	85.3	117.5	45.1	79.1	67.3	82.8	110.7	102.6	100.8
Grapes	43.3	29.3	31.0	9.2	17.6	19.7	14.3	22.7	17.2	18.1
Hay	1097.9	986.2	1001.6	943.3	856.2	906.7	955.8	899.4	905.2	907.5
Fodder	3588.1	3262.3	3316.1	2716.0	1924.7	1009.6	734.0	602.5	552.6	379.3

Source: Natskomstat

Table 13.2.2 confirms the claim in the national food security report of self-sufficiency in wheat, but a decrease in the less important production of barley. The traditional and popular Kyrgyz dish is 'bishbarmak,' a kind of pasta from wheat (in the south sometimes rice) mixed with sheep meat and spices. It is a Kyrgyz word and translated it means 'five fingers,' which explains the way the dish should be eaten!

Another remarkable point is the almost stable production of hay. Private farmers are obviously able to harvest hay from common pastureland to feed domestic animals. The decimation of fodder production confirms the strong drop in livestock production in line with data from other sources. Observations on local markets and talks with citizens reveal that the current economic hardship causes them to reduce their consumption of meat and change to a diet pattern that includes more bread and other wheat-based foods. The most exported agricultural products are currently white sugar, uncombed cotton, ethyl spirits, cattle skins, and unfermented tobacco. It is remarkable that the Kyrgyz Republic exports white sugar, because the supply of raw sugar is not very reliable and Kyrgyz sugar

[1] As mentioned already, the number for wheat in 1993 is obviously a mistake. The actual figure for 1993 will more likely be between 600 and 800

refineries are energy inefficient and technologically obsolete according to WB paper # 394 [58].

Important imports are raw sugar, vodka, molasses and most of the agricultural inputs such as mineral fertilizers, and fuel. Looking at the main products in domestic agriculture, it is reasonable to assume that the changes in production reflect changes in consumption and this will be even more evident over time with the concept of a growing free market economy. Unless there is a considerable amount of food produced that is not consumed – which is not revealed by reports, partially observable phenomena, and questions – then the assumption that the domestic production of foodstuff reflects consumption can be justified as a good proxy.

13.2.3 GROWTH RATE OF THE POPULATION

An important factor in matters of food security is the growth rate of the population. The resident population of the Kyrgyz Republic has increased during the past ten years.

Table 13.2.3 shows an increase in the population of around 13 per cent in the past ten years. It is also interesting to note that there has been no significant occurrence of migration to the cities. On the contrary, the rural population has increased more than the urban population.

Table 13.2.3 Population growth

Number of residents (x 1000)	1989	1999
Kyrgyz Republic	4,257.7	4,829.1
Men	2,077.6	2,385.5
Women	2,180.1	2,443.6
Urban areas	1,624.5	1,684.9
Men	770.1	807.0
Women	854.4	877.9
Rural areas	2,633.2	3.144.2
Men	1,307.5	1,578.5
Women	1,325.7	1,565.7

Source: The Kyrgyz Mass Media Digest of 17 October, 1999

There are 1,103,700 households registered in the Kyrgyz Republic. The average household consists of 4.4 people, in urban areas this figure is 3.5 and in rural areas 5.0. The largest households are in the south and have an average size of 5.5 people.

13.3 FOOD POLICY IN THE KYRGYZ REPUBLIC

13.3.1 FOOD POLICY STRATEGY

The description of the current food security situation in the national food security strategy presented in July 1999 will be used. Food security is reported as being not too positive yet. The final conclusion is that a structural food security situation in the country is still not existent. There is a volatile and only basic situation of national food security; there are imbalances at regional level, and a growing occurrence of food insecurity at household level. Achieving structural food security remains a principal and most urgent issue that the government of the Kyrgyz Republic must address during the years to come. In order to consolidate the country's current basic food security position on a national level into a structural food security position at all levels (national, regional and household), a comprehensive, coherent and integrated strategy is needed. The core of the strategy will focus on the development of the agricultural potential of the country. Agricultural development is crucial in terms of domestic availability of food, income generation for the overwhelming majority of the population and the single most important driving force for the overall economic development of the country.

At independence the Kyrgyz Republic inherited a pattern of depending on large food imports from other FSU republics, mainly wheat and sugar. During the nine years of independence the country has successfully met the challenge of achieving basic national food self-sufficiency. Agricultural production became dominant with wheat production. Bread being the basic food commodity, wheat production and trade are an important indicator for monitoring the national food security situation. In 1990 domestic wheat production was about 450,000 tons. Now domestic wheat production is about 1,200,000 ton annually. However, in 1999 that amount was not produced and according to an article in the Times of Central Asia [88] of 13 April 2000, the Ministry of Agriculture forecasts a 1,145,000 ton harvest for 2000, while about 1,250,000 must be produced to achieve national food security. The Ministry will monitor and analyze the domestic grain market and submit proposals on the export and import of grain to the government.

The second basic commodity in the Kyrgyz diet is meat (mainly mutton and beef). There seem to be sufficient quantities available to meet basic nutritional requirements. Although statistics show a drastic reduction in fodder production, the Kyrgyz Republic nevertheless has become self-sufficient in wheat and in meat products according to the food security policy report. Internal flows of foodstuffs remain fairly modest because most regions have achieved a certain degree of self-sufficiency in basic food commodities (especially in wheat). According to the national food security policy report of July 1999, the country as a whole is marginally food secure.

Michel Petit [64] strengthens the fact that food security is not an incident. He argues that food security can only be achieved by substantial development of human, material, and technological capabilities giving depth and resilience to broad based food availability and access. Implementing long-term policies engendering strong institutions, enhancing the widespread availability of sustainable livelihoods and instilling a capacity to withstand food shocks requires a high level of social organization. To achieve food security, markets must work; property rights to (rural) land must be distributed among the population and policymakers must work also. Taking into account the current persistent economic decline and the poor functioning of markets in the whole country, the Kyrgyz Republic is not yet structurally food secure.

13.3.2 ASSESSMENT OF THE FOOD SECURITY SITUATION

As far as food security is concerned, the measures proposed by the government in the national food security policy report are encouraging (as far as political rhetoric reflects future real activity) and could enhance the basis for a food secure Kyrgyz Republic in the coming years. The population growth is a point of concern, especially because it seems that a considerable portion of it is the result of emigration from neighboring states where the regime is far less democratic than the government of the Kyrgyz Republic. Widespread promotion of and education in use of biotechnology can assist in improving agricultural production. The application of new agro-technology by well-educated farmers will improve the food security situation in the Kyrgyz Republic.

The complexity of the effect of a change in institutional arrangements often makes it difficult to draw clear conclusions. The researchers cannot control the effects by changing some of the phenomena, because the effects of change simply happen. Generally it is difficult to distinguish between the causes or results. For example a higher yield may be the result of more efficient land use, but it can also be caused by spending of resources on better quality seeds or more fertilizers, or by simply expanding the area of land sown. In the case of the Kyrgyz Republic however, the complexity is limited by the circumstances. From the previous chapters it turns out that there is not significantly more land available for agriculture than before transition, although some pastureland has obviously been converted into arable land. The economic development has not (yet) started and farmers will not have the effect of more income to spend. Availability of resources to improve agricultural production is (still) very limited and the use of land as collateral for loans can be ignored.

The application of the model for the project restructuring of the agricultural production shows with both the reported data on crops and rural employment that Kyrgyz farmers used their new opportunities to start farming more efficiently and that rural employment is likely to increase. The model leads rapidly to this conclusion by following a logical pattern to analyze data (via the indicators) revealing the development.

13.3.3 ACCESS, AVAILABILITY, AND UTILIZATION

Consumption does pre-suppose that there is access to food. Access to food is the start of food security but it is not the only component. In paragraph 2.3.2 apart from access availability and utilization are also stated as components of food security. While discussing food security it was found that food production in itself does not provide for food security. But at the same time income generation in rural areas is supposed to come from improvement of productivity in agricultural production although not necessarily food production. Cotton and tobacco are main crops in some areas in the Kyrgyz Republic.

Against the background of most research on food security, the almost one-sided approach with focus almost completely and exclusively on food production in the food security policy of the Kyrgyz Republic is reason for concern

Access to food – the ability to acquire food from earnings and transfers – is the start of food security according to research findings. With emphasis on increased food production it can be assumed that rural incomes will increase as well, providing for the monetary capacity to purchase food in rural areas. In urban areas, however, this is more complex. A policy on increased food production will most likely benefit primarily rural areas, leaving the urban population mainly out of the picture. That is, unless they have access to house plots (of which I have seen hardly any in the bigger cities where apartment buildings dominate the residential areas) to grow some food, food to consume or to sell or to use in an exchange. Here the problem of the generally ignored urban population becomes manifest. When there is no economic development providing for the basic needs of the urban population, the effect of a privatization program linked to agrarian reform will have a negative impact on urban dwellers. Their earnings may drop (and in the Kyrgyz Republic they did drop) leaving them with fewer possibilities to acquire food.

For the population in general a food policy focused on food production might give an assurance of food availability, the second element in food security policy. But here again it is particularly the rural population that will benefit first because of their closeness to the agricultural land where food is produced. In terms of food security the rural population will always have the possibility to rely on subsistence agriculture that is impossible for the majority of urban dwellers.

In several countries of the former USSR an infrastructure to transport food products is inadequate and this will add to the disadvantage of urban dwellers in this respect. A clear sign of this is the number of farmers' relatives traveling (by bus or private car) each day to cities with agricultural products to set up their 'table' shops along the sidewalks.

And what can be said about the third element; utilization of food? Observations in the Kyrgyz Republic show that there is a vulnerable dependency on the supply of natural gas and other energy sources from neighboring countries. During the assignment period the supply of natural gas from Uzbekistan was shut down for several weeks causing a run on electrical appliances. Unfortunately the gas was still not available when the winter season started resulting in a postponed start of the central heating system. (Central heating in most former communist countries is really centralized heating. It means local heating plants where the water is heated and from there supplied to consumers in the buildings.) To avoid uncomfortable low temperatures inside the apartments, many citizens started to operate cheap, and not very efficient, electrical heaters causing regular outages of electricity.

For the preparation of food in suburbs of Bishkek, citizens had to use wood fires in the back yard of their buildings, making the preferred weekend outing a trip to the nearby park to chop some extra firewood. Several project staff members – myself not excluded – clearly suffered from the effects of inadequate utilization of food by insufficient heating. I have been informed that this last winter the situation became similarly difficult because the supply of natural gas was again postponed for some weeks. With, actually, only food availability sufficiently covered in the food security policy of the country, general food security is still at times a real concern in the Kyrgyz Republic. The conclusion is that for the Kyrgyz Republic to become a full food secure nation, a broader based food policy strategy should be developed.

The situation that urban residents are more vulnerable to the effects of land and agrarian reform projects might be a relatively new phenomenon typical for countries in transition. Research from some decades ago in Africa, Asia and Latin America shows that year round access to food in many cities was better than in poorer rural regions (Barraclough [2] p.33). Most poor urban residents had access to nutritionally adequate diets. It has to be mentioned that urban growth was rapid in most cities. It averaged between five to eight per cent yearly. Part of the explanation was the traditional welfare net provided by extended families. Many city residents, especially the poorest, were recent arrivals with close family ties to better-off city residents as well as in the rural communities they had left. Relatives sometimes sent food from the countryside. Kyrgyz citizens seem to have less extensive and less intense family ties. But what is more important, migration from rural to urban areas is absent in the Kyrgyz Republic. Total population grew by 13 per cent between 1989 and 1999; the rural population grew in that same period of time by 19 per cent while urban population grew by only four per cent (See paragraph 3.1.3 and Table 13.2.3).

CHAPTER 14

THE LAND AND REAL ESTATE REGISTRATION PROJECT

14.1 NEW LAND REGISTRATION

14.1.1 CONTRADICTORY DATA AND POOR MAPPING

The project for Land and Real Estate Registration has been considered and planned during the land and agrarian reform project in the Kyrgyz Republic. It was originally intended to be one of the institutional arrangements to be operational before the actual start of land distribution. And although, from the very beginning, the possibility of a new system for land registration had been investigated, the preparation phase for such a project in the Kyrgyz Republic started as a relatively small project about eight years after the process of land reform began in the country. The reality now is that most farmers have taken possession of their land or have distributed the land among themselves on the basis of land certificates prepared and issued by agencies other than the new land registration organization.

Because of low quality of the mapping available in the Kyrgyz Republic and the way documents have been 'interpreted' by several of the new owners, discrepancies are common between the written documentation and the actual situation on the ground. One reason for this is the system of production quota used in the Kyrgyz Republic during Soviet times. The magnitude of that quota increased exponentially with the size of the land holdings. Farm managers often shrank the size of holdings on paper to reduce the quota that had to be produced for the State. In chapter one an example of this practice is given by Katherine Verdery [96] with the 'elasticity' of land in Transylvania. Nowadays surveyors in the Kyrgyz Republic are regularly confronted with land sizes on paper that do not comply with the actual size on the ground. This is an example of non-integrity of land related data. Sometimes informed participants have taken advantage of this knowledge at the time of land distribution. Some people in rural areas have house plots of over one ha, indeed a considerable size. With the poor mapping in some areas, there is ample opportunity for contradictions and this sometimes causes land conflicts and disputes.

Currently the proposal is that new registration offices will use as much as possible the existing documents and will try to register the actual situation as long as that does not conflict too much with the records provided.

14.1.2 RENEWAL OF MAPPING

It was often mentioned during the preparatory phase that after establishing the new system of land registration in the Kyrgyz Republic, the payment of services by users of the system would be allocated toward renewal of the geographical data in the system to improve the integrity of the land related data. Only time will tell if demand for registration services is sufficient to receive enough income not only to pay for the services but also to provide for a surplus in resources; and can demand be placed on an expensive and time-consuming task in a country where so many other expensive priorities put pressure on the budget of the government.

Given the deep rooted bureaucracy, visits for a technical inventory on the ground are still considered to be an essential element because of the assumed responsibility to register only what is actually proven to be true by observation of the registering official. This expensive and time-consuming activity can only be justified when in the very near future such a visit is used for other purposes like the establishment of a real property taxation system or monitoring zoning requirements.

The preparatory phase was completed at the beginning of 2000. It does not make much sense to assess this project with the model at this stage. Nevertheless a few remarks can be made.

14.2 IMPLEMENTATION OF NEW REGISTRATION

14.2.1 NEW OFFICES

At the end of the preparatory phase of the project in early 2000, the authorities had approved the documentation describing the procedures. A schedule for the opening of offices where the new registration system would be implemented had been agreed upon. It showed four offices to be opened in 1999 and 44 more in 2000 and 2001. This schedule of offices to be refurbished – to be made more customer friendly – is given in Table 14.2.1 on the next page. Instructions for staff of the newly opening offices were ready and distributed. The expatriate consultants organized several training sessions with staff of those offices to be the first to open. Selected staff was trained to be trainer for staff of offices to be opened in the year to come. All the relevant forms for land registration had been developed and the maps covering the areas for the newly opening offices were prepared from existing mapping.

Unfortunately the approval process of the regulations for the opening of new offices with all the involved ministries and agencies took more time than initially anticipated by GosRegister. This was undoubtedly a setback for the project, because the opening of offices took place before approval and so had to be a kind of 'low-key' affair, not drawing too much attention. Also mentioned earlier, a scheduled public awareness campaign highlighting the new system of registration

Table 14.2.1 Land registration offices

Нанменованне городов и р-нов	Количе-ство не-движи-мост	Количе-ство сделок *1997*	Количе-ство сделок *1998*	I этал *1999 г.*	II этал *2000 г.*
1 Кара-Сүйкий р-н	253902	1200	1640	III кв	
2 Ыссык-Атинский р-н, г. Кант	26150	1600	1500	III кв	
3 г. Бишкек	258432	–	18329	III кв	
4 Сокүлүкский р-н	28576	1858	1912	IV кв	
5 г. Ош	93466	3608	2534		I кв
6 г. Жалал-Абад	15524	1070	1118		I кв
7 Аламудунский р-н	51552	1946	2073		I кв
8 Чуйтокмакский р-	28932	2225	2160		I кв
9 Иссык-Кульский р-н, Чолпон-Ата	25240	–	–		I кв
10 Ак-Суйский р-н, г. Кара-Кол	204421	1556	1374		II кв
11 Нарынский р-н, г. Нарын	14267	330	318		II кв
12 Жайылский р-н	8696	734	828		II кв
13 г. Кызыл-Кия	20340	660	784		II кв
14 Тюлский р-н	14750	264	197		II кв
15 Таласский р-gн, г.Талас	17629	768	814		III кв
16 Московский р-н	34456	–	1231		III кв
17 Ноокатский р-н	152660	60	120		III кв
18 Узгенский р-н	149837	262	359		III кв
19 Сузакский р-н, Кок-Джангак	37736	166	567		III кв
20 Панфиловский р-н	14206	–	232		IV кв
21 Базар-Коргонский р-н	33240	81	72		IV кв
22 Ноокенский р-н	32460	131	135		IV кв
23 г. Майлуу-Суу	7180	127	101		IV кв
24 г. Балыкчи	7448	1811	1498		IV кв
25 Араванский р-н	89839	111	117	Rest of openings	
26 Кадамжайский р-н	190230	210	345	scheduled in 2001	
27 Лейлекский р-н, г.Сулюкту	105350	211	218		
28 г. Кара-Куль	8435	121	70		
29 г. Таш-Кумыр	6920	155	124		
30 Аксыйский р-н	20024	106	117		
31 Ала-Букиискнй р-н	12831	86	71		
32 Кеминский р-н	12625	1284	1396		
33 Манасский р-н	6232	28	64		
34 Кара-Бурииский р-н	11200	20	30		
35 Бакай-Атииский р-н	4623	55	85		
36 Кочкорский р-н	8958	189	23		
37 Жумгальский р-н	7777	19	23		
38 Баткенский р-н	188231	115	160		
39 Кара-Кульджиискнй р-н	68078	45	90		
40 Жету-Огузский р-н	22064	108	91		
41 Тонский р-н	2807	–	120		
42 Токтогульский р-н	13346	24	31		
43 Тогуз-Торооузский р-н	8217	15	9		
44 Алайский р-н	71970	98	210		
45 Чон-Алайский р-н	14908	54	36		
46 Ат-Башинский р-н	7690	23	26		
47 Ак-Талинский р-н	4612	–	–		
48 Чаткальский р-н	9651	6	4		

Explanation:

1st column = #

2nd column = Town (г.) or Rayon name (р-н)

3rd column = total amount of parcels in the area

4th column = # transfers 1997

5th column = # transfers 1998

Next columns = Opening new offices (кв = quarter)

of rights to real property was postponed due to the continued absence of approval by government agencies for the regulations for opening of new registration offices.

Although this public awareness campaign was specifically targeted at land registration issues, it could have assisted indirectly with more general issues of ownership of real property as well. Thus the opening of new offices became a local affair and general information about the new procedures of registration could only be distributed by the offices themselves (and generally on request of potential customers). It is difficult to estimate the effect of the absence of a larger scale public awareness campaign, but it most likely would have made a difference for the awareness of new opportunity sets among the Kyrgyzstani. Moreover, opening of new registration offices is behind schedule and the streamlining of the registration process is frustrated by government agencies that try to retain some of the profitable activities, which, after formal approval of the regulations for opening of the new offices are projected to be solely a responsibility of GosRegister. For example notaries in the Ministry of Justice charge relatively high fees for transfers of real property (around $40 to benefit the Ministry), while GosRegister recently started to provide competing notary services for around $10. It is hoped that competition will start to work here.

14.2.2 STAGNATING DEVELOPMENT

Recent data that have been reported by the three newly opened offices in 1999 show no significant changes in the number of transactions in real property before and after opening of the office. Only a short time has elapsed since the opening and these results are not too meaningful yet. The numbers are given in Table 14.2.2a and they are only indicative. It will take time for the citizens to get used to the new system. A certain period of at least several years is needed before the stabilization of the new relative economic positions and the possibilities that come with it become common among citizens. The Kant office reported 145 transactions in October 2000, so still about the same level as the previous year (see Table 14.2.1 where on line 2, the numbers for this office are given).

Table 14.2.2a Transactions at newly-opened offices (Spring 2000)

Average number of transactions monthly transactions	Last moths before new office opened	First months after new office opened	Average # 1997-1998
Kant (Issyk-Ata) (open end of October 1999)	133	142	129
Kara – Suu (open mid November 1999)	167	160	118
Sokuluk (open 25 December 1999)	159	112	157

Source: GosRegister (reported Spring 2000)

Table 14.2.2b Actual progress of the Land Registration project

Office location scheduled	Actual opening date	Total of transactions registered	Average # of monthly transactions	Originally opening and # in table 14.2.1
Issyk-Ata (Kant)	30 October 1999	1358	127	III quarter 1999(# 2)
Kara-Suu	12 November 1999	1490	148	III quarter 1999 (# 1)
Sokuluk	25 December 1999	1974	267	III quarter 1999 (# 4)
Osh	8 April 2000	2975	407	I quarter 2000 (# 5)
Chui-Tokmok	4 August 2000	385	82	I quarter 2000 (# 8)
Moscow	14 August 2000	398	113	III quarter 2000 (#16)
Djalal-Abad	9 September 2000	288	78	I quarter 2000 (# 6)
Alamudin	29 September 2000	554	204	I quarter 2000 (# 7)
Issyk-Kul	26 December 2000	2	-	I quarter 2000 (# 9)
Nookat	26 December 2000	2	-	III quarter 2000 (#17)

Source: GosRegister January 2001

It is interesting to notice the progress of the implementation of the Land and Real Estate Registration project. Table 4.2.1 presents the schedule of opening of newly refurbished offices. This scheme was agreed upon with the World Bank. From a report of GosRegister at the beginning of 2001 Table 14.2.2b can be composed. This table lists all new refurbished offices open in January 2001. The last two offices mentioned in Table 14.2.2b, were actually opened on 26 December 2000, so there was hardly any time left in 2000 to register transactions there.

Table 14.2.2c Transactions in newly-opened offices (January 2001)

Office location	Average # of monthly transactions after opening new office	Average # of monthly transactions (table 14.2.1) in 1997-1998
Issyk-Ata (Kant)	127	129
Kara-Suu	148	118
Sokuluk	267	157
Osh	407	55
Chui-Tokmok	82	182
Moscow	113	102
Djalal-Abad	78	91
Alamudin	204	167

Source: GosRegister January 2001

One of the most disappointing developments for the local experts working in the project was the fact that due to disagreement about the location and building the opening of the new office in the capital Bishkek had to be postponed time after time.

Table 14.2.2c contains data as reported by GosRegister in January 2001 and it gives already more insight in the number of transactions registered in the newly opened offices as Table 14.2.2a could give. In the table a comparison with the average monthly transactions registered there in 1997 and 1998 is also given. With only this limited number of new offices operational it is too early to draw some conclusions on the development of a land market, although, it seems that there is a slight increase in the number of transactions.

Table 14.2.2d Systematic registration activities

Office location	Start of systematic Registration	Total of poperties processed	Percentage of total # of properties (see Table 14.2.1)
Sokuluk	8 November 2000	1001	3.5%
Issyk-Ata (Kant)	13 November 2000	1761	6.7%
Kara-Suu	13 November 2000	719	0.3%

Source: GosRegister January 2001

Table 14.2.2d provides first results of the systematic registration of properties. This important activity (described in 6.3.5) is designed to support the newly opened offices in setting up a reliable database of registered properties. Although, anticipated much earlier by the foreign experts assisting with the development of the new registration system, this activity obviously got underway by the end of the year 2000.

The progress of the Land and Real Estate Registration project is clearly less than originally anticipated. It is difficult (and speculative) to look for reasons. Besides, it is not unusual that progress of donor-funded projects is slower than scheduled. During my assignment I did not observe a lack of funding that could be blamed for major delays. Local staff was made responsible by WB rules for taking care of timely funding. One would expect them to be familiar with bureaucratic procedures and red tape, (and funding via the WB not surprisingly has that), but their anticipation toward scheduled funding needs seemed sometimes less than adequate. The (long) discontinuity in expatriate presence in Bishkek that occurred in 2000 might be another cause for the delay in the scheduled opening of refurbished offices and the general slow down in project progress.

On paper regulations for the institutional change have been completed, but execution of the changes is behind schedule. Some of the conditions for an effective and efficient implementation of institutional changes are not yet in place. Moreover, it seems that the new system for land registration in the Kyrgyz

Republic is only a slight improvement of the existing – albeit cumbersome – system of registration of real property. The new system will be welcomed in providing a one-stop-shop for citizens, and it will promote a unified national registration system. That is quite a task in itself. But so far the new system has not solved the continuing need to use relatively expensive services of a notary. Nor did it include identification of the real property by means of adequate mapping as part of the project for land and real estate registration. Neither has it eliminated one of the time consuming and sometimes costly procedures: technical inventory of the real property object as part of the registration process, requiring a site visit to be paid for by the buyer or seller. Officials justified the site visit not only because of establishing a 'pure' and reliable registration system but also because it serves as a way to assess the value of the property for property taxation. Apart from the fact that it is at least doubtful whether a user of property should pay for this, it is certainly an significant expense at a transfer.

The perspective is that the new standardized system for registered alpha-numeric data will improve understanding and usability of the land registration system. It is important to show that it is worth the cost involved. If citizens can be convinced that the information value of the registered data results in a considerable reduction of uncertainty, the land registration project will become a success. But the project for land and real estate registration takes place in almost complete isolation without institutionalized connections with other (donor driven) projects to stimulate the land market or other incentives for development of the economy. During the project assignment there have been no formal contacts with other projects or with government agencies outside the GosRegister organization. It was hard to find out whether there were other more or less parallel donor funded projects going on in the country, and when found out the contacts were always informal.

14.2.3 NOT A SPECIFIC ELEMENT IN THE MODEL

As mentioned in paragraph 5.1.2 Land Registration has not been included as a separate element in the model built in Chapter 5. The main reason for this is that I will not imply that land registration is a sine qua non for land reform. It is not necessary that land reform consists of all three steps as described in 4.3.5; redistribution of land, new legislation to formalize the rights to land, and recording in registers. In several societies communal land tenure provides land tenure security without any form of documentation or formal recording of rights to land.

Whether or not land registration or the establishment of a cadastre is part of the institutional arrangements accompanying land reform is a political decision. It has been stated before that a land reform project is generally motivated by the political situation in a country, while land registration is often donor instigated. However, there should be no doubt about the usefulness of land registration. In countries where a strict formal definition of rights to land is the dominant feature of the property regime, land registration is often legally required to prove rights to land. In those countries, being registered as the owner of rights to land means often the benefit of state guaranteed protection of those rights and the possibility to uphold those rights easily against others. It facilitates dealings with real property when there is a reliable and up to date land registration where all rights to land are recorded. But a land registration is never more than a tool to support the perception of land tenure security among citizens.

14.2.4 PERSPECTIVE OF THE NEW LAND REGISTRATION SYSTEM

The Kyrgyz Republic has is in the process of establishing a sound institutional framework for land registration. By using the documentation of the former BTI offices and land management offices for the new land registration organization gives a stable starting point for the provision of land tenure security. In cases of discrepancies between the available documentation and claims made by applicants for registration of their land, a provisional title can be provided, allowing for the full title to be conferred after a number of years have passed.

Registration is obligatory in order for rights to be enforceable against third parties. The moment of registration is also the moment that the rights become valid. As mentioned before transactions must be notarised, which puts a financial burden on transfers although GosRegister is trying to let competition work by offering notarial services in some cases at reasonable costs.

The index map of parcels is far from complete and there is considerable doubt if the necessary land survey activities can be carried out within a reasonable timeframe because of the limited professional capacity available in Kyrgyzstan for this type of work.

In most of the rural areas the privatization of farmland progresses smoothly. In the fertile areas where land is scarce, new individual parcels are generally too small to start sustainable farming. Agriculture remains a co-operative affair and there is seldom the need to mark the individual parcels on the ground. Boundary markers would soon be destroyed or removed by mechanical farming methods.

During the project assignment some problems occurred in urban areas because of contradictions between available BTI documents and the actual situation on the ground. Obviously there have been cases of intentional or accidental encroachment unnoticed so far during communist times. Building without the proper permission or correct approval of the authorities might have caused such encroachments that are now being revealed. In exceptional cases it even might have been an intentional encroachment by (former) users of the real property. The number of cases that were revealed during the project assignment was relatively small, but recent information points to a serious problem in some urban areas. As mentioned in Chapter 3, recent reports even mention a percentage of up to 50 per cent in application for registration of urban property. For the current user of the real property an unpleasant surprise that also undermines the image of the new registration. It is a pity that the officials dealing with first registration do not have the authority to resolve most of these, often minor, discrepancies immediately, but that a bureaucratic procedure must be followed to correct the situation.

GosRegister strives to be self-sufficient with its new land registration offices. The new more public friendly offices with their open access areas with large counters to serve the public and clear price lists should encourage the general public to use the land registration facility. The new lay-out of the offices makes it more difficult to conduct transactions behind close-doors in small offices and thus limit invitations for extra payments and prevent other tendencies to favor special customers of the system.

The basic elements for an effective land registration institute in Kyrgyzstan are in place. Apart from the earlier mentioned sound legal framework, the introduction of competitive notarial services, a nation wide public awareness campaign and a quick completion of opening of all new style offices for land registration will be the main ingredients to win the public over to use the new land registration system.

CHAPTER 15

IMPLICATIONS OF NON-EVOLUTIONARY LAND REFORM

15.1 A WIDER APPROACH

15.1.1 EMPHASIS ON EQUITY

This chapter contains second thoughts on the effects of land reform; it also reviews the most notable strategy implications of land and agrarian reform. The research in this book primarily focuses on project advisors and expatriate experts working on the ground. It is not the intention to raise political issues, but results of the research and the developed method do provide signals and indications for project strategies. In addition, a number of implications provide background information for consultants and add to the conclusions and statements in the following chapter.

From a research perspective, property is often conceptualized as a resource endowment to be allocated in the most efficient way to alleviate rural poverty and food insecurity. There is an assumed automatic link between commodifying of land and economic development. This assumption often causes a government to turn a blind eye to growing inequity simply because it is accepted as the price to be paid for economic development. Myrdal [60] (p. 51 and 52) remarks that this growing inequity is based on 'the traditional common assumption that a price had to be paid for the egalitarian reforms. *The reforms were argued in terms of reaching greater social justice,* the importance of which was gradually becoming recognized so widely in the developed countries that the political conditions were created for their passing through the parliaments. The reforms were coming to be considered worth their price ... This thought is often rationalized by a saying, which throughout the development of economic thinking has also been popular in developed countries, viz., that 'production goes before distribution.'
But then he argues (in 1970): 'In recent years evidence has emerged that welfare states, instead of being costly for a society, actually lay the basis for more steady and rapid economic development.' Economic development thus should result in political attention for positive change in income among those population groups where poverty is most significant. Since most of the poor live in rural areas, improvement of agricultural production resulting in income improvement in rural areas and improved nutritional status should, in most countries, be the focus points of a development policy. A possible negative result like growing inequity in the

distribution of resources has to be corrected by additional measures of the government.

El-Ghonemy [37](p.1-2) lists three concerns about the decline in land reform since the 1980s. First, from originally being the foundation of rural development, land reform has suffered decline, ironically almost at the same time that countries committed themselves to realize equitable distribution of land, to implement land distribution and to eliminate under-nutrition. (FAO, Rome 12 - 20 July 1979) [28]. The second concern is academic and analytic; there is a growing gap between the institutional and political determinants of rural poverty and the application of analytical economic theory. Economics has changed from a social science to Newtonian mechanics. Quantitative analysis and efficient allocation of resources by a free market economy has had more emphasis than distribution and welfare considerations. The third concern comes from the swift swings in international development. Emphasis on liberalization of trade and structural adjustments of national economies resulted in a delay of land reform implementation, land reclamation and land settlements' schemes, and a decrease of subsidized goods and services in rural areas.

Property rights have a strong political function as an element of power to subordinate people at all levels of socio-political organization. In theory the alleged absolute character of private individual ownership of property rights differs from actual legal regulations. But absolute ownership is a myth because of the public limitations or constraints put on property in most countries. Governments act to safeguard the social function in a property regime. Especially for agricultural land this may require an exploitation pattern not directed at the immediate and full production potential of property. It may require a property system in which more than one owner has equitable rights to the property (in which, for example, trees have a different owner than the land they grow on, and a third person owns the fruit of those trees). It can also become manifest in conditions on transferability imposed by the authorities. Another example of a social orientation in a property regime can currently be found in China where family size determines the size of the land made available for agricultural production. One can think also of a system in which kinship or community relations play a role in the management of the land. Like, for example, in customary systems where transfers of land to 'outsiders' need the approval of the clan or community; or a system in which less fortunate members of the community have a right to a reasonable share in the harvests. All this will require a different approach to property systems that are partly 'western style' while at the same time maintaining some of the social features of most communal tenure systems. With many countries in transition this may be a thought worthy of further consideration and elaboration.

15.1.2 NOT ONLY ECONOMIC EMPHASIS

An important research finding is that economic development cannot be achieved by neglecting other elements in development policy. Technological change and capital accumulation are crucial factors for growth. For rural regions access to sufficient farmland, to capital, to mechanization, to biotechnology, to extension services, to agricultural education, to markets for in- and output, and to information are the most crucial factors to achieving growth.

Ismail Serageldin, [75] international economist and vice-president of the World Bank for special programs, sees an urgent need to increase agricultural production in order to feed a burgeoning world population. At the same time, though, he worries that the growing privatization of biological research could hinder that effort. He states: 'There is no way of dealing with poverty, protection of the environment, or food without transforming agricultural production at the small holder level in developing countries.' The world is, in parallel, on the cusp of a new revolution in the biological sciences. The manipulation of genes opens up all sorts of possibilities such as the application that plants are more drought-resistant, more salt tolerant, more resistant to pests without pesticides. There is an enormous biotechnology investment by the private sector, but private money is only invested if it can be recouped with the protection of intellectual property. This raises issues and ethical questions. Poor farmers who have bred plants over generations get nothing out of a patent for which they supplied the basic ingredients. If the science used to produce the Viagra pill could be applied to produce a malaria pill, we would be able to have the old parallelism of an open access exchange system. There should be a serious dialogue between the private and the public sector in order to ensure that there is adequate attention to the poor, and that the issue of proprietary science does not become a real threat. Preventing science from creating a gap between 'haves' and 'have-nots,' making a 'scientific apartheid' in this century, will be part of that dialogue.

At the start of the new millenium it has been calculated that 840 million people are going hungry and 2 billion are malnourished. The global population grows by 3 per second. Food should be available at affordable prices and production increase in the countries themselves is the best option. India could realize a production growth on almost the same arable land area from 7 million ton in 1961 to 197 million ton in 1990, with biotechnology and green revolution higher yields. Integrated pest management results in less pesticide use and cost of chemicals. Teach people that livestock are not only food and transport, but if corralled during the night, also produce manure.

It is important to educate the poor smallholder farmer to reduce food insecurity and poverty. The conclusion is that the Kyrgyz government should provide specific agricultural education and should strongly stimulate modern agricultural technology to improve agricultural production and to give the Kyrgyz Republic an advantageous position in producing certain export crops.

15.1.3 CAREFUL IMPLEMENTATION OF REFORM

In the abstract (p. ix) of 'Time to Rethink Privatization in Transition Economies,' John Nellis [62] expresses concerns about privatization programs (not only of farm land).

> Worldwide evidence shows that privatization improves firm performance. But in some institutionally-weak transition economies, ownership change has so far not delivered on its promise. Why? Mass and rapid privatization schemes turned over mediocre assets to people lacking the incentives, skills and resources to manage them well. Most high-quality assets have ended up in the hands of the resourceful, agile and well-connected few who for a variety of reasons have tended not to embark on the thorough restructuring that might have justified their acquisition of the assets. In an institutional vacuum, privatization can and has led to stagnation and decapitalization rather than to better financial results and increased efficiency.
>
> What is to be done? Proposals include re-nationalization and/or postponement of further privatization, both to be accompanied by measures to strengthen the managerial and administrative capacities of the state. Neither approach seems likely to produce short-term improvements; the regrettable fact is that governments that botch privatization are equally likely to botch the management of state-owned firms. And there is no need for such measures in a number of Central European transition countries where privatization is (in the main) more or less living up to expectations.
>
> For institutionally weak countries, the less dramatic but reasonable short-term course of action is to push ahead, more slowly, with case-by-case and tender privatization, in cooperation with the international assistance community, in hopes of producing some success stories that will lead by example.

More than 100 countries, on every continent, have privatized some or most of their state-owned companies. The process has not been reversed. On a very small scale some companies have been renationalized. Evidence is mounting that privately-owned firms outperform state owned enterprises.

Research shows significant increases in profitability, operating efficiency, capital investment spending, output and employment and a decline in leverage and an increase in dividends. And yet, despite the ubiquity of divestiture, privatization moved from novelty to global orthodoxy in the space of two decades. Doubts remain and are growing, suspicions and concerns about privatization are resurfacing. There are fears that privatizations have not proven to be beneficial to society (it may well be for shareholders!), or at least for significant groups of generally poor and powerless actors in society. John Nellis' principle findings are (p. 3 and 4) as follows:

- Too much was expected and promised in institutionally weak transition economies;
- For what seemed excellent political reasons, emphasis has been on rapid transactions rewarding with stakes workers and managers in the firms being privatized out of fear that they might block the process;
- The farther east (from the Atlantic that is) one travels the more the required supporting insitutionalization, financial discipline, competition, freedom and promotion of entry to the new businesses have not been attended to. Here the speedy insider oriented forms of privatization have not delivered (yet).

But he also remarks that if these states had retained the firms in public ownership there is no guarantee or even expectation that they would have performed better! If they botch, the botching is everywhere, and 'The key unanswered question is how to go about correcting and improving privatization in institutionally weak settings (p. 4).'

These remarks by Nellis for firms in general can be applied to privatization of farms and farmland. It is important to set a pace of reform that allows the population to cope with changes. Too quick implementation might exclude a large segment of the rural inhabitants because they are yet not familiar (enough) with the new approach. Information from Kyrgyzstan shows for example that especially the more entrepreneurial farm workers have benefited most of the privatization process. By being the first to apply they could safeguard most of the initial incentives for the start of their new private individual farms. A careful and well-timed reform project will create better opportunities for a wider circle of farmers to feel sufficiently confident to respond to the new challenges.

The conclusion is that to be successful, land and agrarian reform must be carried out after extensive investigation of the circumstances in the target country, and with carefully timed implementation of the various interrelating other activities and policies.

15.2 THE STANDARD MODEL

15.2.1 OVERALL PICTURE

The broad framework for economic progress in the prosperity paradigm as developed in this book requires a policy blueprint for the process by which culture, natural resources and institutions create capital and economic progress to alleviate (rural) poverty and food insecurity. Research at the Ohio State University in Columbus, mainly at the department of agricultural economics, has led to a standard model that relates to markets, which allocate goods and services being rival and exclusionary. The standard model is given in a compact scheme in Figure 15.2.1.

When goods are non-rival, consumption by one consumer does not compete with consumption by another, hence, a supplier can charge a high price, which will limit consumption and economic progress. Where goods are non-exclusionary, markets under-produce because a supplier will not be able to capture enough of the monetary benefits to cover his costs. It is assumed that the standard model provides a blueprint outlining the basic elements of a political framework. When it could be implemented as such it is expected to boost economic development.

15.2.2 DETAILS OF THE STANDARD MODEL

The functions of the 'Standard model' (as described by Tweeten [93], [94]) can be elaborated in brief in a description of requirements as formulated in the model.

Macro environment	Honesty and competence in public administration Security, stability and order Property rights (reap what is sown) Competition (limited para-statals, encourage foreign trade)
Sound macro economic policy	Fiscal responsibility (avoid persisting deficits) Monetary restraint (money supply in line with GDP growth rate) Appropriate taxation (preferably VAT, sales tax etc.)
Use foreign markets	Proper foreign exchange rate Openness to trade
Proper infrastructure	All weather 'roads' Bridges, airports, seaports, utilities
High returns public services	Agricultural research Human resource investment Sanitation for food security Health services
Environmental sound	Attention for environmental effects
Food and Income	Minimum level guaranteed by safety net

Figure 15.2.1 The standard model

The macro environment

There must be honesty and competence in public administration. Corruption in government undermines economic progress. The same goes for matters such as security, stability, and order. The rule of law and order needs a judicial system to administer justice and interpret laws. The government needs to strive for an environment where business plans can be made and carried out with minimal transaction costs. To encourage investment and improvements in property, investors must be able to 'reap what is sown.' Property rights allow property to be used as collateral for loans. A favorable investment climate avoids capital flight and attracts foreign direct investment. Governments need to avoid giving protection to firms exercising monopoly power. Open foreign trade to countervail the economic power of domestic firms is often the most effective option. State-owned enterprises need to be avoided where possible. The government role should be inducing the private sector to produce public goods.

Sound macroeconomic policies

Countries need to avoid persistent deficits in their operating account. A deficit is justified in the capital account only for investments with the strong chance of a

return that will pay the principal and interest, plus leave a social dividend. As far as monetary restraint is concerned a useful rule of thumb is to increase money supply at the real GDP growth rate, with appropriate adjustments for foreign exchange and direct investment. A central bank at 'arms length' from political pressure, and with the sole objective of price stability has proven successful in several countries.
There must be appropriate taxation. Charge user fees for utilities and try to tax bad things (over-consumption, tobacco, alcohol, emissions) not the good ones (investment savings, export). Sales tax, value-added tax and property tax distort the economy less than taxes on corporate profits and exports.

A successful developing economy utilizes foreign markets.
The necessary conditions are a proper foreign exchange rate achieved by the market and a sound monetary-fiscal policy, openness to trade in investment, goods and services with allowances for infant industry, national security and sanitary protections.

A proper infrastructure
This requires investment in all-weather roads to allocate commodities for food security and to encourage commercial activity consistent with comparative advantage. (Bridges, seaports, airports, reliable utilities, etc.).

Public services that offer high returns
Some public services offer higher returns than others do, like agricultural research, and human resources investments. Universal elementary schooling is a priority for food security and development and positive externalities of broad-based development for men, women and minorities are essential. There must be a regime of minimum standards of sanitation for food security and health services.

Environment
Sustainable development requires attention to the environment. Do not consume and exploit now the needs of future generations. Invest effort in integrated crop management, conservation tillage, integrated pest management, pest resistant crops and livestock etc.

Food and income safety net
A social safety net for those unable to depend on themselves, the market, family, or other private sources of sustenance is essential. The height and breadth of social services is a political decision.

15.2.3 IMPLICATIONS OF THE STANDARD MODEL

Not all elements of the standard model can be pursued simultaneously. Priorities are policy reform, agricultural technology adaptation, elementary schooling, and infrastructure. The policy reform is an overarching priority because it is essential to most other dimensions of the standard model. Thus the standard model should be

seen as a policy blueprint. It describes the requirements for a society under which the process that alleviates poverty and alleviates food insecurity will flourish.
In the early stages of implementing the standard model, when the economy still has a low base to provide minimal development tools such as improved agricultural technology, foreign assistance is critical (Burnside and Dollar, 1997) [12]. Furthermore foreign assistance can be decisive for countries which want to break the poverty cycle of too little income to support public infrastructure and services necessary to raise income.

The standard model is a set of rules to guide the process by which culture, natural resources and institutions create capital and economic development to decrease poverty and food insecurity. Application of the standard model is not a guarantee, but rather a proven base for sustainable economic development. An advantage of economic development is that it provides resources to fund socially critical functions such as education, research, health care, and infrastructure; and what is perhaps of less importance in former communist countries where – except for some ethnic minorities – families tend to be small, it implicitly reduces population growth.

A high safety net ('welfare state') often means slower economic growth. In an IMF working paper of December 1995, research of Tanzi and Schuknecht (1995) [83] concludes that a public sector of no more than one-fourth of the GDP appears to be adequate for economic progress and food security if military spending is restrained and social security privatized. Most decisions of when, where and what to produce are left to prices reflecting market supply and demand; the standard model calls for a lean public sector doing a few things well. I'd like to add that the reverse seems also to be true; a high safety net slows down economic decline!

The standard model has been successful in nations following its principles. Analytical studies make that case compelling (Kim Holmes and Melanie Kirkpatrick, 1996 [41]; Jeffrey Sachs, 1997 [70]. It must be concluded that in the Kyrgyz Republic today too many elements of the standard model are still insufficiently developed to expect a sustainable economic development.

15.3 INTEGRITY OF LAND RELATED DATA

15.3.1 COMPATIBILITY OF LAND RELATED DATA

Data on land are a necessity to govern properly. In modern societies various, sometimes complex, computerized land data systems supply information for considerations on responsible use of natural resources for decision making on land distribution, for decentralizing the governing in matters of economic regulation, zoning, and physical planning. There is a vivid exchange of data between all levels and disciplines in government. Due to the fact that computerized systems can exchange data easily, strict definitions and a couple of rules have to be followed to make that happen efficiently and reliably. The registered data on land must have integrity, or in other words must be compatible and convertible to a commonly used (and perhaps centrally dictated) data-exchanging format.

Different government agencies use land related data for their own purposes first and will initially build up land data systems without bothering too much about exchange of data and information. The result is a mixture of different systems with different formats and definitions causing problems or impossibilities when it comes to data exchange.

Easily exchangeable data on land does provide governments with important tools for exercising fair, reliable, accountable and flexible governing. Data obtained by citizens from government agencies are in compliance with each other, and will provide citizens with a feeling of security as far as their actions are based on land data storage and retrieval by the government. This also results in positive effects on the level of land tenure security as experienced by the population. In the ideal situation all land related data stored at all government levels should be fully exchangeable and compatible. Data on the who, what, when, where and how should translate into unambiguous and clear (land) information.

15.3.2 A POSSIBLE SOLUTION

It goes beyond the scope of this book to elaborate much further on this point, but let me give a few examples of conditions that provide for the integrity of land related data. A land registration system showing the property rights of the population should be easily comparable with the land tax system showing at least the same subjects and objects without confusion. Data on objects in systems in their alphanumeric form should be comparable with data on the same objects shown on maps in geographical form. Data on subjects related to real property objects should be the same in the land tax system as in the land zoning system. Land data is often multi-functional e.g., used by more than one government agency or other institution. The multifunctional land data must be created or at least designed by one central authority and must have a (preferably the same) central updating authority recognized and respected by each user of land related data. It is my experience – and there is evidence – that it pays (considerably) for the exchange of land related data in a country when multi-functional data are managed in a centralized way.

15.4 NEGLECTED DYNAMICS

15.4.1 VISUALIZATION OF DYNAMICS

The link between land tenure and food security goes beyond direct production. The simple food security model does not explicitly pay attention to the three components of access to food – sufficiency, sustainability, and vulnerability. We can investigate these aspects separately and can do so by introducing an extended scheme, as given in Figure 15.4.1a, for the dynamic system in which decisions about production, marketing, consumption, and investment drive changes and in turn are driven by changes over time in distribution of resources within and among households.

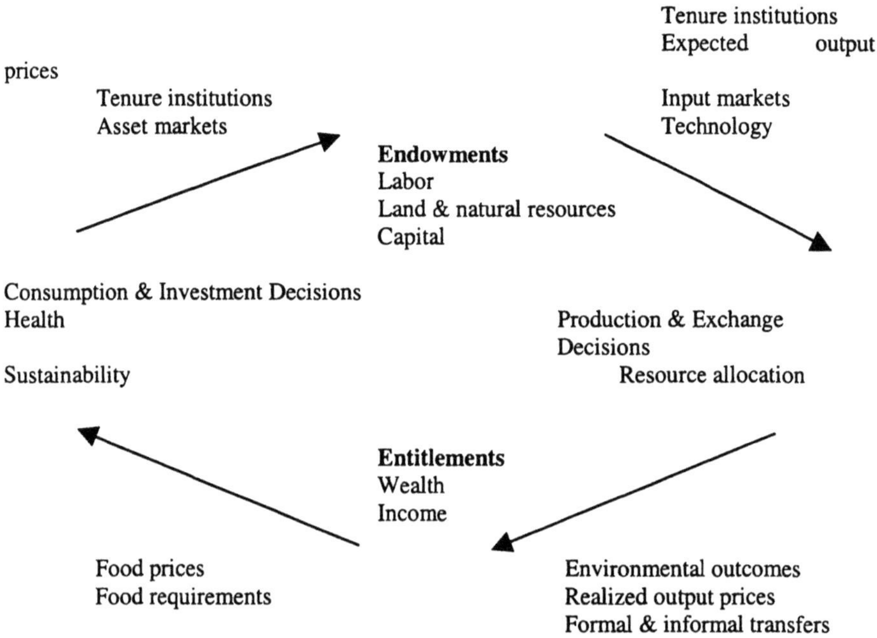

Figure 15.4.1a Extended food security scheme

According to Maxwell and Wiebe [55] Figure 15.4.1a shows the dynamics. Conventional focus of land tenure is represented in the right-hand side of the figure. Food security research generally focuses on the lower half of the figure. The institutional provisions are depicted in the top of Figure 15.4.1a. To understand Figure 15.4.1a, start at the top center and go clockwise. The endowment drives resource allocation decisions on production and/or exchange of commodities; the resulting entitlements (wealth and income) generate the household access and give consumption and investment decisions. Decisions of the household are critical for the household endowment in the next cycle. A household whose members have secure access to sufficient food can consume without drawing unsustainable on its reserves, maintaining its endowments of labor and non-labor resources over the longer term. Other households may be forced to a choice (not free to choose) between maintaining health and labor endowment or maintaining the non-labor endowment. The difference between the two households

described here can be depicted in two figures. Figure 15.4.1b shows household A that is food secure over time because of the sustainability of its resources:
Both Figures (15.4.1b and 15.4.1c) depict the access to resources (Y) over time. Y varies during the year due to seasonality of agricultural production or employment opportunity, and Y varies more than consumption C over the year. The household in the first figure only experiences transitory insecurity, and because most of the year the level of Y is higher than the level of C, the total endowments (E) do increase during the year.

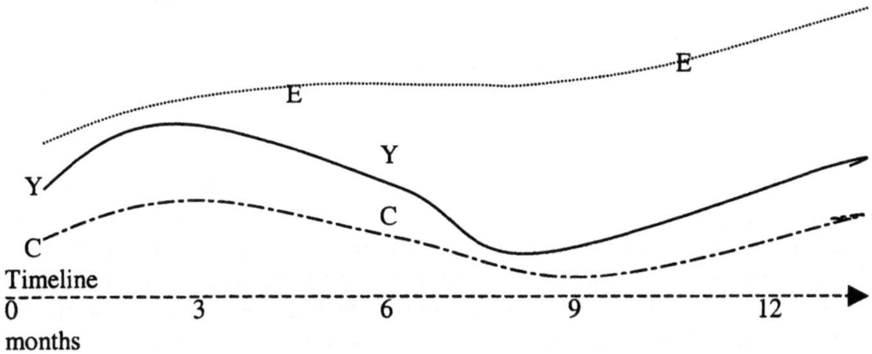

Figure 15.4.1b A food secure household

For a food insecure household B Figure 15.4.1c (with approximately the same seasonal effects) describes the situtaion:

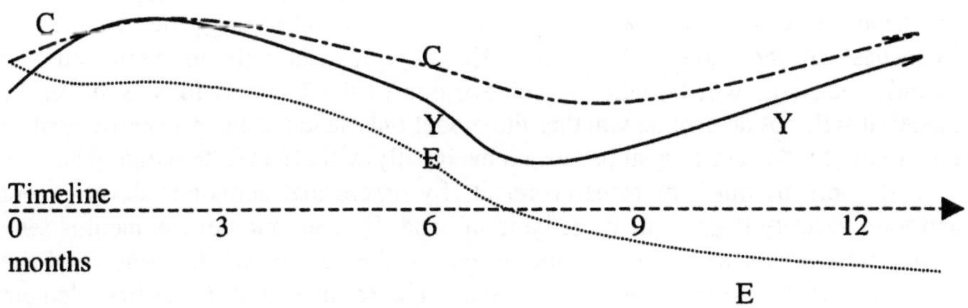

Figure 15.4.1c A food insecure household

Figure 15.4.1c shows that the level of resources Y is insufficient for the purchase of C (the level of C is higher) resulting in a depletion of the endowments depicted by E.

Another dynamic element (Maxwell and Wiebe) comes from vulnerability as mentioned previously. A resource-poor, food insecure household with limited access to credit, will opt for a crop with low returns if that crop is to be trusted, rather than go for a crop with higher returns but with more risk for failure. Expectations about potential long-term tradeoffs between sufficient consumption and investment in non-labor resources affect resource allocation decisions in the short term.

Some important conclusions of dynamics are that if bad years succeed each other and there are not enough good years to restore depleted assets, there is no sustainability in the long run, making any resource poor household food insecure. It also suggests that wealthier households will gain in endowments over the poorer households in due time because of their initial position. Wealthier households can, with less risk, make the choice for a higher return crop (on most of their land), increasing their chances for a higher yield, more than a resource poor household can do.

Over time, the result of a change in land tenure arrangements will most likely not be equally distributed among the households. Resource-poor households will lose to more endowed households and over time the gap between the two can increase considerably. The effect of this growing gap between those who benefit more from reform than those who are less fortunate can be diminished or even be eliminated by specific institutional measures taken by the government, but this is seldom part of initial changes in the institutional arrangements.

15.4.2 INTERDEPENDENCY OF THE TWO PARADIGMS

In chapter 5, a method has been developed to assess the efficiency of land reform projects. At the end of the chapter two paradigms were brought together into one model. Although it is possible to follow completely one of the paradigms, it is actually impossible to separate the two effects of economic development on the one hand and change in food security on the other hand as suggested by the two 'branches' of the model. Although different emphasis will be employed and specific measures will be taken to achieve one of the goals as formulated in the model, it will not determine whether the model only leads to the prosperity goal or only to the food security goal because it eventually will affect both paradigms.

It confirms much of research results by others that economic development and food security improvement go hand in hand. If economic development is seen as the most urgent aim – the prosperity goal – then emphasis in elements of the model should be mainly prosperity oriented. The result is that in the first element of change -institutional change – a legal model should be used that focuses on rapid commodifying of property (property stripped as much as possible from social obligations). The function of property in the new legal system should be toward economic organizations were commodified property has the best ability to be exchanged easily to contribute to efficient and optimal allocation. In such cases imported legal systems that follow the Roman law doctrine of (almost) absolute property rights might do well.

If on the other hand, the first priority is reaching a higher level of food security and increased rural living standards – as in the food security paradigm – the new legal system to be incorporated in the institutions should be more socially oriented. In this case absolute private ownership of property rights, like in the continental Western-European countries, is most likely not the optimal solution.

Rather than transferring property from the State to private individuals, creating absolute property ownership, a more socially mortgaged right to land should be promoted as the primary private right to land. In previous chapters it has become clear that there are always 'losers' in the process of transfer of rights, not only the well-known groups such as women, elderly people, and hunter-gatherers, but sometimes also the urban population, when economic development does not provide for earnings for access to food.

A possible solution could be to develop an inheritable lease right to property at a long term fixed (low-level) lease rate issued and guaranteed by the state (as sovereign owner of property rights) with certain conditions attached to it. Certain obligations for the use of the resource could be attached as part of the contract between the absolute owner (the state) and the hereditary lessee (the private owner of the inheritable right to lease the resource). The state then should use the income of those land leases for redistribution of resources to combat growing inequity. It should be remembered that if ever existing, real absolute property rights are an extreme exception.

So, why not at the beginning of the privatization process distribute socially oriented (thus limited) private property rights? The social function of property is institutionalized by rules, principles and procedures to some degree in all societies, for legitimate control over and access to the means of production (on analogy of Von Benda-Beckmann [5] p. 310/311)

On the other hand, when economic development should rapidly come about – which seems hardly likely in the light of current experiences in most countries in transition – there is nothing inherently wrong with absolute rights of property ownership, as long as there is a secure social safety net for those who benefit less from the change in property regime.

15.4.3 A DIFFERENT PROPERTY REGIME?

When new legislation is imported in a country, it normally takes considerable time for a government to implement an institutionalized and respected legitimate control. In the situation of a country in transition this will most likely not happen simultaneously with the redistribution of land in privately owned separate units. Land redistribution generally comes first. But soon it will be realized that private ownership of property must be restricted for the benefit of a society as a whole. If the legislature is willing to discuss and propose restrictions on the private property rights soon after distributing them, this will surprise and disappoint (or even outrage) new owners of rights to land and it will certainly undermine their perception of land tenure security. When importing a new property regime, the state should create more emphasis on the social function of the property. In that case these restrictions might not be necessary. Design a new property regime in which the state retains certain influence on the use of real property and takes a fair share in the reaping of increasing benefits of redistributed property. This government share must then be used for correction of growing inequities among the population. In former communist countries, where there is a lot of mistrust between the citizens and the state, this could be done by the legal construction of inheritable very long-term lease rights with reasonable lease rates. The lease contract should contain the conditions for the use of the property and thus be known to the lessee before hand without any surprises afterwards created by public law, and interfering with the ownership shortly after it is acquired. In doing so the contract between the state and the lessee will contribute to the latter's feeling of tenure security.

Recently the Kyrgyz government changed the contents of the rights to agricultural land. Originally land certificates and State Acts provided the holder with (inheritable) use rights, but in November 1998 ownership rights replaced these rights. The different land policy in neighboring China, culturally and ethnically Kyrgyzstan's close neighbor, has evidently not influenced the decisions made in the Kyrgyz Republic. This can be visualized in Table 15.4.3. The change from use rights to ownership rights of agricultural land was adopted in 1998, while in 1996 a World Bank development report ('from plan to market') presented some specific comparative data on the GDP growth and inflation in both countries:

Table 15.4.3 GDP growth and inflation rates in the Kyrgyz Republic and China

GDP growth rates	1990	1991	1992	1993	1994	1995
The Kyrgyz Republic	6.9	-9.1	-15.8	-16.3	-26.5	-6.0
China	3.9	8.0	13.6	13.4	11.8	10.2
Annual inflation rates	1990	1991	1992	1993	1994	1995
The Kyrgyz Republic	3.0	85.0	854.6	1208.7	280.0	45.0
China	1.6	3.0	5.4	13.0	21.7	17.0

Source: WB 1996

The growth in China has been achieved without transferring agricultural land to private individual owners, by using the system of re-adjustable use rights without full protection of the exclusiveness and duration of property rights (see 2.5.3).

The Kyrgyz government has made all property subject of absolute ownership rights in a Western fashion. Safeguarding some of the social functions of property will most likely soon force the government to introduce limitations on the use of property by public law. After just having granted full ownership rights to private individual owners, this will undoubtedly cloud the relationship between government and citizens.

In my opinion, more emphasis on the social function of property in the rural areas of former Soviet states is a necessity simply because of the lack of an adequate social security net. The urban population cannot fall back on subsistence agriculture when the motor of economic development stalls. Older urban inhabitants and people incapable of being agricultural employees in rural areas are dependent on all kinds of survival techniques. They should have some extra possibilities like a garden plot, allowance for grazing a beast in the margin of fields, in parks, or along roads, picking up left over harvest on the field and collecting firewood, because there most likely is no sufficient government resource for adequate social support for them.

Some thirty years ago researchers (re-)discovered the benefits of a more socially oriented approach for tenure regimes, but until today little attention has been given to this aspect in the terms of reference of international donor-sponsored projects. In almost all former Soviet states the population is quite used to a concept where the state owns all real property, and 'inheritable' use rights are given to individuals. A conditioned inheritable lease right to real property might be well accepted in those countries, providing the state with possibilities to condition socially acceptable use of the real property. Statistics on agricultural production in the Kyrgyz Republic from the last decade, in which the inheritable exclusive use right was the dominant land tenure mode for farmland, show that such land tenure did not impede the development of agricultural production in a significantly negative way.

CHAPTER 16

CONCLUSIONS

16.1 CONSTRAINTS

16.1.1 PERSONAL CONSTRAINTS

There are limiting factors of a personal nature for the research in this book. Personal time and resources form the main constraints. As expatriate consultant I am also constantly reminded of the restricted level of communication that is possible. One can learn a language, one can use interpreters, but even with good knowledge of the language and with the best interpreters available, it is impossible to fully understand and appreciate the conceptual approach of native inhabitants to new circumstances in their country. I am more and more aware of the fact that research is only an attempt to describe factual occurrences. It means that research is limited to a personal perspective and the concept that guides personal activities and personal conclusions. Moreover, the data collected is sometimes contradictory. I have tried to eliminate, as best as possible, inconsistencies in data by comparing data from various sources and by using and evaluating research results of others.

16.1.2 GENERAL CONSTRAINTS

General limitations are that obviously national statistics in former communist countries do not always use the same definitions for the same terms and that statistical data are difficult to compare in time because of implicit factors that are ignored or used differently in later statistics. The population is not accustomed to being involved in research and is generally reluctant to submit data on their economic situation and resource use patterns. Familiarity with considerable control on the use of real property by the government will provoke citizens to avoid answering questions on actual or intended use of real property and this results in evasive answers. Expatriates becoming more or less familiar with local experts and interpreters can be surprised that sometimes the same person does easily change an opinion in the course of time depending on the circumstances although this is not done intentionally. There is another factor, farmers in communist countries are more or less accustomed to stretching or shrinking the size of land and the cooperative bending of statistical data in favor of the former Soviet farm; for them questionnaires are just another tool to rewrite reality.

16.2 THE METHOD

16.2.1 CHARACTER OF THE METHOD

The method developed in this book for rapid assessment of a land reform project has been used to evaluate the land and agrarian reform project in the Kyrgyz Republic. The method does not claim exclusiveness of the indicators, statistics, and observations used. On the contrary, it is expected that indicators and observations being available for each particular project can assess such projects. Moreover, the method does not claim to provide absolute proof of the current situation or future developments. The added value of rapid assessment with the method lies not in its guarantee of effects of the land reform project that are about to occur, but rather in the signal function of effects that might occur. Using the method for rapid assessment gives the assurance that some effects easily overlooked or ignored during the busy time of project implementation will get attention. Effectiveness of the project will increase because inconsistent expectations of assumed relations can be corrected by additional supportive measurements.

16.2.2 EFFECTIVENESS OF THE METHOD

A relative simple set of macro-economic indicators and field observations can provide useful signals about what supplementary supportive activities should be developed to make a land reform project (more) effective. It signals for example – as was the case in the Kyrgyz Republic – that the expectation of the development of a real property market without additional supportive measures will not soon come about. It also indicates that the food security situation did not yet reach a satisfactory level. It suggests that agricultural infrastructure for marketing of farm products is needed to enable farmers better market access and information and to decrease informal trade with 'table-shops' in cities and small towns.

The method also provided insight in some less desired developments and supported measurements taken by the government to improve effectiveness of the project. Whether desired or not, the increasing subordination of women is a signal of re-appearing customs from before the Soviet times. This is not in-line with a 'western' style model to develop a market economy. As for food security, it give signals that the food security situation for the urban population still is a matter of concern.

Finally the method could encourage project staff to recommend additional helpful activities and to pursue (donor funded) supportive projects to insure a more rapid sustainable benefit of the land and agrarian reform. Examples in the Kyrgyz case are a renewed emphasis on land market development, strengthening of the social safety net, facilitating credit possibilities, a wider approach to improvement of food security than focus on food production, etc.

16.3 EFFECT OF LAND REFORM

16.3.1 THE TIME FACTOR

It will take substantial time and effort to verify the results of the land and agrarian reform project to its full extent in the Kyrgyz Republic. The effect of the new relationship to land, expressed by private ownership, is still alien to most citizens and it must be assumed that a context-specific 'mapping' of the full extent of possibilities will take time to result in a behavioral change in the rural population. As mentioned before, normally a generation will pass before results of land reform projects are clearly visible. Particulars of behavioral effects resulting from land tenure change are difficult to measure. There is a danger in using once proven but possibly outdated or irrelevant concepts to justify current actions. Indolent linking of context specifics with concept dependencies easily immunizes itself against verification.

The assumption that change to more individual and private land tenure will stimulate economic performance in a positive way has increasingly failed to deliver on its promises. The high expectations of change in property regime measured against the objectives of attaining specific social and economic goals have turned out to be more or less failures in the last decades. Nevertheless the expectation that economic performance is an automatic result of a change to individualized commodified private property rights, can often be found in contemporary donor sponsored projects as motive for land tenure change. It is linked to the strong belief that individual private ownership in modern western societies evolved naturally from primitive communism (as the previous existing various communal property regimes can be characterized), thus freeing the individual from bureaucratic controlling processes and procedures. But this belief has turned out to be at least speculative. It is not substantially supported by hard evidence and this research, once again, shows that disappointment can easily be triggered by uncritical use of unsubstantiated expectations. I have expressed my concern not only because of possible disappointment among the politicians in countries in transition, but even more because I observed so many ordinary people living in relatively poor conditions. When land reform does not deliver expected results, those same people can be confronted with prolonged poverty before recovery will start.

16.3.2 ONCE AGAIN, A MORE SOCIALLY ORIENTED LAND TENURE REGIME?

Western observers noticed a more socially oriented way of life in the communist society. But as far as I could observe, this hardly influenced their thinking when considering suitable property regimes in those countries after gaining independence. One can question whether such societies – only a few years after independence – are yet ready for the individualistic capitalist type of society and its individualized private property relations proclaimed as the most suitable way to achieve economic development and progress. In several of my assignments I could not avoid the impression that donors encouraged a post communist society too quickly into a direction toward capitalism and free market economies. Donors generally permit insufficient time for the population – and thus for their society – to make necessary social and ideological adjustments.

Why not create and introduce a new form of communal property regime with similarities to (primitive) communism instead of the individual private ownership contrasting with the concept of a property regime the population has lived with for so many years under Soviet rule? For the Kyrgyz Republic this argument is even more poignant. Initially the distributed land was granted to individuals in either rent or lifetime inheritable tenure. It would have been relatively easy to 'transform' this type of tenure to registered land tenure, with conditions attached to it, in order to establish a property and land tenure regime that would benefit the population as a whole and not only tenants of property rights. One can only guess at the reasons for the Kyrgyz Parliament to convert the land certificates to ownership documents introducing a typical Western style ownership right to agricultural land with the capitalistic commodified notion of land tenure. It now is to be hoped that the process of increasing individualization is not going to weaken the social and economic function of property by an aggressively promoted land registration program of the vast area of commonly used pastureland in the Kyrgyz Republic.

Bibliography

1. Aiken, William and Hugh, LaFollette (1996), *World Hunger and Morality*, Prentice Hill; Upper Saddle River New Jersey. Second edition.
2. Barraclough, Solon (1991), *An End to Hunger? The Social Origins of Food Strategies*, Atlantic Highlands (Zed Books), London.
3. Benda-Beckmann F von (1989), 'Scapegoat and magic charm; Development theory and practice.' *Journal of Legal Pluralism* 28.
4. Benda-Beckmann F and K von (1994), 'Property Rights and Economic Development', Chapter 1, Kegan Paul International London.
5. Benda-Beckmann F von (1995), 'Antropological approaches to property law and economics; ' *European Journal of Law and Economics* 2, 309-336 (1995)
6. Berry, Albert et al. (1979), *Agrarian Structure and Productivity in Development Countries*, John Hopkins University Press, Baltimore.
7. Bledsoe, D.J. and R. L. Prosterman (2000), 'Policy, the Rule of Law, and Rural Land Reform in China.' *Rural Development Institute (RDI) reports on Foreign Aid and Development* 101, February 2000.
8. Bloch, Peter et al. (1996), 'Land and Agrarian Reform in the Kyrgyz Republic.' *LTC research paper 128*, July 1996. Madison Wisconsin.
9. Bruce, John and Louise Fortmann (1998), *Whose Trees? Proprietary Dimensions of Forestry*, Westview Press, Boulder/London.
10. Bruce, John and Shem Migot-Adholla (1994), *Searching for Land Tenure Security in Africa*, Kendall/Hunt Dubuque, Iowa.
11. Bruce, John (1998) 'Review of tenure terminology.' *Tenure Brief* 1, July 1998, LTC publication, University of Wisconsin, Madison.
12. Burnside, Craig and D. Dollar (1997), 'Aid, Policies and Growth' *Working Paper* 1777 World Bank, Washington D.C..
13. Carter Michael et al. (1994) 'Tenure Security for whom? Differential effects of land policy in Kenya.' *(Chapter 7 in Searching for land tenure security in Africa* edited by John Bruce and Shem Migot-Adholla).
14. Carter, Michael R. (1984), 'Identification of the inverse relationship between Farm size and Productivity; An Empirical Analysis of peasant Agricultural Production' *Oxford Economic papers* 36: Pp. 131-145.
15. Chambers, Robert (1988), 'Sustainable Rural Livelihoods: A Key Strategy for People, Environment and Development.' *'The Greening of Aid'* edited by Conroy and Litvinoff, London: Earthscan.
16. Chatwin, Bruce (1988), *The Song Lines*, Penguin Books USA Inc, New York, 1988
17. Crevecoeur, J Hector St. John (1782), *Letters from an American farmer*.
18. Crook, Frederick E. (1999), 'An Analysis of China's Food Grain Security Policy.' *Agriculture in China and OECD Countries; Past Policies and Future Challenges*. Paris.
19. Csaki, Csaba (1994), 'Where is Agriculture heading in Central and Eastern Europe?' *Agricultural Landownership in Transitional Economies*, edited by Gene Wunderlich

20.Deininger, Klaus and Squire Lyn (1997), 'Income Growth and Income Inequality.' *Finance and Development,* March 1997 pp. 38 - 41.

21.Denman, D.R and Prodano S. (1972), *Land Use, An introduction to Proprietary Land Use Analysis*, Allen and Unwin, London.

22.DeSoto, Hernando (1994), 'The missing ingredient' in *World Politics and Current Affairs* pp. 10 - 14; July.

23.DeSoto, Hernando (1988), *The Other Path,* (original title: 'El Otro Sendero') London.

24.Dorner, Peter and Kanel Don, (1971), 'The Economic Case for Land Reform: Employment, Income Distribution, and Productivity.' *'Land Reform, Land Settlement, and Cooperatives';* 1971 no. 1; FAO 1971.

25.Dorner, Peter (1991), *Latin American Land Reforms in Theory and Practice; a retrospective analysis*, The University of Wisconsin Press.

26.Doolittle, Amity (1998), 'Historical and contemporary Views of Legal pluralism in Sabah, Malaysia (North Borneo).' *'The Common Property Resource Digest* 47 pp. 1 - 9, December.

27.Dubois, Olivier (1998), 'Does Title Really Matter? Rights and Wrongs of Rights to land and Forest Resources in sub-Saharan Africa; Bridging the gap between customary and formal rules.' *Forestry and Land Use program of the International Institute for Environment and Development* 10, London.

28.FAO (1979), 'Declaration of Principles and Program of Action' of the World Conference on Agrarian Reform and Rural Development FAO, Rome 12 - 20 July.

29.FAO (1996), The Rome declaration on World Food Security and the World Food Summit Plan of Action. Rome.

30.Feder, Gershon (1985), 'The Relation between Farm Size and Farm Productivity; The Role of Family Labour, Supervision and Credit Constraints.' *Journal of Development Economics.*

31.Feder, Gershon et al. (1988), 'The Economic Implications of Land Documents in rural Thailand;' *Agricultural Administration and Extension*, Elsevier Applied Science Publishers 1988 (pp. 123 - 133).

32.Feder, Gershon (1988), 'Economic aspects of Land Registration and Titling.' Paper presented at Cadastral Congress Warsaw, Poland September.

33.FIG Symposium papers 'Cadastre and Environment in the Countries of Central and Eastern Europe with application of GIS/LIS, GPS and RS,' 15 - 18 November, Sofia, Bulgaria 'The Cadastre in Central and Eastern European Countries and recent developments in Bulgaria' and 'Evaluating the concept of 'Multi-Purpose' Cadastre' by Henri Dekker.

34.FIG (1995), Féderation Internationale dès Geomètres (FIG) Statement on the Cadastre, February.

35.Galbraith, John (1983), *The Anatomy of Power*, Houghton Mifflin Company Boston.

36.Galbraith, John (1994), *A Journey through Economic Time*, Houghton Mifflin Company, Boston.

37.Ghonemy, Riad El- (1990), *The Political Economy of Rural Poverty; The Case for Land Reform*, Routledge New York .

38.Granberg, Leo and Imre Kovach (1998), 'Actors of the Changing European Countryside' Proceedings of a Conference on rural Development. Budapest, Hungary.

39.Hanson, Victor D (1999), *The Land was Everything; Letters from an American farmer*, The Free Press.

40.Hoekema, André J. (2000), Texts on legal pluralism and development. Text used at Amsterdam Law School: Sociology and Anthropology of Law. (Revised in 2000).

'Keuzevak Rechtssociologie: Rechts-pluralisme en Ontwikkeling. (University of Amsterdam Law program; Faculty of Law).

41.Holmes, Kim and Melanie Kirkpatrick (1996), 'Freedom and Growth' in *'The Wall Street Journal'* Monday, 16 December. p. A12

42. Hongyu, Zhang (1999), 'Land Tenure Policy in Rural China; Development and Prospects a Re-evaluation of the Institutional Reform of Rural Land Use.' *Agriculture in China and OECD Countries; Past Policies and Future Challenges.* Paris.

43.Jianwen, Liu (1999), 'Utilization of Land and Water Resources in China; Resource Endowment, Institutional Arrangements.' *Agriculture in China and OECD Countries; Past Policies and Future Challenges.* Paris.

44.Kyrgyz Republic

Law on Peasant Farms (PF) of 2 February 1991

Law of the Kyrgyz Republic on Enterprises in the Republic of Kyrgyzstan 6 February 1991

Law of the Kyrgyz Republic on Land Reform 19 April 1991

Presidential Decree, on Emergency Measures for Ensuring Realization of Kyrgyz Republic Laws Regulating Land and Other Relations in Agriculture 10 November 1991

Law of December 1991 On privatization of housing stock in the Republic of Kyrgyzstan

Decree of the President of the Kyrgyz Republic on Measures for Continuing Implementation of Land and Agrarian Reform in the Kyrgyz Republic 10 December 1992

Presidential Decree on Measures for Enhancement of the Land and Agrarian Reform in the Kyrgyz Republic 22 February 1994

Regulation on Reorganization of Agricultural Enterprises 22 August 1994

Regulation on order of Finding Out the Land Share of Citizens and Giving Certificate of Land Use 22 August 1994

Law of November 1994 On Destatisation and Privatization of State Ownership in the Kyrgyz Republic

Draft Land Code of the Republic of Kyrgyzstan November 1994

Law of November 1998 On State Registration of Rights to Immovable Property

Constitution of the Kyrgyz Republic as amended 16 February 1996 and Amendments on the Constitution of 1998

Regulation on State Agency on Immovable property rights registration under Kyrgyz Republic Government 12 April 1999

Land Code of May 1999 (passed in June 1999)

National Food Security Policy report to be presented at seminar in Bishkek, 27 July 1999.

(Draft) Regulation on procedure for state registration of rights to immovable property and transactions with it. Fall 1999.

45.Lambert, Virginia et al. (1994), 'Investments in Agriculture: Asset Distribution and Access; Land Tenure Programs' *ETS project for A.I.D.*, February.

46.Lappe, Frances and Joseph Collins (1986), *World Hunger: Twelve Myths*, Grove Press New York.

47.Lastarria-Cornhiel, Susana (1997), 'Impact of Privatization on Gender and Property Rights in Africa.' *Paper presented in Budapest* 1997, Elsevier Science Ltd, Great Britain.

48.Lemel, Harold (1998), *Rural Property and Economy in Post-Communist Albania*, Berghahn Books Oxford-New York.

49.Lerman, Zvi (1995), 'Changing Land Relations and Farming Structures in Formerly Socialist Countries.' *Agricultural Landownership in Transitional Countries.* Ed Gene Wunderlich 1995 University Press of America, Lanham, Maryland pp. 54 - 81.
50.Lin, Justin Y, Fang Cai and Zhou Li (1996), 'The China Miracle; Development Strategy and Economic Reform.' The Chinese University Press, Hong Kong.
51.Lin, Justin Y, Burcoff R, and Feder G, (1992) 'Agricultural Reform in a Socialist Economy: The Experience of China', *The Agricultural Transition in Central and Eastern Europe and the Former USSR.*
52.LTC (Land Tenure Center) The Land Tenure Center of the Wisconsin University, Madison. Research papers no. 120, 128 and 129.
53.Lynch, Owen and Kirk Talbott (1995), *Balancing Acts; Community Based Forest Management and National Law in Asia and the Pacific*, A world resources institute book.
54.Maslow, Abraham (1962), *Toward a Psychology of Being.*
55.Maxwell, Daniel and Kieth Wiebe (1998), 'Land Tenure and Food Security: A review of concepts, evidence and methods' *LTC research paper* no.129; University of Wisconsin-Madison.
56. Molnar, Joseph. J. (1998), 'Sound Policies for Food Security: The Role of Culture and Social Organization,' Auburn University Auburn AL. *Second contribution in a Trilogy of papers on international food security.* Columbus, Ohio State University.
57.Moore, Barrington Jr. (1968), *Social Origins of Dictatorship and Democracy, Lord and Peasant in the Making of the Modern World*, Beacon press, Boston, 1968.
58.Mudahar, Mohinder S. (1997), Kyrgyz Republic Strategy for Rural Growth and Poverty Alleviation. *World Bank discussion paper* no. 394.
59.Myrdal, Gunnar (1968), *Asian Drama: An Inquiry into the Poverty of Nations*, (Volume 1) Twentieth Century Fund Study; Pantheon Books, New York.
60.Myrdal, Gunnar (1970), *The Challenge of World Poverty. A World Anti-Poverty Program in Outline*, Pantheon Books, New York.
61.Nabli, M. K and J.B. Nugent (1989), 'The New Institutional Economics and its Applicability to Development.' *World Development 17*, no. 9 pp. 1333-1347.
62.Nellis, John (1999), 'Time to rethink privatization in transition Economies?' *International Finance Corporation discussion paper* no. 38.
63.OECD Proceedings (1999), 'Agriculture in China and OECD Countries. Past Policies and Future Challenges.' OECD paper Paris.
64.Petit, Michel (1993), 'Determinants of Food Policy: An attempt to understand Government Behavior.' *'The Political Economy of Food and Nutrition Policies;'* pp. 22 - 33. John Hopkins University, Baltimore.
65.Platteau, Jean-Phillippe (1992) 'Land reform and structural adjustment in sub-Saharan Africa: controversies and guidelines' FAO-report 107, Rome 1992.
66.Platteau, Jean-Phillippe (1996), 'The Evolutionary Theory of Land Rights as Applied to Sub-Saharan Africa: A Critical Assessment.' *'Development and Change' Volume* 27.
67.Place, Roth and Hazell (1994), 'Land Tenure Security and Agricultural Performance in Africa.' *'Searching for Land Tenure Security in Africa'* edited by John Bruce and Shem Migot-Adholla; chapter 2.
68.Prosterman, Swarzwalder and Jianping (2000), 'Implementation of 30-Year Land Use Rights for Farmers under China's 1998 Land Management Law: An Analysis and Recommendations Based on a 17-Province Survey.' *RDI Reports on Foreign Aid and Development* no. 105. Rural Development Institute Seattle, Washington. March 2000.
69.Rowton Simpson S. (1976), *Land Law and Registration*, Cambridge University Press.
70.Sachs, Jeffrey (1997), 'The Limits of Convergence' *The Economist* 14 - 20 July, 1997.

71.Schmid, A. Allan (1987), *Property, Power and Public Choice; An Inquiry into Law and Economics,* Second Edition. Praeger, New York.

72.Seattle Chief of the Puget Sound tribe (1855), 'Our people are ebbing away like a rapidly receding tide.' *'How can one sell the air?'* Book Publishing Company, Summertown, Tennessee. *First published in 1980 by Ekologische Uitgeverij Amsterdam and Aktie Strohalm Utrecht.*

73.Sen, Amartya K. (1981), *Poverty and Famines: An Essay on Entitlement and Deprivation,* Clarendon Press Oxford UK

74.Serageldin, Ismail (1998), 'World without hunger, hopes for the new millennium' *Paper presented at Ohio State University, Columbus Ohio,* November.

75. Serageldin, Ismail (1998), 'Can we Feed our World?' *Interview in Newsweek 1998*

76. Slaats, Herman (1999), 'Land Titling and Customary Rights: Comparing Land Registration Projects in Thailand and Indonesia' *Chapter 3 in 'Property Rights and Economic Development'* Edited by Toon van Meijl and Franz von Benda-Beckmann, Kegan Paul International London and New York.

77.Smith, Adam (1776),'(An Inquiry into the Nature and Causes of) *the Wealth of Nations.*'

78.Spoor, Max (1999), 'Agrarian Transition in Former Soviet Central Asia: A Comparative Study of Kazakhstan, Kyrgyzstan and Uzbekistan.' *Institute of Social Studies, The Hague, The Netherlands Working Paper 298,* September 1999.

79.Stanfield, David (1995), 'Insecurity of Land tenure in Nicaragua' *LTC research paper 120,* University of Wisconsin-Madison, 1995.

80.Stanfield, David (199), 'Creation of Land Markets in Transition Countries; Implications for the Institutions of Land Administration.' *LTC working paper* no.29 Madison Wisconsin.

81.United Nations report (1978), 'Our Common Future,' *Report of the Brundtland Commission* UN; New York.

82.Tabyshalieva, Anara (1999), Social Assessment of Land Registration Project in the Kyrgyz Republic. *(Draft) report,* December 1999

83.Tanzi, V and L. Schuknecht (1995), 'The Growth of Government and the Reform of the State in Industrial Countries.' *IMF working paper December 1995* International Monetary Fund, Washington D.C.

84.Thiesenhusen, W and J. Melmed-Sanjak (1990), 'Brazil's Agrarian Structure: Changes from 1970 through 1980.' In *World Development 18.* pp. 393 - 415.

85.Thiesenhusen, William (1995), 'Landed Property in Capitalist and Socialist Countries: The Russian Tradition' *'Agricultural Landownership in Transitional Countries.* Edt. Gene Wunderlich. University Press of America, Lanham MD pp. 27 - 53

86.Thiesenhusen, William (1995), 'Review: Land Reform Lives!' *European Journal of Development Research 7,* pp. 193 - 209.

87.Thiesenhusen, William (1995), *Broken Promises; Agrarian Reform and the Latin American Campesino,* Westview Press, Boulder, Colorado

88.Times of Central Asia (the) *Weekly newspaper in the English language* (website www.times.kg)

89.Tisenkopfs, Talis (1998), 'Post-Collectivist Farmers as Social, Economic and Political Group.' *'Actors on the Changing European Countryside,* edited by Granberg and Kovach Budapest. pp. 131 - 143.

90.Tshuma, Lawrence (1998), 'Colonial and Post-Colonial Reconstruction of Customary Land Tenure in Zimbabwe.' *'Social and Legal Studies,* Volume 7.

91.Tuan, Francis C. and Bingsheng Ke (1999), 'China's Agricultural Policy' *'Agriculture in China and OECD Countries; Past Policies and Future Challenges.'* Paris.

92.Tweeten, Luther and George Brinkman (1976), *Micropolitan Development,* Ames: Iowa

State University Press.
93.Tweeten, Luther et al. (1997), *Promoting Third World Development and Food Security*, Preager New York, 1997.
94.Tweeten, Luther (1998), 'The Economics of Global Food Security' *First of Trilogy of papers on international food security*. Columbus, Ohio State University.
95.VanAtta, Donald (1994), 'The 18th Brumaire of Boris Yeltsin: Agrarian Reform, Macroeconomic Policy and Rural Political Interests in Post-Soviet Russia' *Post Soviet Affairs*, 1994.
96.Verdery, Katherine (1994), 'The Elasticity of Land, Problems of Property Restitution in Transylvania.' *Slavic Review 53* no. 4.
97.Wheeler, Rachel (1998), 'Past and Present Land Tenure Systems in Albania: Patri-lineal, Patriarchal, Family Centered.' *Working Paper* no.13 LTC Madison, Wisconsin.
98.World Bank (WB) (1986), Poverty and Hunger: Issues and Options for Food Security in Developing Countries Washington D.C..
99. World Bank (WB) (1993), Binswanger Hans P. et al. 'Power, Distortions, Revolt, and Reform in Agricultural Land Relations' *Working Paper,* World Bank, Washington D.C.
100. World Bank (WB) (1998) Discussion Paper no.394 '*Strategy for Rural Growth and Poverty Alleviation*' by Mohinder Mudahar.
101. World Bank (WB) (1999), Project Information Document of 3 June 1999; Land and Real Estate Registration Project in Kyrgyzstan by Edward Cook.
102.Wunderlich, Gene (1995), 'Creating Private Ownership and Markets in the Agricultural Land of Formerly Socialist Countries.' '*Agricultural Land Ownership in Transitional Economies.*' University Press of America, Lanham/New York.

GLOSSARY

(partly based on John Bruce [11])

Access to land	The ability to use (landed) property.
Access to food	The ability to acquire available food from earnings and transfers.
Architectura	Offices of the State Committee on Architecture and Construction (Gosstroi), a government agency for city and regional planning. It registers urban owners and users of immovable property and reports this information to the rayon tax office.
Associations of peasant[1] farms	A category of farming enterprises devised to cope with the fact that peasant farmers often worked cooperatively (and typically under old management structures).
BTI	Bureau of Technical Inventory concentrates all information on immovable property (construction plans of houses, apartments, etc.) in urban areas.
Bundle of rights	The several rights that constitute a tenure; alternatively, all the rights belonging to various persons or groups in a piece of property.
Cadastre	A system of recording different forms of land tenure such as ownership, leasehold, easements, mortgages and different types of common, communal or customary land tenure.
Command economy	An economy in which not prices but (governmental) commands and directives determine production.
Common property	A commons from which a community can exclude non-members and over which the community controls use.
Commons	Land or another natural resource used simultaneously or serially by the members of a community.
Communal property	See common property.
Deeds registration	A registration of deeds on property.
Food security	Sustained and assured access by all social groups and individuals to food adequate in quantity and quality to meet nutritional needs – to live an active and healthy life (This definition used by FAO and UN does not

[1] Note that 'peasant' in this context does not have the connotation of 'backward' or 'subsistence'. It is used for individually operated farms as the result of poor translations and censorship.

	mention two other important determinants of food security: Availability and Utilization, see paragraph 2.3.2).
GosRegister	Institute created to develop and implement a new unified system of Land Registration in the Kyrgyz Republic, as a result of the November 1998 Law on State Registration of Rights to Immovable Property.
Immovable property	Property in land and attachments (European Civil Law)
Imported tenure system	Tenure system copied from another country.
Individual property	Property held by a natural person or legal entity.
Inheritable use rights	System of tenure under which use rights pass from a deceased owner to his or her heirs.
Institutions	The established rules and customary relationships of a social organization.
Land	Any part of the earth's surface which can be owned as property, and everything annexed to it, whether by nature or by hand of man. (In legal terms also a thin layer of earth beneath the surface and a certain layer of 'air' above this surface is considered property and the rights to land can be executed as the same rights in those layers).
Land Administration	A rayon level office organization of the State Institute for Land Resources and Land Management (Kyrgyzgiprozem). Compiles annual inventories of land resources with detailed data on land holdings and agricultural land users. (Also called offices of Land management or offices of Land Engineering).
Land Certificate	A formal document and proof of land tenure issued a by rural committee showing the size of each individual and family land share and the initial cost of the land in soms. (The certificate must be registered in the land cadastre of the rayon land management office to become valid).
Land reform	The attempt to change the land tenure (and often improve the distribution among right holders to support a certain goal).
Land share	An individual property share in rural property of a former state or collective farm, prorated according to the labor contribution of the individual on the farm.
Land survey	Determining the boundaries of rights to land and fixing the location of a parcel of land.
Land tenure	In short: Right(s) in land. Formally: The institutional arrangement of rules, principles, procedures, and practices, whereby a society defines control over, access

	to, management of, exploitation of, and use of means of existence and production.
Land tenure security	Tenure perceived as held without risk of loss except for customary rulings or formalized expropriation with fair compensation.
Land tenure system	All the tenure types provided for by a statutory or customary (legal) system, taken together.
Landed property	Property rights of land held under ownership rights.
Livelihood	Adequate stocks and flows of food and cash to meet basic needs.
Mortgage	A contract by which a borrower commits land as security for a loan.
Opportunity set	An individual's physical and emotional capacities plus legal or customary understandings of potential options that are conditioned by actual choices of others.
Parcel	A contiguous area of land acquired as a unit under one title.
Peasant[2] Farm	An independent farming complex operated by a single family or operated by more than a single family in which case family members, relatives, and other individuals can jointly run the farming unit (Art. 2 of the Law of Peasant Farms of the Kyrgyz Republic).
Personal property	Property other than real property (Anglo-American usage).
Plan economy	An economy in which the production is determined by central planning. Usually referred to as a central plan economy because generally the state determines an annual national economic plan.
Private property	Property held by natural or legal private persons.
Property	A set of rights and responsibilities concerning a thing, often stated as rights in a thing, to show they are rights against everyone.
Property regime	A complex of rules, principles, and procedures that regulates legitimate control over, access to, and conditions of use of, means of existence and production.
Public property	Property held by any level of government
Re-adjudication	To come to a judicial decision about restitution by study and investigation.
Real property	Property in land and attachments (Anglo-American usage).

[2] Note that 'peasant' in this context does not have the connotation of 'backward' or 'subsistence'. It is used for individually operated farms as the result of poor translations and censorship.

Regime	A complex of rules, principles and procedures that regulates legitimate control over, access to, and conditions of use of things.
Restitution	The act of restoring to the rightful owner something that has been taken away, lost, or surrendered.
Sporadic registration	Registration of property separately from others in the area, voluntarily and generally at the expense of the owner of rights to the property.
Sustainability	The maintenance or enhancement of resource productivity on a long-term basis.
Systematic registration	Registration of all property in an area at the same time, usually compulsory and without charge to the owners of rights to the property.
Tenure	In short: Right(s) in a thing; Formally: The institutional arrangement of rules, principles, procedures, and practices, whereby a society defines control over, access to, management of, and use, of a thing.
Title registration	A land registration system that confers a guarantee of the title by the registration authority.
Ugodia	Rural land specifically designated for agricultural production and initially subject to a different tenure system in Kyrgyzstan.

INDEX

(number refers to subparagraph; *P* = preface)

Annex A

PART OF (English translation of) THE LAW OF REPUBLIC OF KYRGYZSTAN 'On privatization of housing stock in Republic of Kyrgyzstan' Enforced by the Supreme Soviet Resolution of Republic of Kyrgyzstan as of 20 December 1991 # 682-XII

Chapter I

General provisions

Article 1. Idea on dwelling privatization

Dwelling privatization means free transference and transference on payment basis of living accommodation to individuals' ownership.
Dwelling privatization will be conducted on voluntary base.

Article 2. Privatization object

Dwelling houses of state and communal housing stock, apartments within blocks of houses (apartment, dwelling house here and after), as well as hostels and houses of hotel character will be objects of privatization.
The following will not to be subject to privatization:
Apartments, that do not meet standard sanitary and technical requirements and acknowledged as inappropriate for living and are not subjects to repair;
Official dwelling houses. Apartments excluding housing stock of state farms and other agricultural enterprises equal to them;
Houses which are to be subject to demolition; houses within the closed cantonments;
Apartments with two and more families without blood relations, if a dispute arises between them
Dwelling houses, having historical, cultural and architectural significance, as well as apartments within such houses will be subjects to privatization only with the consent of appropriate state administration organs or organs of local self-administration by signing contracts, providing for security of these living accommodations.
Local state administration will attach the status of dwelling houses to hostels, houses of hotel character in accordance with the decision of general meeting of the individuals, living in these houses. In this case privatization will be conducted in

the order, established by the law for dwelling privatization that is on the balance of enterprises, organizations, agencies.
Hostels and houses of a hotel character, owned by joint-stock companies, based on state enterprises, will be privatized in the order, defined by the Part 4 of his article.

Article 3. Privatization subjects

Organs, carrying out apartment and dwelling house privatization (sellers) will be:
Appropriate organs of local state administration;
Enterprises, organizations, agencies to which apartments and dwelling
Houses have been assigned as the right to full economic management or as the right to efficient management;
Joint-stock companies, based on state enterprises, having on their balance dwellings, constructed before enterprises' re-organization.
Apartment and dwelling house buyers can be:
Citizens of Republic of Kyrgyzstan;
Juridical entities, not based on state property;
Non-residents, residents of other countries permanently living within the territory of Republic of Kyrgyzstan;
Individuals and juridical entities of other states in the order, established by the Government of Republic of Kyrgyzstan.

Article 4. Methods and order of house stock privatization

State and communal housing stock privatization will be executed as free and payment based transference of apartments and dwelling houses.
Apartments and dwelling houses will be freely transferred to:

- Great Patriotic War invalids and participants, families of perished and missing warriors, died invalids, war participants and equal to them individuals, in the established order;
- Families of persons, died while carrying out official and civic duty; families with 4 and more children;
- Invalids of I and II group regardless reasons of becoming an invalid;
- Educationalists, health care, culture workers, employees of organs of the Ministry of Home Affairs, Ministry of National Security and servicemen in accordance with the existing legislation;
- Persons, having illnesses caused by sequels of the Chernobyl Atomic Electro Station accident, persons, participated in Chernobyl AES accident sequels liquidation, as well as persons, evacuated in 1986 to Republic of Kyrgyzstan out of the estrangement zone;
- Persons, illegally convicted during punitive measures, directed by Stalin, and their families (spouses, children);
- Officers, ensigns and warrant officers, transferred to the reserve or retired

according to the age, health status, staff reduction or family and other important circumstances and having period of service of 20 and more calendar years, occupied or assigned to them state -owned apartments;

- Employees of heath care organizations in the order, established by the Government of the Kyrgyz Republic;
- Educationalists in the order, established by the Government of Kyrgyz Republic;
- Employees of the organs of Home Affairs and persons, retired according to the age, health status, staff reduction and having period of service no less than 20 calendar years, as well as family members of employees of organs of Home Affairs perished or died executing official activity.

Payment based transference of apartments and dwelling houses will be based on using by dwellings' buyers special legal tenders of Republic of Kyrgyzstan, their allotment will be regulated by the Regulation, approved by the decree of the President of Kyrgyz Republic.

In accordance with the decision of the local state administration, meetings, conferences of working groups, part of the owned released and new dwellings can be sold on competitive base and through auctions.

Order of registration of individuals, whose living conditions are needed to be improved, and lease of living accommodations will be defined by the Housing code of Republic of Kyrgyzstan.

Free or payment based transference of living accommodations to persons being on the book for dwelling assigning, will be executed in the methods and order, established for the people having dwelling.

Article 5. Conditions of payment of apartment, dwelling house

If amount of special legal tenders does not cover apartment's, dwelling house's cost, there will be additional paying to the sum that is difference between apartment, dwelling house cost and amount of special legal tenders used.

In case, if sum of special legal tenders is enough and there is a surplus, it can be used when paying off another state and communal owned property, that is subject to privatization.

Payment of apartment, dwelling house can be made through long-term credits, by installments in the order, defined by the Government of Republic of Kyrgyzstan. The initial fee should be no less than 20 per cent of the apartment; dwelling house cost and period of installments should not exceed 10 years. For those, having many children, young and low income family according to their will, amount of the initial fee will be lowered to 15 per cent, and period of installments will be increased up to 15 years.

Article 6. Right to acquire apartment or dwelling house into the ownership

Lessee of the apartment or dwelling house will have the right to acquire apartment

or dwelling house into the ownership by the written permission of all living together members of the family of age, including those being temporary absent and persons on the book for apartment acquisition.
Application for apartment or dwelling house acquisition will be presented by the person, mentioned in the first part of this article to the appropriate organ of the local state administration. In case, if apartment or dwelling house has been assigned to enterprise, organization or agency as the right of full economic or efficient management - to the administration of these enterprises, organizations, agencies.
Individuals' applications on apartment and dwelling house privatization will be examined within 2 months since the day of presentation.
In case of unfounded denial to privatize an apartment or dwelling house, violation of taking decision on privatization terms, the guilty officer should be imposed a fine in accordance with court decision in the amount of up to 20 minimal month wages.
Acts, made by enterprises, organizations, agencies of any forms of property on dwelling issues, should not contradict this Law.

Chapter II
Main conditions of apartment privatization

Article 7. Means for apartment, dwelling houses acquisition

To acquire an apartment and dwelling houses special legal tenders of Republic of Kyrgyzstan, individuals' money, including foreign currency and borrowed funds will be used.

Article 8. Determination of cost of dwelling privatized

Cost of privatized apartments and dwelling houses will be determined by commissions under local state administration, enterprises and organizations with obligatory participation of peoples' deputies, representatives of financial organs, banks, housing service organizations, working teams, trade unions and individuals, acquiring apartment or dwelling house.
Cost determination of privatized apartments and dwelling houses, put into operation before, 1 January 1991, will be in the prices of 1984, and since 1991 - in prices of 1984 using increasing coefficients, developed by the State Republican administration organ, dealing with architecture and construction issues on the base of indices of capital investments changes, approved by the Government of Republic of Kyrgyzstan regardless property forms of organs, dealing with dwelling privatized.

Etc.

For Product Safety Concerns and Information please contact our EU representative GPSR@taylorandfrancis.com Taylor & Francis Verlag GmbH, Kaufingerstraße 24, 80331 München, Germany

Batch number: 10726370

Printed by Printforce, the Netherlands